OTHER PUBLICATIONS FROM THE DRUCKER FOUNDATION

Organizational Leadership Resource

The Drucker Foundation Self-Assessment Tool

The Drucker Foundation Future Series

The Leader of the Future, *Frances Hesselbein, Marshall Goldsmith, Richard Beckhard, Editors*

The Organization of the Future, *Frances Hesselbein, Marshall Goldsmith, Richard Beckhard, Editors*

The Community of the Future, *Frances Hesselbein, Marshall Goldsmith, Richard Beckhard, Richard F. Schubert, Editors*

Video Training Resources

Excellence in Nonprofit Leadership Video, *featuring Peter F. Drucker, Max De Pree, Frances Hesselbein, and Michele Hunt. Moderated by Richard F. Schubert.*

Lessons in Leadership Video, *with Peter F. Drucker*

Leading in a Time of Change Video Package, *featuring Peter F. Drucker and Peter M. Senge*

Journal and Leaderbooks

Leader to Leader Journal

Leader to Leader: Enduring Insights on Leadership from the Drucker Foundation's Award-Winning Journal, *Frances Hesselbein, Paul Cohen, Editors*

The Collaboration Challenge: How Nonprofits and Businesses Succeed Through Strategic Alliances, *James E. Austin*

Online Resources

www.leaderbooks.org

LEADING
BEYOND THE WALLS

**DRUCKER FOUNDATION
WISDOM TO ACTION SERIES**

ABOUT THE DRUCKER FOUNDATION

The Peter F. Drucker Foundation for Nonprofit Management, founded in 1990, takes its name and inspiration from the acknowledged father of modern management. By providing educational opportunities and resources, the foundation furthers its mission "to lead social sector organizations toward excellence in performance." The Drucker Foundation believes that a healthy society requires three vital sectors: a public sector of effective governments; a private sector of effective businesses; and a social sector of effective community organizations. The mission of the social sector and its organizations is to change lives. It accomplishes this mission by addressing the needs of the spirit, mind, and body of individuals, the community, and society. This sector also provides a significant sphere of effective and responsible citizenship.

In the ten years after its inception, the Drucker Foundation, among other things:

- Presented the Drucker Innovation Award, which each year generates several hundred applications from local community enterprises; many applicants work in fields where results are difficult to achieve.

- Worked with social sector leaders through the Frances Hesselbein Community Innovation Fellows program

- Held over twenty conferences in the United States and in countries around the world.

- Developed seven books: a *Self-Assessment Tool* (revised 1998) for nonprofit organizations; three books in the Drucker Foundation Future Series, *The Leader of the Future* (1996), *The Organization of the Future* (1997), and *The Community of the Future* (1998); *Leader to Leader* (1999); *Leading Beyond the Walls* (1999); and *The Collaboration Challenge* (2000).

- Developed *Leader to Leader,* a quarterly journal for leaders from all three sectors.

- Established a Web site (drucker.org) that shares articles on leadership and management and examples of nonprofit innovation with hundreds of thousands of visitors each year.

To realize its vision for the next ten years, the Drucker Foundation will bring together the best leadership and management voices from across the world with a focus on providing social sector organizations with the ideas and tools that enable them to better serve their customers and communities.

For more information, contact:

The Peter F. Drucker Foundation for Nonprofit Management
320 Park Avenue, Third Floor
New York, NY 10022-6839
Tel: (212) 224-1174
Fax: (212) 224-2508
E-mail: info@pfdf.org
Web address: www.drucker.org

LEADING BEYOND THE WALLS

FRANCES HESSELBEIN
MARSHALL GOLDSMITH
IAIN SOMERVILLE

EDITORS

JOSSEY-BASS
A Wiley Company
San Francisco

Jossey-Bass books and products are available through most bookstores. To contact Jossey-Bass directly, call (888) 378-2537, fax to (800) 605-2665, or visit our website at www.josseybass.com.

Substantial discounts on bulk quantities of Jossey-Bass books are available to corporations, professional associations, and other organizations. For details and discount information, contact the special sales department at Jossey-Bass.

TCF Manufactured in the United States of America on Lyons Falls Turin Book. This paper is acid-free and 100 percent totally chlorine-free.

Jacket design by Paula Goldstein
Cover design by Yvo Riezebos Design

Credits are on page 298.

Library of Congress Cataloging-in-Publication Data

Leading beyond the walls / Frances Hesselbein, Marshall Goldsmith, Iain Somerville editors. — 1st ed.
    p. cm. — (Wisdom to action series)
    "The Peter F. Drucker Foundation for Nonprofit Management."
    Includes bibliographical references (p.   ) and index.
    ISBN 0-7879-4593-5 (hardcover)
    ISBN 0-7879-5555-8 (paperback)
    1. Leadership. 2. Organizational change. 3. Management
I. Hesselbein, Frances. II. Goldsmith, Marshall. III. Somerville, Iain. IV. Peter F. Drucker Foundation for Nonprofit Management. V. Series.
    HD57.7 .L4374   1999
    658.4'092—dc21   99-6508

HB Printing   10 9 8 7 6 5 4 3 2   FIRST EDITION
PB Printing   10 9 8 7 6 5 4 3 2 1

CONTENTS

PREFACE

In 1996, the Drucker Foundation published *The Leader of the Future*, the first book in its *Future Series* trilogy, which also includes *The Organization of the Future* and *The Community of the Future*. The Drucker Foundation *Future Series* brought together global thought leaders to detail the challenges we will face as leaders, organizations, and communities in the twenty-first century. The *Future Series* books met with an enthusiastic response in business, government, and the social sector domestically and were translated into sixteen languages for publication around the world.

Leading Beyond the Walls is the inaugural volume in the Drucker Foundation's *Wisdom to Action Series*. The *Wisdom to Action Series* brings together remarkable thought leaders and practitioners from around the world to articulate how we can meet the challenges that were presented in the *Future Series*. As the name implies, the focus is on action, on the steps we can take today to build a better future. Each book in the *Wisdom to Action Series* will provide guidance for effective change, describe strategies for learning and development, and offer examples of leaders and organizations that are exploring new frontiers across all sectors of society.

Leading Beyond the Walls focuses on the first requirement of leadership in the twenty-first century. In the chapters that follow, leaders at all levels will find inspiration and practical advice on building effective organizations that focus on their strengths and employ the resources of individuals, organizations, and communities beyond their walls. This book explores what is needed to transcend the personal walls that inhibit effectiveness and the organizational, social, and political boundaries that inhibit reaching out. It will help all leaders to achieve personal excellence and high performance and to lead beyond the old boundaries to forge partnerships that are essential in the increasingly challenging period ahead.

Leading ourselves and our organizations *beyond the walls* is the first requirement for success in the years to come. It's a call for engagement; one each of us must answer.

Acknowledgments

This book results from the effort and commitment of many people. First are the thought leaders who contributed their expertise and insight by writing the chapters in this book in service to the Drucker Foundation and its mission. We owe these authors our deepest gratitude for their gifts of time, talent, and commitment.

We thank the staff of the Drucker Foundation: Andrew Fenniman, who coordinated the efforts of the widely dispersed editors and authors; Paul Typaldos, who was tireless in his support of this project; and Rob Johnston, Suzanne Sousa, Hillary Strilko, and Patrick Waide. We thank our able colleagues at Jossey-Bass: Alan Shrader, who lent his sure eye and hand to the work; Paul Cohen, who provided "beyond the walls" assistance at critical junctures; Xenia Lisanevich, who coordinated the production as if she were building a cathedral; Erik Thrasher; and Johanna Vondeling.

June 1999

Frances Hesselbein
Easton, Pennsylvania

Marshall Goldsmith
Rancho Santa Fe, California

Iain Somerville
Santa Barbara, California

LEADING
BEYOND THE WALLS

FRANCES HESSELBEIN

INTRODUCTION

The Community Beyond the Walls

Frances Hesselbein is chairman of the board of gover-
nors of the Peter F. Drucker Foundation for Non-
profit Management. She served as founding president
and CEO for nine years. She is editor in chief of the
foundation's Leader to Leader *journal and is coeditor*
of the Drucker Foundation Future Series. She
received the Presidential Medal of Freedom, the
United States' highest civilian honor, in 1998 in
recognition of her leadership as CEO of Girl Scouts
of the U.S.A. from 1976 to 1990 and her current
national and international role in leading social sector
organizations toward excellence in performance.

The development of productive partnerships has been a passion
of the Drucker Foundation's work since its founding in 1990.
Distilling this passion into compelling, spare, *urgent* language became a true challenge. As we tried to find the few words that would
communicate the imperative faced by all three sectors—moving
from concentration only on internal operations to partnership in
building community—"beyond the walls" emerged as a message we
could embrace, share, adapt, and build upon. For the foundation

1

and most of the people we reach, "beyond the walls" has become synonymous with efforts to build a viable, relevant organization of the future and an inclusive, cohesive community through new partnerships. "Beyond the walls" is a battle cry that mobilizes. Commitment to the people, organizations, and world within and beyond our walls makes us full participants in the growing network society and offers us new certainty in an uncertain world.

As we explored this theme—and many times it awakened me at 3:00 A.M.—I came to understand more clearly that the walls that surround us, protect us, and embrace us can also inhibit movement, limit understanding, restrict engagement, and diminish our relevance in the wider world. I realized that my walls, and the walls of leaders everywhere, were not only the walls of current policy, practice, procedure, and assumption but also the walls of the past—safe, familiar, and secure. This recognition was just the first of several as we worked through a process to take ourselves and our organizations beyond the walls to new levels of performance and positive changes in the lives of people.

Moving Beyond the Walls

Following are requisite steps for moving beyond the walls. These steps represent major commitments; they require significant investment of time and attention.

Prepare for Adventure

It is hard work to appreciate, examine, confront, and move beyond the familiar walls that surround us. Making this move requires the courage to embark on an emotional, cultural, and intellectual leadership adventure. We make a tough, impassioned examination of where we are and where want to be; it cannot be a cool and clinical review. This adventure is not for the faint of heart; the future belongs to the courageous, risk-taking, passionate how-to-be leader.

The job demands this deeply felt investment; as Peter F. Drucker has said, "I have never seen results accomplished without passion."

Trust in People

Moving beyond the walls, we have a vision of the future we desire, and we hold that vision before the people of the enterprise. Whether in a government agency, a corporation, or a social sector organization, we are leaders who truly believe that the organization is its people. This belief is embodied, for example, by Bill Pollard, chairman of the ServiceMaster Company, when he says of that company's 240,000 people, "Every employee is a person of great worth and dignity," and by the United States Army when it says, "Soldiers are our credentials." This trust is held by all leaders who can answer in the affirmative the question Jeffrey Pfeffer asks in *The Human Equation* (1998), "When you look at your people, do you see intelligent, motivated, trustworthy individuals—the most critical and valuable strategic assets your organization can have?" Leaders beyond the walls say yes and move into the exploration.

Get the Organizational House in Order

Before working as a productive partner with organizations in our sector or across sectors, we work to be sure we have our own house in order. We undertake with our organization an examination of where the organization has been, in a celebration of the past, and an examination of where we are, in affirmation of present relevance and viability. We examine the present mission, present customers, present performance and results, and our vision of the future. The values and soul of the organization undergird the exploration, the change.

A positive response to this revisiting of our status separates the leaders of the past from the leaders of the future. It separates those of us who choose to remain within the walls of the past and the present—a safe haven for the moment—from those who dare to venture beyond the walls on the journey to transformation. This is a transformation to greater significance and contribution in the future and indeed to being present when the roll is called in 2010 or 2020.

Challenge the Gospel

We've revisited the mission, and in a powerful, compelling way, we beam the message of why we do what we do—our purpose. But now the exacting, tough examination of the infrastructure and the organization's governance begins. We challenge the gospel of "how we've always done it." We challenge every policy, procedure, practice, and assumption and eliminate all that worked in the past but will be of little relevance in the future. Peter Drucker calls this "planned abandonment." Through this process we streamline the structure, scraping off the old barnacles that impede movement into the future.

Communicate

With clearly differentiated governance and management, with mission and vision the driving force, and with a flexible, fluid structure and infrastructure as the organizational support, the walls that once contained us are moved aside. If we hesitate, we can remember the great biblical communication challenge: "Should the trumpet give an uncertain sound, who shall gird himself for the battle?"

A few clear, compelling messages—messages of viability, relevance, and new significance—mobilize our people and lead them and the organization beyond the walls where the community calls for a new kind of collaborative leadership. In this beyond-the-walls community, partnerships of social sector organizations with corporations or with government agencies and sometimes partnerships representing all three sectors identify the critical needs and issues and, together, address them with their people and combined resources. This team approach to confronting community challenges reaches new heights of performance and results.

Results Beyond the Walls

Many of today's organizations have made the journey beyond the walls and have delivered visible, measurable results others can learn from.

In Baltimore, two organizations serving homeless people established a common headquarters. Through this facility sharing they reduced the costs of operation. In addition, they rented space to a third organization serving the same customers. The result is a collaborative, effective operation that provides better service to all customers.

An environmental organization protecting tropical rainforests has been successful in working in alliance with the industries usually considered the enemies of environmentalists. By building collaborative programs that define the practices and processes used in cultivating and harvesting wood and tropical agricultural products, they have protected rainforest areas and provided a basis for sustainable use of such areas. For this organization, working beyond the walls has replaced the practice of short-term confrontation with more productive long-term collaboration.

The Drucker Foundation, with a staff of seven and a board of fifteen, calls itself, as something of an inside joke, a "virtual foundation." To deliver conferences and develop publications, it is dependent on a network of over a hundred remarkable thought leaders in the United States and abroad who contribute their unique skills and talent. They write and speak for us and travel with us when the foundation takes a team abroad. The foundation operates without the security of an endowment, so for its continued success it must build and sustain its network of relationships with great leaders of thought and action. Like many social sector organizations, it is an example of an organization that exists because of the generosity of individuals and organizations beyond its walls.

The growth of communication technologies is supporting the development of beyond-the-walls operations and outreach. A noted technology company has for three years been operating an e-mail mentoring program. Working with public school teachers, the company matches trained individuals with students in the fifth through twelfth grades. They communicate by e-mail, across the country and the world, working on specific projects defined with the teacher's support.

Succeeding Through a Web of Relationships

The security of the old walls and the relevance of the gated enterprise are slowly diminishing. There is a new energy as leaders of the future embrace the vast opportunities for leadership in this wider world of building community where the old barriers and boundaries, both psychological and physical, are fading. Even leaders not ignited with the passion for changing lives are now participating out of enlightened self-interest, knowing that a sick and ailing community cannot provide the healthy and energetic workforce the competitive organization of the future demands.

Wherever we look the walls are coming down. The old barriers are fading. Partnerships are defining a new order that is marked by open lines of communication among organizations working to build a healthy, vibrant society. As leaders move beyond the walls, they find in the new partnerships the ultimate leadership challenge. They contribute to building communities that nurture all of their people, and the people of all the partners celebrate with the community they have helped renew.

Part I

NEW STRATEGIES FOR A WORLD WITHOUT WALLS

---

1   PETER F. DRUCKER

THE NEW PLURALISM

*Peter F. Drucker has been a teacher, writer, and
adviser to senior executives for more than fifty years.
Author of thirty-one books, he is honorary chairman
of the Drucker Foundation and Clarke Professor of
Social Sciences at the Claremont Graduate University in Claremont, California.*

Society in all developed countries has become pluralist and is
becoming more pluralist day by day. It is splintering into a myriad of institutions each more or less autonomous, each requiring its
own leadership and management, each having its own specific task.

This is not the first pluralist society in history. But all earlier pluralist societies destroyed themselves because no one took care of the
common good. They abounded in *communities* but could not sustain
community, let alone create it. If our modern pluralist society is to
escape the same fate, the leaders of *all* institutions will have to learn
to be *leaders beyond the walls*. They will have to learn that it is not
enough for them to lead their own institutions—though that is the
first requirement. They will also have to learn to become leaders in
the community. In fact they will have to learn to create community.
This is going way beyond what we have been discussing as *social*

responsibility. Social responsibility is usually defined as doing *no harm* to others in the pursuit of one's own interest or of one's own task. The new pluralism requires what might be called *civic responsibility*: giving to the community in the pursuit of one's own interest or of one's own task.

There is no precedent in history for such civic responsibility among institutional leaders. But there are, fortunately, signs that the leaders of our institutions in all sectors are beginning to wake up to the need to become leaders beyond the walls.

A Brief View Back

The last pluralist society in the West existed during the early and high Middle Ages. The Roman Empire tried, quite successfully, to create a unitary state in which Roman law and the Roman legions created political uniformity throughout the empire while cultural diversity was preserved. But after the collapse of the Roman Empire, this unity splintered completely. In its stead arose a congeries of autonomous and semiautonomous institutions: political, religious, economic, craft oriented, and so on. There was the medieval university, autonomous and a law unto itself. But there were also the free cities, the multinationals of the medieval economy. There were the craft guilds, and there were the all but autonomous major orders and great abbeys of the Church.

There were any number of landowners, from small squires to great dukes, each all but independent. Next to them were autonomous bishoprics, paying at best lip service to both the pope in Rome and the local prince. At its height, medieval pluralism in western and northern Europe alone must have been embodied by several thousands of such autonomous institutions, ranging from small squires to great landowners, and from small craft guilds and equally small, local universities to transnational religious orders. Each of these pluralist institutions was concerned only with its own welfare and, above all, with its own aggrandizement. Not one of them was concerned with the community beyond its walls.

Statesmen and political philosophers tried throughout the Middle Ages to re-create community. It was one of the main concerns of the Middle Ages' greatest philosopher, Saint Thomas Aquinas, in the early thirteenth century. And it was equally the concern of the Middle Ages' greatest poet, Dante, in his late-thirteenth-century work, *De monarchia*. Both preached that there should be two independent spheres: the secular one, centralized in and governed by the emperor, and the religious one, centralized in and governed by the pope. But by 1300 it was much too late to restore community. Society had collapsed into chaos.

Beginning in the fourteenth century and enduring for five hundred years, the trend has been toward abolishing pluralism. This tendency underlies all modern social and political theory, all of which preaches that there can be only one power in society: a centralized government. And one by one, over five hundred years, government either suppressed the autonomous institutions of pluralism—such as the free cities of the Middle Ages and the craft guilds—or it converted them into organs of government. This assumption of power is what is meant by *sovereignty*—a term coined in the late sixteenth century, by which time, in most of Europe, government had already become the dominant though not yet the only power. By the end of the Napoleonic Wars following the French Revolution, there were no autonomous institutions left on the European continent. The clergy had become civil servants everywhere. The universities had become governmental institutions everywhere. By the mid-1800s, there was one organized power, the government, and there was a society consisting of individual molecules, without political or social power. This is still the accepted political and social theory of today.

The only exceptions to the universal centralization of power that we mean when we talk of *modern society* existed in the English-speaking world and especially the United States. Religious diversity, especially in the United States, maintained a substantial sphere of pluralism, and out of this then grew the uniquely American independent college and university, the equally uniquely American nongovernmental hospital, and so on. But even in the United States the trend ran strongly toward centralization in which one political institution, the government, has a monopoly on power whereas society itself consists of very large numbers of independent individual or small enterprises, each with considerable freedom but without any power. In fact, modern economic theory, whether Keynesian or post-Keynesian, denies that these individuals have even economic autonomy. Their economic behavior is assumed to be determined by the government's fiscal, monetary, and tax policies.

As said before, the United States was an exception all along, something on which all foreign observers commented: for example, Tocqueville in the early years of the nineteenth century and Lord Bryce in its closing years. But even in the United States the trend was toward increasing centralization of power, with the peak reached in the Kennedy and Johnson years of the 1960s. By that time, prevailing ideology in the United States had come to believe that government could and should take care of every problem and every challenge in the community—a thesis that clearly no one believes anymore but that only forty years ago was almost universally accepted.

The trend toward the total monopoly of power by one institution, the government, still dominated the first half of the twentieth century. The totalitarian regimes, whether Nazism in Germany or Stalinism in the Soviet Union, can be seen as the last, extreme attempts to maintain the unity of power in one central institution and to integrate all institutions—down to the local chess club—into the centrally controlled power structure. Mao in China tried to do exactly the same with a major effort to destroy the prime autonomous power in Chinese society, the extended family.

By the middle of the nineteenth century, political theory and political practice in Europe—and in the West altogether—proclaimed that the task, begun five hundred years earlier, had been accomplished. Government, to be sure, was subject to severe limitations on its power. But nobody else had any power; all institutions with power had either been abolished or had been made government agencies.

But just then a *new pluralism* began.

The first new institution that was not part of government was the large business enterprise, made possible around 1860 to 1870 by the two new technologies of transportation and information. The large business enterprise was not subordinated to government, and it had to have substantial autonomy and substantial power. Since then, modern society has become totally pluralistic again. Even institutions that are legally governmental now have to be autonomous, have to be self-governing, have to have substantial power. Only thirty years ago, education in France was so totally controlled by government that the French minister of education could know at every moment what every teacher in every French school was teaching. By now even the French schools are heavily decentralized. And the European university, although still legally a government agency, has increasingly had to become autonomous, in control of its own research, its own faculty, its own disciplines, its own degrees. And just as the late Middle Ages tried to accommodate the reality of pluralism by preaching the existence of two autonomous and separate spheres of influence, the secular sphere and the religious sphere, twentieth-century social theory has tried to salvage the political and social theory of the unitary state with its sovereign government by talking of two sectors, the *public sector* of government, and the *private sector* of business.

By now we know that government cannot take care of community problems. We know that business and the free market also cannot take care of community problems. We have now come to accept that there has to be a third sector, the *social sector* of (mostly nonprofit) community organizations.

But we also know that all institutions, no matter what their legal status, have to be run autonomously and have to be focused on their own tasks and their own mission. We know, in other words, that it is almost irrelevant whether a university is private or is tax supported and owned by the state of California. However funded, it functions like other universities. We know that it makes little difference whether a hospital is a nonprofit institution or owned by a profit-making corporation. It has to be run the same way, that is, as a hospital. And the reality in which every modern society lives is therefore one of rapidly increasing pluralism, in which institutions of all kinds, sizes, values, missions, and structures constitute society. But we also know that this means that *no one is taking care of the community*. In fact the same degenerative tendencies that led to the revolt against pluralism in the fourteenth century are clearly at work in developed societies today. In every single developed country, single-cause interest groups are dominating the political process and are increasingly subordinating the common good to their own values, their own aggrandizement and power.

And yet, we need pluralism.

Why We Need Pluralism

There is one simple reason why the last 150 years have been years in which one institution after the other has become autonomous: the task-centered and autonomous institution is the only one that *performs*. Performance requires clear focus and narrow concentration. Multipurpose institutions do not perform. The achievements of the last 150 years in every single area are achievements of narrow focus, narrow concentration, and parochial self-centered values. All performing institutions of modern society are specialized. All of them are concerned only with their own task. The hospital exists to cure sick people. The fire department exists to prevent and to extinguish fires. The business enterprise exists to satisfy economic wants. The great advances in public health have largely been the result of freestanding organizations that focus on one disease or on one part of the human body and disregard everything else (consider the American Cancer Society, the American Heart Association, the American Lung Society, the American Mental Health Society, and so on).

Whenever an institution goes beyond a narrow focus, it ceases to perform. Hospitals that tried to go beyond sickness care into "health education" and "illness prevention" have been miserable failures. There are many reasons why the American public school is in trouble. But surely the one reason that stands out is that we have, of necessity, tried to make the school the agent of social and racial reform and social and racial integration. Schools in all other countries, including countries that have serious social problems of their own (for example, France, with its large immigrant population), have stuck to the single goal of teaching children to read. And they are still successful in this single endeavor. One may argue (as I have) that the present concentration on "creating shareholder value" as the sole mission of the publicly owned business enterprise is too narrow and in fact may be self-defeating. But it has resulted in an improvement in these enterprises' financial performance beyond anything an earlier generation would have thought possible—and way beyond what the same enterprises produced when they tried to satisfy multiple objectives, that is, when they were being run (as I have to admit I advocated for many years) in the "best balanced interests" of all the stakeholders, that is, shareholders, employees, customers, plant communities, and so on.

A striking social phenomenon of the last thirty years in the United States, the explosive growth of the new "mega-churches" (now beginning to be emulated in Europe), rests on these institutions' dedication to a single purpose: the spiritual development of the parishioners. The decline of their predecessors, the liberal Protestant churches of the early years of the twentieth century, can largely be traced to their trying to accomplish too many things at the same time—above all, in their trying to be organs of social reform as well as spiritual leaders.

The strength of the modern pluralist organization is that it is a single-purpose institution. And that strength has to be maintained. But at the same time the community has to be maintained—and in many cases it has to be rebuilt.

How to balance the two, the *common good* and the special purpose of the institution, is the question we must answer. If we cannot accomplish this integration, the new pluralism will surely destroy itself, the way the old pluralism did five hundred years ago. It will destroy itself because it will destroy community. But if at the same time institutions abandon their single purpose or even allow that purpose to weaken, the new pluralism will destroy itself through lack of performance.

Leadership Beyond the Walls

We know that this integration can be achieved. In fact there are already a good many success stories. What is needed is for leaders of *all* institutions to take leadership responsibility beyond the walls. They have to lead their own institutions and lead them to performance. This requires single-minded concentration on the part of the institution. But at the same time the members of the institution—and not just the people at the top—have to take community responsibility beyond the walls of their own institution.

There is a *financial* dimension to this integration: the financial support of autonomous community organizations by both government and business. There is a *performance* dimension to it: the organization of partnerships for common tasks among various types of institutions. There is a *personal* dimension to it: work as volunteers in community organizations by the people of institutions; development of second careers by successful people who in middle age switch from, for example, being division controller in a big company to being controller in a nonprofit hospital; and development of parallel careers by people who in the second halves of their lives take on a major task and a major assignment outside while keeping on with their original work.

But above all there is need for a *different mind-set*. There is need for the acceptance of leaders in every single institution and in every single sector that they, as leaders, have *two responsibilities*. They are responsible and accountable for the performance of their institutions, and that requires them and their institutions to be concentrated, focused, limited. They are responsible also, however, for the community as a whole. This requires commitment. It requires willingness to accept that other institutions have different values, respect for these values, and willingness to learn what these values are. It requires hard work. But above all it requires commitment, conviction, dedication to the common good. Yes, each institution is autonomous and has to do its own work the way each instrument in an orchestra plays only its own part. But there is also the *score*, the community. And only if each individual instrument contributes to the score is there music. Otherwise there is only noise.

And this book is about the score.

2 JIM COLLINS

AND THE WALLS CAME TUMBLING DOWN

Jim Collins is coauthor (with Jerry I. Porras) of Built to Last, *a* Business Week *best-seller for more than four years. In his management research and teaching laboratory in Boulder, Colorado, he is conducting a multiyear project that will be the foundation for his next book. Previously, he taught at the Stanford University Graduate School of Business, where he received the Distinguished Teaching Award.*

A few years ago, while staying at a Marriott hotel in Houston, I walked by a large conference room rollicking with noise—hoopla, yelling, almost a revival session. Curious, I peered through the door and witnessed a congregation of women, all wearing pink, putting forth testimonials about how their relationship with their company had changed the way they lived, giving them confidence, responsibility, self-direction, and control over their lives. I had dropped into a Mary Kay meeting. Say what you will about the pink Cadillacs and unusual culture of Mary Kay, you cannot deny the company's success. And the more I learned, the more impressed I became with the degree of commitment and energy these people displayed. Then a remarkable fact dawned on me: none of the people in that room had jobs with Mary Kay. They had a contractual relationship with the company, and the opportunity to do well within the boundaries of the contract, but they didn't have a job. They had no stable salary, no office to go into every day, none of the traditional mechanisms that would make them "part" of the company. And yet they displayed tremendous commitment and every sense of being part of Mary Kay. Mary Kay has created a remarkable blend of tight psychological attachment and extreme operating autonomy, in which the organization and its people connect in the spirit of partnership and freedom, not ownership and control.

I start with this story because it foreshadows the organization of the future, one in which the walls that have traditionally defined organizational boundaries—what you own, what you control, whom you employ, where they work—will cease to have any significant meaning. Instead, the defining boundary will be a permeable membrane defined by values, purpose, and goals; organizations will be held together by mechanisms of connection and commitment rooted in freedom of choice, rather than by systems of coercion and control. Executives will need to accept the fact—always true but now impossible to ignore—that the exercise of leadership is inversely proportional to the exercise of power. Indeed, they will need to accept the fact that the whole idea of walls is becoming an unproductive concept and that the most highly productive relationships are all, at their core, mutual partnerships. I elaborate on these points in this chapter, looking at them from the point of view of four shifts executives need to make in order to be effective in the next century.

First, executives must define the inside *and the* outside *of the organization by reference to core values and purpose, not by traditional boundaries.*

Every great organization is characterized by dual actions: preserve the core and stimulate progress. On the one hand it is guided by a set of core values and fundamental purpose—which change little or not at all over time—and on the other hand it stimulates progress—change, improvement, innovation, renewal—in all that is not part of the core values and purpose. Core values and core purpose in enduring great organizations remain fixed while their operating practices, cultural norms, strategies, tactics, processes, structures, and methods continually change in response to changing realities. Indeed, the great paradox of change is that the organizations that best adapt to a changing world first and foremost know what should *not* change; they have a fixed anchor of guiding principles around which they can more easily change everything else. They know the difference between what is sacred and what is not, between what should never change and what should be always open for change, between "what we stand for" and "how we do things." The best universities understand, for example, that the core value of freedom of inquiry must remain intact as a guiding precept while the operating practice of tenure goes through inevitable change and revision. The most enduring churches understand that the fundamental values and purpose of the religion must remain fixed while the specific practices and venues of worship change in response to the realities of younger generations. Core values and purpose provide the glue that holds an organization together as it expands, decentralizes, globalizes, and attains diversity. Think of them as analogous to the principles of Judaism that held the Jewish people together for centuries without a homeland, even as they scattered during the Diaspora. Or think of them as analogous to the truths held to be self-evident in the U.S. Declaration of Independence or the enduring ideals of the scientific community that bond scientists from every nationality together through the common aim of advancing knowledge (for a more detailed discussion of this concept, see J. C. Collins and J. I. Porras, *Built to Last*, 1994, and "Building Your Company's Vision," *Harvard Business Review*, Sept.–Oct. 1996).

Core values and purpose define the eternal character of a great organization, the character that endures beyond the presence of any set of people or individual leaders. In the long run, individual leaders do not hold an organization together; core values and purpose do. In the best organizations, leaders are subservient to the core principles, not the other way around. Furthermore, an individual's *membership* in the organization is ultimately defined by shared core values and common purpose, establishing a form of connection that often endures beyond that individual's formal activities with the organization. Consider the U.S. Marine Corps. It is a tightly aligned, high-performance organization, and yet it has a highly permeable membrane of membership. Those who survive boot camp forever carry the core values of being a Marine, remaining connected to the family of Marines by the fundamental principle that "Marines take care of Marines." Marines almost never say, "I was a Marine." They say for the rest of their lives, "I *am* a Marine." I know of a prosperous businessman who took special interest in the plight of a homeless man for the simple reason that they had both served in the Marine Corps decades before. They had not served in the same unit; they were not of the same generation; they had never even met. And yet once a Marine, always a Marine, and Marines take care of Marines. That is a lifetime connection that transcends an individual's active participation as an enlisted soldier.

As we move into the next century, core values and purpose as a defining boundary will become even more important. Given the obvious trends in organizations—greater decentralization and autonomy, wider geographical dispersion, increased diversity, more knowledge workers, technology and travel that make going into the office a less relevant activity—the bonding glue that holds organizations together will increasingly be in the form of shared values and common purpose. No matter how much the world and its organizing structures change, people still have a fundamental need to belong to something they can feel proud of. They have a fundamental need for guiding values and a sense of purpose that give their lives and work meaning. They have a fundamental need for connection to other people, sharing with them beliefs and aspirations to form a common bond. More than at any time in the past, people will demand operating autonomy—freedom plus responsibility—and will simultaneously demand that the organizations they are part of *stand* for something.

Second, executives must build mechanisms of connection and commitment rooted in freedom of choice, rather than relying on systems of coercion and control.

Of course you can't just establish shared values and common purpose and then expect everything to hold together; you also need tangible mechanisms that foster the commitment required to produce results. However, unlike the systems of the past, these mechanisms will increasingly rely on commitments freely made and will grant wide operating autonomy, rather than relying on coercion and control.

Allow me to use my research laboratory as an example. My large-scale research projects require the contributions of highly dedicated and talented research assistants. The research teams, usually four to six people, operate in a high-performance, high-energy climate characterized by a powerful sense of team unity and work ethic. During the summer session, team members frequently work more than forty hours per week, putting forth whatever it takes to accomplish objectives on time with thoroughness, accuracy, and quality. They generally feel that they've produced some of the best—if not the best—work of their lives while working on these teams.

And yet this high-performance environment relies almost not at all on the traditional methods of coercion and control. We have no offices or fixed hours; researchers attend team meetings, but otherwise they work on their own, managing their own time. If they want to work intensely for three days a week and take four-day weekends, fine; if they want to work from midnight to 6 A.M., fine; so long as they meet their commitments, they are completely free to arrange their own time. They have no budget constraints; if they need something to get their work done, they simply buy it and get reimbursed. They're not coerced by the carrot of a career path or long-term employment, as the lab operates under a strict "no permanent full-time employees" model. There is no direct impact on assistants' graduate study requirements (for example, no threat of grades), as the lab operates as an independent entity in an informal joint venture with the University of Colorado. And money is not a controlling factor; although they're paid better than other graduate research assistants, they earn less per hour than they would if they spent their summer at a corporation or consulting firm.

The whole key to the high-performance climate on the research team is our use of mechanisms of commitment and connection rooted in freedom of choice. We operate off a clear set of deadlines and project objectives, yet team members generally select their own deadlines, as people feel much more committed to a deadline that they have had a hand in setting. We break the research projects into discrete chunks and then have a *draft* in which individuals bid for the pieces they would most like to work on, a process that creates much greater commitment than preassigned responsibilities. We have weekly gatherings at the lab in which team members interact with each other, and we assess overall progress and discuss emerging ideas; the meetings serve as a glue, bonding the team members together. Most important, we design the work process so that team members must draw from each other's work as the project progresses. This creates more commitment to perform than anything I could say, as no team member wants to let his or her comrades down or look inadequate relative to peers. When team members request to miss a key team meeting, they do not ask me for permission; rather, they must personally call each team member and get his or her consent, thereby delegating the power of consent to the team. And as a precursor to all our mechanisms of commitment and connection, each person invited to join the team receives a written and verbal orientation on team values, purpose, and performance standards and is asked to join *only* if he or she can commit to those principles.

Before joining, each person is told, "If you have any doubt about whether this is the right place for you, then it is in our mutual interest that you decline this opportunity."

The commitment plus freedom model requires heavy up-front investment in selecting the right people. It does not try to mold people to be what they are not. People often ask, "How do we get individuals to share our core values?" The answer is, "You can't." You can't open somebody up and install new core values in his or her belly. The key is to find, attract, and select people who have a *predisposition* to sharing the core values, and to create an environment that consistently reinforces those core values, buttressing it with mechanisms of connection and commitment. If you select the right people in the first place—and they select your organization—then you don't need to control them. They don't need fixed hours. They don't need to come into offices where they can be watched. They don't need rules. You need to guide them; you need to teach them; you need to provide direction; you need clear objectives; you need mutually agreed deadlines; you need mechanisms of commitment and connection. But you don't need control. Most organizations underinvest in the selection process, and then try to correct for bad choices through control and overmanagement. If you select the right people, you don't need to mold them. Indeed, the moment you feel the need to control and mold someone, you've made a selection mistake.

Third, executives must accept the fact that the exercise of true leadership is inversely proportional to the exercise of power.

The best and most innovative work comes only from true commitments freely made between people in a spirit of partnership, not from bosses telling people what to do. Leadership cannot be assigned or bestowed by power or structure; *you are a leader if and only if people follow your leadership when they have the freedom not to.* I've always been impressed with the mechanisms that W. L. Gore & Associates, Inc., has put in place to create a climate of leadership.

Gore uses the twin mechanisms of *lattice structure* and *natural leadership,* which give every individual the freedom to establish working relationships with any other individuals without regard to any chain of command. In addition, any individual can by self-initiative assume leadership for an objective, again without regard to any hierarchy, so long as others freely commit to follow. To facilitate this flexibility, no one at Gore has a formal title; there are no vice presidents, no directors, no chief this or chief that; *everyone* has the simple title *associate.* The beauty of these mechanisms is that they allow those with true leadership potential to quickly rise to positions of responsibility. Conversely, those without leadership skill will quickly be rendered impotent as associates simply bypass them and align around those who can lead. In effect these mechanisms allow groups of associates to fire their boss.

If you're uncomfortable with the idea of vesting people with the power to fire their boss, then you're not ready for the task of leadership in the next century. As people become increasingly comfortable with ambiguity, they will increasingly trade the single-job model for a multiclient model, thus granting to any single organization or leader less power over their lives and livelihood. All those people who lost their jobs at IBM in the 1990s, for example, suddenly came to understand that low ambiguity (a single job) comes at the price of high risk (all eggs in one basket). You can already see this change to the lower-risk, multiclient model happening as older executives bemoan the "lack of loyalty" in the younger generation. And yet there is no less loyalty in the younger generation. They are simply granting less power to any single organization; they are less subservient because they have more degrees of freedom. And the moaning executives are simply confusing subservience to power with loyalty to cause. But they are very different concepts indeed, and executives will need to cultivate the latter and relinquish dependence on the former in order to be effective. Eventually we will look back at single-job employment structures as a somewhat barbaric form of organization, much the way we view indentured servitude today. We will increasingly see a shift away from ownership of people in any form, including the traditional job, which is nothing other than an advanced form of owning people by owning their time. In the future every relationship, at least in the best organizations, will be viewed conceptually as a joint venture.

Fourth, executives must embrace the reality that traditional walls are dissolving and that this trend will accelerate.

We are moving toward a world in which the concept that walls are necessary is becoming archaic and is no longer useful. The most progressive corporations have jettisoned the idea that they can exist in a walled-off cocoon of private activity. The customer revolution, for example, reflects a dissolution of the walls companies once tried to construct between customers and themselves. One leading company, Granite Rock, has taken this change so far as to extend to its customers the power to decide for themselves whether and how much to deduct from an invoice if they feel dissatisfied. Granite Rock customers work in partnership with Granite Rock people toward the mutual goal of continually improved Granite Rock products that benefit both customer and company. The quality revolution is also about dissolving artificial walls. For instance, a central tenet of any good-quality effort is that suppliers and producers will operate in partnership to create a better end result.

All around us we can see signs of tumbling walls. Technology allows us to access Harvard lectures without being admitted inside the exclusive gates of the Harvard student body. The Internet allows us to share databases directly with colleagues at organizations around the world, without being on the staff of those organizations. And the dissolution of walls is not limited to the work world but is occurring in all aspects of life and society. The walls around the traditional family are dissolving. It's not uncommon, due to divorce and complex family histories, for an adult to be parenting children with whom he or she has no genetic link or to be mentoring genetic offspring who live in someone else's household. This may not be ideal, but it is a fact of modern life. At the national level the scale and impact of manmade systems, both economic and technical, are making national boundaries less relevant. A German academic colleague has told me that the most psychologically significant event for the German people in the past decade was not the tearing down of the Berlin Wall but the failure of the Chernobyl nuclear reactor, which made it clear that the problems and disasters of one nation cannot be contained within that nation's legal boundaries. Racial walls, although still visible and oppressive where they exist, have become less concrete. Political leaders in the both the southern United States and the nation of South Africa have no choice but to learn to be effective across racial lines, else they have no hope of holding major political office.

In part we are simply seeing a fulfillment of the promise of the Enlightenment, particularly in the tradition of John Locke, which sought to dissolve the walls between sovereign and subject and emphasize the rights and dignity of the individual. But what is happening today is more than a philosophical shift. It is also a reflection of a practical fact: the most productive relationships are in their essence mutual partnerships rooted in a freedom of choice vested in both parties to participate only in that which is mutually beneficial and uplifting. Moreover, the social systems best suited in the long run to meeting the material and spiritual needs of the majority of people tend to distribute, rather than concentrate, power. Unless we see a resurgence of tyranny (always a threat, as dictatorship is a highly efficient form of organization), there is every reason to believe that this trend will continue, and accelerate.

3

C. K. PRAHALAD

PREPARING FOR LEADERSHIP

C. K. Prahalad, Harvey C. Fruehauf Professor of Business Administration at the University of Michigan Business School, Ann Arbor, is a specialist in corporate strategy and the author of The Multinational Mission *(with Yves Doz, 1987) and* Competing for the Future *(with Gary Hamel, 1994). He has been named one of the top business professors in the country by both* Business Week *and the* Wall Street Journal.

I n the new millennium, managers are likely to live and work in a new competitive environment characterized by the coexistence of intense global competition and increased global opportunities. Emerging geographical markets, such as China, Brazil, and India, will change the competitive landscape. Simultaneously, digital convergence will create new businesses. No firm will have the resources or the skill base to compete in this emerging marketplace as a stand-alone entity. A wide variety of collaborative arrangements will be necessary. Firms will have to collaborate with other firms and governments to *create value* (wealth). Simultaneously, they will compete with each other to *extract value*. Collaboration and competition, rapid change and volatility, pressure for innovation and efficiency, demand for global and local capability will be the norm. What kind of leadership will this competitive milieu demand? How prepared are we?

Although there is a wide variety of literature on globalized companies, alliances, and networked corporations, comparatively little attention has been focused on the nature of leadership in all these organizations, especially on the *personal qualities of leadership*. In this chapter I propose to outline some of the personal traits of leaders in the new millennium.

The Emerging Competitive Landscape

Leaders are partly creatures of the environment in which they find themselves. However, they also fundamentally reshape that environment. A discussion of the role of leaders in the new millennium must therefore start with a perspective on the nature of the competitive environment.

First, the emergence of global competition during the late 1970s and early 1980s in a wide variety of industries, such as textiles, shipbuilding, consumer electronics, semiconductors, and automobiles, created a new pressure for efficiency because firms now had to transcend *local* standards. For example, Ford could not derive satisfaction by comparing itself with General Motors; it had to compare itself with Toyota. A *global* standard for efficiency—be it in quality, cost, or cycle time—became a critical ingredient for sustaining competitiveness. Corporate initiatives such as downsizing, reengineering, improving quality, and reducing cycle time resulted. Firms searched for new levels of efficiency but within the existing business model. The basic business model, for example, in the auto industry, did not change. I see *no letup in the pressure for improvements in cost, quality, cycle time, and price-performance*.

Second, deregulation of industries and privatization of firms around the world is creating a different demand on management.

The focus here is changing the business models. Business models that developed under regulatory regimes and that allowed protection from competition, privileged access to customers, low to no cost pressure, and passive customers are incapable of coping with the demands of an open and competitive marketplace. Deregulation destroys local monopolies. It often results in excess capacity. Significant merger and acquisition activity results. We see this already in telecommunications, utilities (including water), airport management, and defense. In these industries, managers have to *change business models*, moving from one applicable to markets with restricted or no competition to one that can function in open and global markets.

Third, the convergence of computing, communications, consumer electronics, and entertainment is creating a new set of competitive demands. This blurring of industry boundaries results in patterns of competition that can best be characterized as *new games with new rules*. For example, collaboration among current and potential competitors is required to establish industry standards, to shape expectations of consumers, and to seek appropriate regulatory frameworks. Various competitors would like to shape the new industry boundaries to suit their resource endowments. As a result, competition is as much concerned with the migration patterns of clusters of firms (for example, TV companies moving to PC technologies or PC firms moving to a focus on TV) as it is with the strategies of individual firms.

Fourth, the new age of information is likely to create new and untold opportunities as well as to destroy many of the old ways of competing. For example, the Internet will create new modes of economic transactions resulting in new opportunities. Breakthroughs in biotechnology may change the practice of medicine. These breakthroughs drive an *evolving game with evolving rules of competition*.

The effects of the four competitive forces I have just outlined are often commingled. Collectively, these forces will generate an enhanced demand for leaders. However, it is unlikely that all managers will fit the needs of leadership in the new millennium. The emerging competitive landscape is likely to break the managerial ranks within established firms down into cautious administrators, managers, and leaders. Needless to say, there will be a real shortage of leaders.

The Underlying Demands on Leadership

Although the specific future needs and functions of a firm or an industry can be difficult to predict, the broad dimensions of the leadership task in the new millennium are not. First, leaders will have to *cope with the imperatives of being global*. They will have to cope with multiple locations, multiple perspectives, and multiple cultures. Second, as no firm will have the resources to meet the total demands imposed on it, leaders will be forced to *work within a wide variety of collaborative arrangements*. They will need to learn and share information with others as they simultaneously protect their proprietary knowledge. The question they will have to answer is, How do we as an organization become open to learning and at the same time opaque enough to protect our intellectual property? Third, organizations, and thus leaders, will need to *respond with speed*. Leaders have tended to associate speed with easily measured phenomena such as inventory turns or product development cycle time. They now need to associate speed with the rate at which new knowledge is created, codified, and deployed within the organization. Finally, leaders will have to continually *reinvent their businesses* as markets evolve and as competitors become different and more numerous.

The Determinants of Leadership in the New Millennium

We can look at leadership requirements in two categories: the staples of leadership that cut across all industries and are generic and the context-specific requirements of leadership, that is, the needs of specific positions and industries. I believe that both are important.

Generic Capabilities

The changing, evolving, and new games of competition force leaders to confront an extraordinary range of ambiguities and uncertainties. For example, the role of biotechnology breakthroughs in food production, processing, preservation, and healthfulness represents a major discontinuity. In addition to technical uncertainties this sector will be plagued by regulatory and ethical concerns. No single firm or group of firms can manage this evolving competitive game. The focus of debate can change radically and rapidly. Leaders must be sensitive to this evolution and at the same time provide strategic direction. They must *cope with ambiguities*.

The source of competitive advantage is an evolving phenomenon. Traditionally, organizations saw their strategic choices in terms of quality versus low cost and low cost versus differentiation. Global versus local is one of the current debates. Increasingly, however, we know that high quality, low cost, time compression, differentiation, and resource conservation are all compatible. In fact they are an integral part of a high-performance management process. Leaders must first mentally *reconcile the coexistence of apparent opposites*. Then they must *convince the people of the organization to accept this coexistence and build systems capable of delivering on all these dimensions*.

As globalization affects the way firms are managed, leaders must *have the ability to be not just interpersonally competent but also interculturally competent*. It is conceivable that about 40 to 50 percent of the total market for many firms such as Motorola, Hewlett-Packard, Asea Brown Boveri (ABB), or Cargill may be in the developing markets of China, India, Indonesia, and Brazil. The pervasive influence of such globalization of business forces leaders to be sensitive to such intercultural questions as: What are the values that are nonnegotiable in a global company? How and how much should a global company allow local business practices?

Development effort as well as investments will flow into emerging markets. The composition of senior leadership teams in the global firm of 2010 may be very different from that of today's teams, with significant numbers of non–Anglo-Saxon and non-European managers. Managing in such an environment will also call for intercultural sensitivity.

Increasingly, convergence of technologies—such as we are seeing in PC-TV (for example, Sony), cosmetics and pharmaceuticals (for example, Revlon), chemicals and electronics (for example, Eastman Kodak), and food and pharmaceuticals (for example, Unilever)—will demand that leaders understand the different intellectual traditions of the technologies being bonded together. This implies that in addition to intercultural issues, leaders will have to cope with a diversity of intellectual traditions. In short, managing diversity will be a major challenge, and it has many dimensions. In addition to age, race, and gender, leaders will *confront cultural and intellectual diversity.*

Leaders will continue to need the staples of leadership all during our recorded history. Personal integrity will continue to be a key ingredient of leadership. We look to leaders to have a higher standard of personal integrity than other people, and we value it as well. A *sense of "selflessness"* is critical to leadership. Leaders are imbued with a mission bigger than themselves, bigger than any one individual. They are out to change the status quo. It is difficult to ask for sacrifices, loyalty, and dedication when the goal is not worthy or when the leader is seen to be seeking the goal for personal glory. Leaders will *have to be accountable* for their performance. Given the extreme volatility of the marketplace and of the fortunes of firms (for example, the success of Netscape in 1996 and its difficulties in 1998 or the former success of Motorola and its current difficulties) all leaders will need to *exhibit a sense of humility in success and courage in failure.*

Context-Specific Capabilities

All leaders in business need to cultivate these generic skills. However, these skills are not enough. *Great* leaders also have context-specific capabilities.

As a result of major discontinuities in industry structures, new knowledge is becoming a key to providing direction to a firm and to navigating it through an evolving and indeterminate industry setting. This is like navigating through fog. Further, industries are becoming technologically sophisticated, and a deep knowledge of the evolving technological landscape is critical for providing a sense of direction. Seeing beyond the mountain and leading the troops there needs intuition, but a sense of what exists beyond the mountain is critical as well. *A point of view about the future based on substantive knowledge* is a fundamental requirement for leaders in the new millennium. All leaders will be required to forget some of the old ways of competing and to invent new ones. Therefore, the components of substantive knowledge will have to include forgetting as well as learning.

Creating the future requires that leaders have the ability to selectively co-opt others to support their points of view, to facilitate the setting of industry standards, and to participate in shaping the expectations of consumers. This means that leaders must *become an integral part of the evolving network of firms.* For example, the entertainment industry—movies, television, and video games—may prove to be the pacing industry for the development of the next round of computer graphics. Does this mean that the leaders of Intel or Silicon Graphics must forge relationships with Disney, Nintendo, and Sony? The answer may be yes. Increasingly, understanding the network of relationships required to create the future and becoming involved in it is a critical aspect of leadership.

Finally, leaders must understand that the exercise of authority is context specific. Authority has at least three dimensions: administrative (or positional), charismatic (or individual), and intellectual. In an established firm, administrative positions are identified with leadership. Often the leadership team is the senior management team. In emerging industries undergoing rapid change, hierarchical positions do not necessarily equate with the ability to exercise authority. Often, intellectual authority is respected and can override administrative authority. In each industry context the mix of intellectual, charismatic, and positional authority can vary. Leaders must be sensitive to this contextual influence.

Conclusion

The challenge of developing leaders for the new millennium is upon us now. The complexities of the competitive environment demand leaders and not cautious administrators. The function of management must focus on people who are willing to take responsibility for accomplishing complex tasks and who exhibit intellectual and emotional strength. Leaders have to inspire others and expect to receive others' best efforts always.

LEADING THE DISTRIBUTED ORGANIZATION

William Bridges is a management consultant who helps organizations deal with change, particularly its human side. He is also the author of Transitions, Managing Transition, JobShift, *and* Creating You & Co. *The* Wall Street Journal *has named him among the ten top independent U.S. executive development specialists. Prior to 1974, he was the Aurelia Henry Reinhardt Professor of American Literature at Mills College in Oakland, California.*

B eing a leader today is challenging in all sorts of ways. Leading followers who have been confused and frightened by unexpected changes is no picnic. Yesterday's strategies are out-of-date before they get a fair test. Government regulations, even when they are meant to help business, represent new hoops for you to jump through. Then there's turnover . . . and the tight labor market . . . and the fallout from the Asian crisis. Oh, yes, and then there's the prospect that your computers will melt down on January 1, 2000.

But the biggest challenge isn't even on that list. It is the new way in which organizations—or at least many of today's most successful organizations—get their work done. Their strategies challenge the very idea that a leader has followers in the traditional sense, because followers used to be employees, people whose livelihood depended on employment. And employment was normally full-time, long-term employment. But today most innovative organizations are rethinking who should do their work, and a steadily growing number of them are turning that work over to people who aren't employees but who work for other companies or for themselves.

The Distribution of Work

These new-style companies distribute work across the borders that used to separate "us" from "them." And in so doing they challenge the customary idea of where the leader's organization starts and stops. Look at Dell Computer. It has fifteen thousand employees, but the volume of product it sells would require eighty thousand workers if all of them were employed in-house. The common view is that Dell *outsources* 80 percent of its work, but Michael Dell denies that the term fits: "Outsourcing . . . is almost always a way to get rid of a problem a company hasn't been able to solve itself. The classic case is the company with 2,000 people in the IT department. Nobody knows what they do, and nobody knows why they do it. The solution—outsource IT to a service provider, and hopefully they'll fix it. . . . That's not what we're doing at all. We focus on how we can coordinate our activities to create the most value for customers" (Joan Magretta, "The Power of Vertical Integration," *Harvard Business Review*, Mar.–Apr. 1998).

Dell isn't just quibbling over definitions here. For what his company is doing is to systematically and strategically distribute its work to workers outside its borders who technically belong to an altogether different organization—and, theoretically, follow another leader. But the situation is more complicated even than that, for it isn't just that Dell Computer distributes its work elsewhere. Dell's clients do too—and in so doing they include Dell workers inside their boundaries.

Who is today's leader leading? He or she leads employees and others—at Dell, many others. On the one hand, of the ten thousand technicians that service Dell products in the field only a very small number are actually Dell employees. On the other hand, thirty Dell employees don't see the inside of their home organization because they work full-time at Dell's big client, Boeing. There, says Michael Dell, they "don't [function] like a supplier [but] more like Boeing's PC department. We become intimately involved in planning their PC needs and the configuration of their network." They are, he argues, the equivalent of a Boeing "IT department for PC's."

Dell isn't unique. Boeing, for example, uses the same principle in building its airliners, which have more component sources than a patchwork quilt. Wings made here, tail assembly there, and the motors way over there. And then there is Volkswagen. Its new Brazilian automobile assembly plant has hardly any VW employees because the whole operation is staffed by the employees of the supplier organizations, where the various components of the car are actually made. Hamilton Standard Corporation carries the VW principle even further in its role as the company that coordinates the efforts of the eighty subcontractors that make the parts of the $10.4 million space suits worn by U.S. astronauts on their space walks. The suit itself, incidentally, is assembled not by Hamilton but by the customer, NASA.

It's no wonder that Peter Schwartz, the former head of planning for Royal Dutch Shell, has said recently (Robert McGarvey, "Tomorrow Land," *Entrepreneur*, Feb. 1996):

> It's plausible to me that in 10 years we will not see today's multinationals but, rather, large "umbrella" organizations that act as hosts for many small companies that come together for brief periods to do short-term but big projects—for example, the production of a new car. But the umbrella organization may not be an enduring organization in the way, say, GM has been. The model is more like a movie studio, where the studio coordinates

a project but doesn't actually do it. The work is done by
many small contractors who come together for a project
that may last three years, from the time a movie is born
as an idea until its release.

This analogy suggests that the emerging leader may be more like
a studio head who selects projects to underwrite than like the traditional leader who actually heads up projects. Similarly, another
way to see the new leader is as the producer who orchestrates the
whole project but doesn't direct it.

The new circumstances leaders must face exist not only at the
level of the organization as a whole but within its component units.
For example, when Greg Garrison was asked to head up a product-
testing effort at Reuters, he was given only two employees and told
to draw the remaining talent for his *sustainability team* from outside
firms. By the time he finished, he had used eighty outsiders from six
different organizations. Garrison's leadership involved building an
integrated team out of people with different organizational identities. "We went from a Microsoft team, an Admiral team, and a
Reuters team," he wrote later in "Profiting from Flexible Working"
(*Human Resources*, Sept.–Oct. 1995, p. 42), "to a team with Neil
Walker, Ian Clowes, and Wendy Aldred. The chemistry of the people joining together broke down the barriers, and we became our
own entity. . . . Over time, we ended up with consultants that identified with the sustainability team more than with Reuters or their
[original] consultancies."

Garrison's account suggests one outcome of such work distribution: the resulting entity is an entirely new one; it doesn't see itself as
just the-company-plus-vendors. The new leader is going to have to
be comfortable with that outcome and have the skill to produce it.

Taken to its extreme, distributing work creates a virtual organization. Consider the operations at Monorail, a new but rapidly
growing personal computer maker that is currently the fourteenth
largest shipper of computers in the United States. A retailer, say a

CompUSA outlet, orders a machine, transmitting the order electronically through FedEx logistics services, which routes it to one of Monorail's many contract manufacturers. The manufacturer assembles the PC from an inventory of Monorail parts and ships it directly to the appropriate CompUSA outlet, again by FedEx. The entire process takes between two and four business days. Meanwhile, FedEx wires an invoice to SunTrust Bank in Atlanta, whose factoring department handles Monorail's billing and its credit approvals. Monorail quickly receives a cash payment from SunTrust (at a discount from the face value of the invoice), and the bank assumes the risk of collecting the funds from CompUSA. Customers who need help call Monorail's phone-in service center—which is staffed and run by Sykes Enterprises Inc., a call center outsourcing company based in Tampa, Florida. Customers who want to upgrade their hardware simply call a toll-free number. FedEx picks up the computer the next day, delivers it to an upgrade center, and returns it to the customer—all within four days (Heath Row, "This Virtual Company Is for Real," *Fast Company*, Dec. 1997–Jan. 1998, p. 50).

There are all sorts of pitfalls in the path of doing business in this way, and leaders need to learn to spot and avoid them. But it is undeniable that such operations produce stupendous results. Monorail is in fact so successful that it is growing 50 percent a quarter (yes, a quarter!). And incidentally, as of the beginning of 1998, it did all its work with only fifty employees. Talk about low overhead!

Forces Affecting Organizations

The distribution of work and the consequent migration of work across what used to be considered fixed organizational boundaries are the logical outcomes of a cluster of forces affecting organizations everywhere.

1. Organizations face huge pressure to improve financial results, particularly as these results are defined by shareholders and the investment professionals who advise them. Over the past several

decades other yardsticks for measuring organizational success have lost ground to the narrowly financial measures of shareholder value. In this environment organizations are choosing low-cost solutions even when these solutions create new problems. The leader of today cannot overlook the challenge of competitors who achieve huge profits by distributing work. (Dell, incidentally, ranks first among all U.S. corporations in total shareholder return from 1995 to 1997 and second in total performance for 1997.)

2. The popularity (driven by the need to improve financial results) of activity-based accounting, decentralized profit and loss, and economic value added (EVA) as a measurement of success has grown. All these measures make the effectiveness and the real price of different organizational forms and relationships more transparent and make it harder to resist the call to abandon strategies and arrangements that increase costs without adding value.

3. The rapidly changing markets in which today's organizations operate make variable costs preferable to fixed costs, no matter how valuable the results of those fixed costs may have been in the past. Distributed work is contract work, so it can be discontinued if conditions change. Further, it does not tie an organization to a level of employment that it may not be able to sustain if its business climate changes.

4. The pace of change and the competition between producers has shortened the cycle time during which organizations can secure a profit from the goods and services they provide. This cycle is being further shortened by the ease with which modern technologists can *reverse engineer* another firm's innovative offering and duplicate it. As this window of opportunity narrows, firms can benefit from not taking the time to do everything themselves.

5. The same technological sophistication that permits reverse engineering allows companies to integrate projects across space and time. Just as it is no longer necessary to bring workers together in huge factories to get the work done, it is no longer necessary to pull

work together inside a single organization. The supply chain planning software produced by i2 and the Manugistics Group, for example, permits Cummings Engine's Jamestown, New York, diesel plant to assemble engines 30 percent faster than before and Dell to cut inventory turnover from three weeks to one week. The old argument was that integrated operations cost less because they avoided the so-called transaction costs of doing business across organizational borders, but electronic invoicing, electronic data interchange, and on-line banking have changed the equation.

6. The repeated downsizings of large organizations have resulted in clusters of independent workers of great skill and experience, and the tendency of these groups to seek a market niche where they can best use their skills has led to the proliferation of specialized suppliers of goods and services. An organization seeking to distribute its work has options today that it never had before.

7. A whole new style of partnership is being practiced by companies in response to the environmental forces just described. In fact the very concept of partnership has moved from the wings to the center of the stage in management writing, which is focusing on not only the partnership between allies in joint ventures but the in-house partnership between operations and support services and between organizations and their suppliers. Lew Miller, who manages Westinghouse's $640 million radar contract with Boeing, describes the present style of operation as one in which his people feel "like part of the team," whereas in the old system they were just "given a specification and monitored" (Evan Ramstad, "Firms Boost Suppliers' Speeds, Win Investors' Hearts," *Wall Street Journal*, Apr. 6, 1998, p. A20).

8. In some industries, like aerospace, the distribution of work to suppliers in another country greatly increases the likelihood that the big industrial purchasers in that country will buy the product. Asian countries, for example, have sometimes tied the purchase of airplanes by their airlines to the provision of jobs manufacturing parts for those planes.

9. In the drive for results and reduced costs many companies have tied the compensation for work done on a project to the results of the project. When Perot Systems took over Swiss Bank Corporation's computer operations, it agreed to be paid in part by a share of the money it saved. Needless to say, this kind of agreement binds so-called outside workers to the contracting organization much more closely than traditional fees for services did.

10. Finally, the rapid growth of companies in hot industries can be managed much more effectively when certain organizational functions are distributed. Michael Dell alluded to this result when he commented: "If we had to build our own factories for every single component of the system, growing at 57 percent per year just would not be possible. I would spend 500 percent of my time interviewing prospective vice presidents because the company would have not 15,000 employees but 80,000."

Once again, the leader who seeks to follow the path of distribution will encounter plenty of pitfalls, and I am not urging it as a route of choice for everyone. But I am saying that given the success of the Dells, the VWs, and the Monorails of the world, all companies are now playing in a much faster league than they were. And I am saying that most organizations are going to opt for some degree of distribution—the only question is how much? So leaders do need to understand both the promises and the problems of the distribution option.

Leaders' New Partnerships with Followers

The result of the movement of work is that yesterday's tightly integrated organization, which could be governed like an autonomous political entity, is today turning into a diverse constituency in which it is harder and harder to say who is inside the organization and who is outside. It is not just that today more and more organizations are getting their work done through joint ventures and formal alliances. It is that the relation a leader has to his or her followers is getting less and less like *governance* and more and more like *alliance* or *partnership*.

Today's leader requires a whole new way of thinking about delivering products and services. In fact the pressing *strategic* issue of the new organization is how to leverage the organization's resources to get the most out of them rather than what markets to enter and what products to launch. The latter, it can be argued, have become *tactical* issues.

As leaders work to achieve this leverage in a rapidly changing environment, their ability to form and reform partnerships is becoming absolutely critical. This partnering can take place within a company between temporary groupings of workers. It can take place between insiders and outsiders temporarily lodged inside the company to get a project done. It can take place between the company and its external suppliers. And it can take place between the company and its joint venture partners in projects that are too big or risky or complex to undertake alone.

A couple of examples will illustrate the new importance that executives are attaching to partnerships in many of their endeavors.

G. Kelly Martin, senior vice president and chief technology officer of Merrill Lynch's corporate and institutional client group, has remarked: "We're trying to integrate Macintosh security in Australia, we have an expansion plan in Brazil, we've got changes in the UK markets and in NASDAQ. I can't staff all these projects. . . . Software companies want to sell [me] software; I don't want to buy software. Technology companies are interested in inventing new products all the time . . . I [get] all these business cards of people saying 'I've got this product, that product, a new version of this.' I don't need products. I need partners that can help me solve my problems" (Seth Schiesel, "Bull's Eye: Strategic Partnerships Are Keeping Merrill Lynch at the Forefront of the Financial Services Industry," *Continental Magazine*, Apr. 1998, p. 44).

And Swiss Bank Corporation CFO Gene T. Martin has said of the success of the bank's arrangement with Perot Systems, "From the moment we began discussing the project, I felt I had a partner. The others seemed to be vendors selling their services" (Wendy

Zellner, "Gearing Up at Perot Systems," *Business Week*, Nov. 18, 1996, p. 178).

It goes without saying that an otherwise good executive may be very poor at partnering, so among the critical items on any leadership development agenda are the skills that partnering requires. The details of how executives can develop these skills must be the topic of another essay, but briefly, such development must address the following issues:

1. The habits of the commander do not serve the partner well. A partner must create a climate of mutual trust and respect—something that requires empathy for the other party, an understanding of the concerns and aspirations that the other party brings to the table. The focus on one's own purposes and goals must give way to a much more mutual outlook.

2. There must be an experience of equity and parity in the relationship. This does not mean that the parties must be equals in all tangible characteristics, just that they have equal rights to have their needs met and their values respected.

3. The roles and responsibilities of each party must be very clear from the beginning. A partnership in which these things cannot be worked out at the start is heading for trouble. The rule is no surprises. There will be enough that is unknown about any new venture without making assumptions about the rules part of the confusion.

4. Each party must expect not only to surrender some autonomy to the other in forming the partnership but also to grant to the partnership itself some autonomy. As Greg Garrison found with his Reuters project, it is the project itself to which people must develop their commitment. For that reason the partnered project must have the right to its own values, its own practices, its own spirit, and its own style.

5. Because the partnership is a whole new enterprise, it needs to be treated as a little start-up and allowed to build the internal systems and structure that it needs, including policies and reward

systems, communication practices, and all the other characteristics of a separate organization.

6. Finally, the managers within each partnered service or product area need to attend more to that area's interfaces with outside entities than to locales within the area. In the distributed organization, boundaries can proliferate, and how they are managed becomes critical to the success of each place where distributed work is being done.

Leadership During Transition

One last thought: the move from the traditional organization to the distributed organization involves very large changes, and change puts people into transition. In transition people go through three phases.

1. They let go of the old way of doing things and the old identities and assumptions that went with that way of doing. They are likely to experience this as a loss. And the people who were best adjusted to the old way will experience the biggest loss. Unless this loss is handled effectively, it will disrupt the whole organization.

2. Next, people go through the *neutral zone*, an in-between state where everything is up in the air and people feel they are lost. Leaders must also have a plan for managing this state, or else the organization will lose many of its good people and suffer a serious drop in productivity.

3. Finally, people must make a new beginning. You can bring in a new IT service on a particular day, but the building of a partnership will take months. People may say, yes, they understand what is being done on day one. But they will not get on board and feel comfortable with the new arrangements for months. Beginnings take time, and they occur only after phases 1 and 2 have taken place.

Getting people through the transition may prove to be the hardest part of any shift to distributed work and partnership—transition is usually more difficult than change—and it will not happen at all unless the organizational changes that I have been describing are managed well in the first place. And managing them well means managing them consciously. These aren't the kind of changes that just happen whether you understand them or not. Companies like Dell understand exactly what they are doing, and that is why they are so far ahead of the pack.

Indeed, many of Dell's less successful competitors are doing some of the same things Dell is: outsourcing, establishing joint ventures, managing the supply chain, creating virtual task forces. But they have no integrative plan based on a new organizational vision. Without such a vision they have no frame to give contextual meaning to the particulars. Without such meaning the initiatives are just a pile of changes. And as today's employees will tell you, they already have more piles of changes than they know what to do with.

5 SALLY HELGESEN

DISSOLVING BOUNDARIES IN THE ERA OF KNOWLEDGE AND CUSTOM WORK

Sally Helgesen is a consultant, best-selling author, and popular speaker whose studies of changing technology, demographics, and the economy have had a profound influence on how people work. The Wall Street Journal *named her book* The Web of Inclusion *one of the five best books on leadership of the 1990s, and her book* The Female Advantage *is considered "the classic work" on women's management styles.*

Organizations and institutions at the end of the second and the beginning of the third millennium are increasingly character-ized by a breakdown—a blurring—of clear boundaries. These include the boundaries that distinguish who is and who is not a part of a par-ticular organization; the boundaries that separate those who make decisions (executives, managers, generals) from those who simply execute them; the boundaries that differentiate a product from a ser-vice; the boundaries that define distinct disciplines in the academy; the boundaries that separate work and home, public and private, men and women. Only those who understand the phenomenon of dissolving boundaries and its implications for the future will be able to shape events as they unfold; only those comfortable in the zone beyond the walls will be able to assume leadership in the years ahead.

Why is this so? Why are so many barriers eroding at this particular time? And how is this phenomenon transforming the demands on leadership? To understand what is occurring, we need first to look at three of the major forces that are transforming our world at this millennial time, because the confluence of these forces is changing how we all live. I emphasize the notion of confluence here because each of these trends is influencing, and being influenced by, the others. It is above all the simultaneity of these changes and the myriad results of their interaction that is creating a shift of historic proportions.

Three Forces Breaking Down Boundaries

The first major change transforming our world is a social or demographic change: the inclusion of women in every arena of public life—business, legal, medical, educational, political, military, and religious. The number of women entering the public realm has grown steadily for over thirty years, and women have now begun to assume positions of real authority and influence in what were formerly male bastions. We have to some extent grown accustomed to this change, so it is easy to underestimate its impact. To do so would be a mistake, however, because the implications are both numerous and profound. *The Economist* recognized this at the start of the 1990s decade when it examined the major events of the twentieth century in terms of their potential impact on the twenty-first. The magazine looked at everything from World War II to the rise and fall of Communism to the invention of television. And its editors concluded that the single most significant event of the last hundred years, *in terms of its potential to affect the next century,* was the change in the status of women.

This change has been particularly instrumental in breaking down barriers and dissolving boundaries. Indeed, the rigid divide between work and home, public and private, that prevailed until recently was based upon the fundamental divide between men and women, a divide that assumed each gender belonged to and governed a different sphere. This divide is now being breached, not only because women continue to enter the workforce and exercise authority in all areas of public life, but because men are in consequence becoming more intimately and actively involved in the private world of domesticity. And so men and women have more in common than they did in the past in terms of the scope of their concerns and the shape of their days.

One fascinating, though little remarked upon, consequence of the spread of personal computers, which are now ubiquitous in the home as well as at work, is that they mark the first time in human history that men and women have shared the same primary tool of production. From the hunter-gatherer period to the agricultural era and through to the establishment of factory and then office life, men and women have been distinguished by their use of different tools. Sharing a primary tool now gives men and women a common language of work, the consequences of which will grow more clear as a younger generation whose members have used computers almost from babyhood enters the workforce and begins to assume power in public life. In addition, because personal computers serve as an instrument for bringing work into the home (and for enabling people to pursue private interests, from playing bridge to searching for a babysitter, at work), they further undermine the divide between domicile and workplace, returning us to the more integrated ways of living and working that characterized most of our human past.

At the same time that this social revolution is taking place, we are also undergoing a profound economic shift, moving from an industrial economy to an economy based on knowledge, an economy in which knowledge has a greater value than capital, equipment, natural resources, or land. Peter Drucker has observed that if knowledge is indeed the primary value in an organization, then it follows that workers—employees—must own the primary means of production, because the most valuable organizational asset resides inside their heads and is theirs to use or not use and to take away with them if they choose. This is why Drucker calls ours the "postcapitalist" era: those who hold and supply capital are no longer supreme. The markets, of course, acknowledge this primacy of knowledge: for example, they value Microsoft at far in excess of its revenues while they value General Motors, with its prodigious assembly plants, its chains of production, its massive holdings of land, at far less than its total revenues.

The most revolutionary aspect of the value our economy places on knowledge is that, in Drucker's succinct formulation, it begins *to reverse the balance of power between organizations and individuals*. The increasing importance of entrepreneurial ventures in the economy and the evolution of what has been called a *free agent nation* are expressions of this reversal, which is only in its early stages. As more value is vested in knowledge, organizations will find it ever more difficult to retain individuals whose personal goals are at odds with requirements that the organization believes serves its best interests. Inexorably, the balance of power will continue to shift, and organizations will be confronted with the need to work with individuals who no longer want generic career paths but paths customized to meet their needs.

The third major change that is transforming our world is the development of new technologies that are entirely reconfiguring how we do our work. The architecture of today's technology—flexible, organic, interactive—pushes information and thus power down to those on the front lines and thus facilitates and even demands direct communication. The very shape and structure of information technology serve to undermine hierarchical arrangements and to dissolve the rationale for rigid chains of command. We watched this vividly played out during Operation Desert Storm, when it became clear even to those merely watching events unfold on the television news that smart tanks, by integrating reconnaissance and operations, required troops on the ground to make strategic decisions. Something similar is happening in organizations of every variety, as new technologies empower those who formerly only executed tasks to formulate them as well, thus eroding industrial-era barriers between heads and hands.

Powerful and ever-cheaper technologies have also fueled the entrepreneurial boom, which is further exacerbating the shift of power from organizations to individuals by giving individuals ways to reach the marketplace directly and to create ways of working that are relatively independent of formal structures but more dependent than ever upon relationships. Women especially have benefited from and participated in the shift to self-employment and entrepreneurship that today's technology enables and today's emphasis on finding and satisfying ever more specific niche markets requires. With more choices than ever, women have been able to exert pressure on organizations to help them find more customized ways of working that allow them to balance work with domestic demands. And early evidence suggests that men of the next generation will be as eager as women of the present generation have been to find work that fits their lives, rather than fitting their lives around their work.

Results of the Confluence of Forces

The confluence of these major changes is creating a new frontier for organizations as we move into an era different from anything we have known. The emphasis on variety, diversity, options, and choice that we presently find in products and services will increasingly become a workforce issue, as skilled knowledge workers demand and create more customized paths. It makes no sense in the knowledge era for employees of organizations simply to fill slots or to create customized products and services in jobs that are not themselves customized. There is no longer such a thing as a typical American with generic needs: we all have different needs, and these needs change throughout the course of our lives. I like to think of this relentless emphasis on individual preference and demand as the "Starbucks syndrome" of American life. Whereas we used to walk into a coffee shop and order a "regular coffee," we now find ourselves specifying "a tall double decaf skinny latte with flat foam." And whereas we used to define ourselves as simply mothers or organization men, we are now parents, volunteers who run small companies on the side, executives who go back to school at midlife, teachers who give private seminars and do training. In short, our lives increasingly resist easy categorization, and this will become increasingly true in the future.

Leadership Considerations

What kind of leadership will thrive in this new environment? I would like to suggest several considerations. First, leadership in the future will be less derived from and based on positional power than in the past; in this it will reflect the shift in the balance of power from organizations to individuals that Peter Drucker describes. Personal charisma, broad connections, and the ability to establish powerful and fruitful relationships and to reconcile competing or disjunct points of view will become essential characteristics of leaders as the relevance of hierarchy and the mystique of the chain of command declines. With knowledge (and thus power) vested more broadly throughout an organization, a talent for consensus building and an ability to listen and learn from others will become ever more important. The military model of leadership will evolve into a model more in sync with the quieter, more subtle skills of the diplomat. It is a change that the U.S. military has in fact been early to recognize as necessary.

In addition, leaders in the years ahead will have to manage employees, customers, clients, and suppliers who see no reason that their individual goals, preferences, and timetables should not be taken into account, given the paramount value of their knowledge and the highly customized environment in which they live and work. Thus again, leaders in the future will need to be skilled at drawing ideas from people, helping them to identify, articulate, and satisfy their own particular and often changing needs. Because of this imperative, an understanding of and flair for the techniques of Socratic dialogue will be an important aspect of leadership in the years ahead.

Socratic dialogue is noninterventionist: whoever leads it does not make direct suggestions but rather elicits suggestions from others, balancing and harmonizing them and so shaping something new. In medical terms the model is one of care rather than cure, homeopathic rather than allopathic; it is more akin to traditional Chinese medicine than to Western conventions. Chinese practitioners differ from Western doctors in that they do not treat individual organs or diseases in isolation but work *with* the body to restore harmony throughout. The principles are holistic rather than compartmentalized: a good metaphor for how organizations will work in the new millennium as they are transformed by social, economic, and technological forces.

The highest principle in Chinese medicine is that of *wu wei*, or noninterference. That principle is also key in the great Chinese work on leadership, Lao-tzu's classic *Tao of Power*. In that text we discover a theory of leadership that is above all nonheroic, the precise opposite of the leader-as-celebrity syndrome that has become so prevalent. The effective leader, according to that work, is one who objectively observes the way in which the world works, and helps the organization to adapt to the larger reality. The leader does this by coaxing forth the best ideas from other people and creating an atmosphere in which they can thrive: a perfect description of Socratic dialogue. And so we find, in a new and very different era, that the oldest wisdom from Western and Eastern civilization has the most to teach us.

6 CHARLES ROUSSEL

DECISION MAKING BEYOND THE BOUNDARIES

Charles Roussel is a partner in Andersen Consulting's Strategic Services competency, where he directs its global thought leadership program. He also leads the firm's Organization and Change Strategy practice in the eastern United States. He has authored several articles on strategic partnering.

You are CEO of a global corporation. It's 3 A.M., and you're lying awake in a Paris hotel. Your mind races over the speech you'll deliver today at your annual shareholders meeting—a three-year plan to maintain growth and improve earnings. But will it allay the concerns of anxious investors or silence a critical press? And can you implement it?

The last few years have been difficult. You lead in most of your target markets, thanks to revenues boosted by bold acquisitions, but earnings haven't kept pace. You've cut costs, but at the expense of employee loyalty; restive unions won't make further concessions. You've formed some groundbreaking strategic alliances, but they require far more attention than you expected. Your leadership team is on the verge of burnout, and you find it increasingly difficult to recruit and retain management talent with the vision and operational savvy a market leader demands.

Of course, this has all occurred under the highly critical glare of twenty-four-hour global media coverage. Such immediate and efficient information flow has kept your stock price constant. Rumors of a hostile takeover abound and speculation that you may retire early runs rampant.

So as you contemplate the next three years, you wonder whether the new plan will fare better. After all, the last three-year plan looked good. But that planning didn't matter much when events overtook you and you struggled to put the best spin on circumstances you couldn't control. The next years will bring even more uncertainty—economic cycles, new competitors, workforce changes, technology shifts, and regulatory hurdles. You stare at the ceiling and wish you were in Tahiti.

Is this scenario implausible? Hardly. Every few generations, corporate leaders must find new ways to make it through the night—discovering that their predecessors' prescriptions no longer cure the organization's ills. The leaders who will guide their companies into the twenty-first century face this challenge.

Our experience at Andersen Consulting, working with clients across industries and around the world, suggests that an expanded conception of corporate governance, what we are calling "new governance," may be the most important factor in market success for today's large, global organizations. New governance is a broader, deeper, and more flexible framework for deploying, managing, and monitoring corporate resources.

But why do they need a new concept of governance? Isn't governance fairly straightforward, and don't most companies govern fairly well? Not really. During the past dozen years, leading multinational corporations have transformed themselves into global networks of joint ventures, strategic partnerships and alliances, spinouts, carve-outs, distant divisions, and unintegrated acquisitions. The average Fortune 100 company now has forty-two alliances, accounting for 21 percent of revenue. This translates into tens of billions of dollars of shareholder value. Governance hasn't kept pace.

In a survey of 214 alliance executives, we found that only 66 percent of firms regularly use formal alliance governing bodies. In related interviews with over 300 executives, we found that less than 5 percent of alliance governing bodies ever take a formal vote to decide anything. Yet our research also showed that eight of the ten most common causes of alliance failure are governance related. The time has come to rethink the governance paradigm.

The subject of corporate governance has been thoroughly reviewed in both the popular press and academic literature. Shareholder activism and very visible efforts by CalPERS (the California Public Employee Retirement System) and others investigating governance ensure it will remain subject to much discussion and debate. My goal here is to share insights into how some leading companies are expanding and deepening governance to cope with the demands of the networked global enterprise.

A New Concept of Governance

Throw out your preconceptions of governance. Governance is not about how the board deliberates or how the CEO and the leadership team make decisions and hand them down the organization. That is a paternalistic and deterministic view of corporate stewardship almost entirely at odds with the realities of decision making in a global marketplace. Of necessity, a new concept of governance is starting to emerge.

New governance is about decision making beyond the boundaries of the traditional corporation. It encompasses

- The formation, maintenance, and disposition of complex, partly owned global assets

- Both the formal and informal grants of authority and the decision routines needed to respond to crises emerging in any part of the global corporate network

- All levels of decision makers, extending to the geographical and organizational frontiers of the corporation, where many of the most critical decisions are made

- New corporate roles and responsibilities, such as decision expediters, whose sole job is to speed decision making across far-flung and disparate global corporate networks

- Many forms; governance models within a global network may vary greatly to accommodate local market needs

In its application, new governance represents a break with the past (see Table 6.1). Three elements of new governance most clearly distinguish it from old governance: a broader scope and charter; new structures, routines, and behaviors; and a flexible scale to suit different organizational entities and classes of decisions within a diverse global network.

A New Governance Charter

New governance has a much broader charter. It is more than the formal system of checks and balances found in most companies today. While serving the traditional governance purpose of ensuring fiscal integrity, new governance has a more encompassing mandate, consisting of six key responsibilities:

- *Ensure fiscal prosperity and integrity:* meet the primary fiduciary obligations of corporate officers to maximize shareholder value and minimize downside risk through goal setting, performance monitoring, and accurate reporting.

- *Allocate scarce capital:* make the best choices along the "build, buy, borrow" growth continuum (that is, the organization may choose to build a capability, relying on its own knowledge and resources, or to buy or borrow capabilities through acquisitions or alliances, respectively). These decisions are made in the context of a global operations portfolio and require clear understanding of the relative short- and long-term value of internal and external growth options.

- *Value complex assets:* value and revalue tangible and intangible assets in light of market developments

---

**Table 6.1. How New Governance
Differs from Old Governance.**

Old Governance	New Governance
Maximizes control to minimize risk	Ensures high performance as it optimizes senior management involvement
Relies on small group of senior leaders to apply codified policies and procedures	Relies on larger numbers of managers to act within clear decision-making parameters, using timely and accurate information
Applies sanctions to ensure compliance	Uses incentives and personal accountability to motivate action
Engenders bureaucratic complacency	Motivates global market vigilance and local market awareness

(for example, if a new drug compound has a higher-than-anticipated toxicity profile during clinical trials, the alliance partners revalue it in their licensing agreement). Planning assumptions and performance targets change to reflect new valuations.

- *Redirect resource flows:* redeploy resources (such as personnel, physical assets, or knowledge capital) toward more productive ends as conditions change. Resources may or may not be owned by the company (employees may come from a strategic alliance partner, for example).

- *Expedite work relationships:* make decisions speedily across all parts of the organization, including allied and outsourced businesses. Decision makers are truly empowered and decisions proceed with few "pass-ups" (in which one organizational level passes a decision up to the next level despite having authority to make the decision).

- *Establish durable links across national and corporate cultures:* establish a common frame of reference for all employees in the form of shared aspirations, operating principles, and values that link global operations. Leadership encourages local variations and interpretations of operating principles.

Although the first two responsibilities of new governance are now universally accepted and are supported by appropriate systems, the other four are not. Yet with global corporations relying more heavily on *borrowed* than *owned* assets—assets that may exist only electronically and belong to a distant, foreign partner—it will become increasingly difficult for companies to meet their fiduciary obligations without a broader governance framework.

With its broad charter, new governance may seem to overlap with management—the daily, often routine processes and actions that make any organization run. If so, it's because many operating decisions in today's global, alliance-intensive companies are no longer routine. The purchasing manager who sells a $150 million overstock of components to reduce year-end inventory may be thinking of reducing costs yet may in reality be damaging the viability of the company's new alliance with an overseas manufacturer who was promised those parts to meet annual production targets. The purchasing manager is part of a complex global network; his or her actions fall within the realm of new governance.

New Structures, Decision-Making Routines, and Behaviors

New governance depends on an interlocking system of decision *structures* and *routines* that cascade through the organization, enabling management to chart and periodically reaffirm the company's direction, manage operations, monitor progress, and make major course corrections.

Decision structures consist of individual and team roles and responsibilities that define who makes key decisions. While maintaining traditional governance structures such as the board of directors, the executive team, and steering and operating committees, new governance adds several new roles:

- *Decision expediters*—either individuals or groups—own and ensure implementation of critical mandates. The head of global supply chain operations is a decision expediter when executing a mandate to reduce the corporate cost of goods sold by outsourcing key distribution and manufacturing operations to alliance partners.

- *Alliance champions* and *alliance managers* marshal outside resources to support their company's and the

alliance's growth objectives. They often work as part
of a venture liaison group established to link parental
governance systems together seamlessly.

- *Frontline employees* provide the first and best defense
  against customer dissatisfaction, once given the information and authority to fix problems that arise.
  They are part of the governance system as imple-
  menters of and commentators on critical customer-
  related decisions.

Decision routines define how decisions are made about growth
and profitability—the essential drivers of corporate value. Traditional decision routines are corporate strategic planning, annual
budgeting and capital expenditure planning, and borrowing and div-
idend planning. New governance incorporates these additional
decision routines:

- *Governance planning:* deciding how best to oversee
  operations given the company's unique operating
  requirements

- *Portfolio and alliance planning:* choosing the best use
  of scarce capital, whether inside or outside the firm

- *Alliance management:* guiding the efforts of two organizations to work together to deliver some unique value

- *Adverse events management:* identifying and ameliorat-
  ing contingencies as they arise (for example, product
  tampering or alliance partner malfeasance)

Today these four decision routines are tangential to most corporate governance systems.

New governance acknowledges the importance of both formal
and informal structures and routines. This sets it apart from traditional governance. Our experience suggests that informal sources of

communication and control materially affect the quality of governance. This *shadow governance* is exercised by power brokers who have become the de facto decision makers in the organization. They flourish because existing governance channels don't reach far enough into the organization or because the volume of decisions is too great for formal channels.

New governance implies new ways of acting for all who participate in the governance system—from the executive team through frontline employees. Employees must be willing to share information quickly and freely. They must learn to work with and trust distant colleagues—especially when different cultures and operating practices are involved. They must become adept at collective problem solving and decision making in a virtual environment. Finally, they must be willing to accept responsibility for actions and outcomes. Hiring, training, and culture-shaping programs can help align behaviors with new governance approaches and priorities.

A Flexible Model

Underpinning new governance is the premise that governance practices can and must change for different decisions. This too is a major departure from current practice.

Today, flexible governance mostly means adjusting budgetary authority to organizational position (for example, a senior vice president can approve any project costing less than $50,000). In the future, governance must be flexible in other ways. It must be scalable—narrow and limited when decisions are relatively straightforward (extending an existing supplier agreement, for example) and broad and inclusive when decisions are more complex (entering a new R&D alliance, for example).

Governance must also be flexible enough to evolve over time. Two global industrial product manufacturers have continually modified governance structures as their product development and cross-selling alliances have matured. Although they initially relied on a formal joint venture board to make key decisions, over time they supplemented the board with an operating committee to deal with more tactical issues. They also added weekly conference calls among sales personnel and engineers to enrich the shared decision-making process.

The logic of flexible governance may seem obvious, but the governance models of most organizations are rigid. One form, one size fits all. So a fledgling alliance is typically subjected to the same onerous oversight as an ongoing project in a well-established internal business unit. Senior management often controls a product's promotional mix, despite lacking practical knowledge of and proximity to targeted customers. Just as common, a local office struggles to manage a major crisis, yet the executive suite stays silent.

In a flexible governance model, *decision complexity* and *decision value* provide the context for deciding who makes what decisions, how, and when. Figure 6.1 illustrates a decision-making matrix based on complexity and value and shows what a flexible governance model implies.

Quadrant I contains highly complex decisions that directly affect shareholder value. These decisions are made by small groups of specialized, experienced executives. Information is tightly controlled and interaction among the governors is episodic. Communication is carefully polished and monitored for impact. Outside parties such as investment bankers and regulators offer opinions on governance processes and results. Here, governance processes focus on minimizing risk.

Quadrant II comprises highly complex decisions with relatively little immediate impact on market perceptions. These decisions are made by small groups of specialized personnel who study the marketplace for context and reach down into the organization for operating data on which to base decisions. These decisions take the form of guidelines, policies, and procedures, which are modified as events warrant. Governance processes focus on creating a harmonious set of operating standards to ensure consistent performance across the organization.

Figure 6.1. A New Governance Decision-Making Matrix.

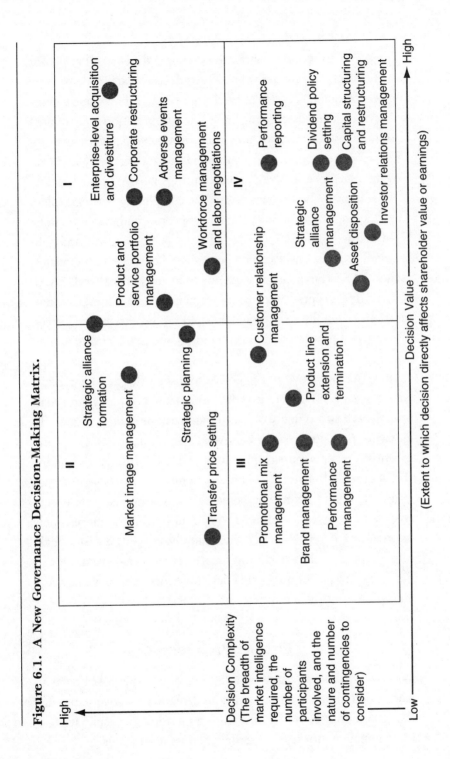

Quadrant III consists of relatively simple decisions that do not directly affect shareholder value. These decisions are made by large numbers of middle- and lower-level managers who have timely information and detailed operating knowledge. Information is distributed broadly to foster consensus, and interaction among governors is frequent. Communication is likely to be ad hoc and relatively informal. Governance processes focus on maximizing operating performance.

Quadrant IV holds decisions of low complexity but high value. These decisions are made by the fewest people, and they tend to be highly skilled professionals in the legal, tax, accounting, and public relations functions. Decision processes follow accepted standards, such as FASB (Financial Accounting Standards Board) and GAAP (Generally Accepted Accounting Principles) guidelines. Communication is carefully scripted and directed toward external audiences. Governance processes focus on building and maintaining market confidence.

In short, new governance begins to dismantle the hierarchical, cumbersome, and convoluted decision making so prevalent today. Success will strain many old corporate structures and systems. To motivate new governance behaviors, performance tracking and incentive systems must change to encourage informed risk taking and shared responsibility. These systems should also emphasize longer-term performance outcomes. To strengthen actions, executive support systems will need to deliver better and more timely information to key decision points. Finally, to speed decision making, new approaches to communication will be essential. Governance can't wait for quarterly board meetings; new governance is an on-line, weekly, if not daily, occurrence.

Future Prospects

What will it take to usher in a new age of governance? I have already asserted that market conditions demand new governance and that communication and information technologies make it possible. But beyond these, some other changes must occur.

Today governance is implicit and exceptional; in the future it must be explicit and routine. Ask fifty employees to define governance, and you'll get fifty different answers. This must change. Companies must educate employees about the often hidden mechanisms of governance, develop a new language of governance, and begin an extended dialogue with employees on how to apply new governance principles. Having provided this critical context, the organization can impose governance obligations on employees.

Today governance is the prerogative of a few; in the future it must be the responsibility of many. Although leadership must set priorities and structures, it cannot comprehend, let alone act wisely on, the plethora of performance data and competitive intelligence spewing forth from today's management information systems.

At a point of unprecedented global growth and prosperity for the industrialized world, but also one of great and subtle complexities, organizations and leaders are on the brink of a commercial paradigm shift—a fundamental rethinking of how businesses must govern resources. It will be born of competitive necessity.

Merger and acquisition activity is rapidly stripping excess capacity out of all global marketplaces. Process and structural redesigns have reduced organizational assets and headcounts; further cuts would impose unacceptable social welfare costs. Information efficiency is improving exponentially. These traditional sources of competitive advantage will soon have run their course. Subsequent gains in productivity and value creation will require a tectonic shift in commercial conduct.

Those organizations that anticipate and help define an emerging paradigm realize enduring benefits. The first organizations to embrace new governance can expect similar advantages—and their CEOs will sleep more peacefully.

Part II

TRANSFORMING ORGANIZATIONS FOR NEW REALITIES

7

PETER M. SENGE

LEADERSHIP
IN LIVING
ORGANIZATIONS

Peter M. Senge is a senior lecturer at MIT and chair
of the Society for Organizational Learning (SoL), a
global community of corporations, researchers, and
consultants dedicated to building knowledge about
fundamental institutional change. Noted for trans-
lating abstract ideas of systems theory into tools for
change, he is the author of many articles and of the
best-selling book The Fifth Discipline: The Art and
Practice of the Learning Organization, *named by*
the Harvard Business Review *in 1997 as a seminal*
management book of the past seventy-five years.

A ll societies are a product of their age and in turn create their age.
We live today in a period of extraordinary transition. We are
trapped between two worlds, an old world and a new world. The industrial age was dominated by the myth of unending material progress and
the image of the machine. The new age remains unnamed because
it is as yet unformed. Regardless of how we label it—information age,

The ideas expressed in this chapter are based on the Fifth Discipline fieldbook, *The*
Dance of Change: The Challenges of Sustaining Momentum in Learning Organizations, 1999.

systems age, or simply postindustrial age—it will not be more of the same. It is not possible to sustain indefinitely a continuing increase in material throughput on a finite planet. Nor can we continue to expand population and resource consumption in an increasingly crowded world of people who do not know how to get along with one another. And the metaphor of the machine, which has given us incredible material affluence but also rigid bureaucracies, assembly-line jobs and schools, and an ever more frenetic, disconnected way of living, must be superseded by the image of the living system.

Nature operates through cyclic processes. The industrial age has operated, by and large, through linear processes: take, make, waste. Nature generates diversity. The industrial age has generated homogeneity, relentlessly eradicating both biological and cultural diversity. Nature focuses on means, allowing ends to emerge. The industrial age has focused on goals, allowing them to justify whatever means were needed.

What kind of society will emerge in and shape the new age? What possibilities will it afford? What new ways of living? None of these questions are answerable. Yet each must be pondered. "History does not follow the path of opportunities but the path of desires," says Chilean biologist Humberto Maturana. How we humans go about discovering, articulating, and manifesting our desires will shape the future.

In particular the practices of a society are embedded in the practices of its institutions and evolve with them. This is why changes in how institutions of business, education, government, and social services operate matter—and why leadership, the energy that enables such change, is so important.

What Do We Typically Mean When We Speak of Leaders?

In everyday colloquial usage, *leader* is typically used as a synonym for *top manager*, as in, "Our leaders will never go for that" or "All change starts with the leadership." This way of thinking poses at least two problems.

The first is evident when someone says, "Great idea. But what do the leaders think?" This question (and the assumption behind it) is disrespectful and disempowering to everyone in the organization who is not a top manager. It constrains innovative thinking and actions.

The second problem is more subtle: if leadership is defined as top management, then it has no real definition at all. Having two terms to describe the same thing means that one is redundant. But there are few other working definitions that would be widely agreed on. This is why even after organizations decentralize decision making, people still tend to speak of leaders as "the people at the top."

This confusion affects every aspect of organizational practice, including the development of future leaders. What corporation does not spend copiously for *leadership development*? High-potential managers are identified early in their careers. They are "fast-tracked," "mentored," and sent off to countless expensive programs intended to develop them for prospective senior management positions. This is undoubtedly important. But why not call this what it is: executive development. By calling it leadership development, we again reinforce the notion that responsibility for the future of the enterprise lies in the hands of a chosen few. And who knows what opportunities for real leadership development, more broadly construed, we miss by focusing exclusively on the elite?

Our choice of words is not academic. Our language shapes our perceptions. It also shapes our actions, making us aware of some possibilities and blind to others. Definitions are especially important when the experience and concerns we are pointing to are something that matters deeply.

What Do We Typically Think Leaders Do?

Leaders drive change. That is what is expected of *real* leaders today. However, when combined with the definition of leader as top manager, this view leads to a continual corporate search for the hero-CEO—the person (read "man") who can deliver for the shareholder, who can energize change-resistant employees, and who is not afraid to make "tough decisions." Gradually, this thinking is spreading to other institutions as well, which are likewise becoming trapped in a search for their own heroic figures to drive change in their recalcitrant, inward-focused, noncompetitive organizations.

But might this very thinking be a key reason such institutions are so prevalent? Might not the continual search for the hero-leader to drive change divert our attention away from building institutions that by their very nature continually adapt and reinvent themselves?

In all types of institutions a disturbing pattern is emerging. Faced with practical needs for significant change, we opt for the hero-leader rather than eliciting and developing leadership capacity throughout the organization. The new hero-CEO then pumps new life into the organization's suffering fortunes, typically by cutting costs (and usually people) and boosting productivity and profit. But the improvements invariably do not last. Many of the leader's grand strategies never get implemented; instead, people cling to habitual ways of doing things. New ideas do not spring forth from people on the front lines because they are too intimidated to stick their necks out. Energies are not released to create new products or new ways to meet customer needs because people are too busy competing with one another in order to please their bosses. Invariably, new crises ensue, spurring a search for a new hero-leader. In effect, the myth of the hero-leader creates a self-reinforcing, vicious spiral of dramatic changes imposed from the top, increasing fear and diminishing leadership within the organization, leading eventually to new crises and calls for more heroic leadership.

Worshiping in the cult of the hero-leader who drives change is a surefire way to maintain change-averse institutions. In fact one can hardly think of a better strategy to achieve precisely this goal. The price that we all pay in the long run is incalculable: institutions that lurch from crisis to crisis, continual stress on the members of those institutions, mediocre (at best) long-term performance, and further reinforcement of the point of view that "common people" are powerless to change things.

A Shift of View

Ironically, despite our continual struggles to drive resisting organizations to change, we are surrounded by a world of continual change. Little in nature seems to stay put. Everything is in motion, continually changing, forever adapting—everything, that is, that is alive.

Herein lies the fundamental failure of most leadership strategies. We fail to understand that what we are seeking to change is alive. Instead, we see our organizations as if they were machines.

It is impossible for us, as products of the industrial age, to know the extent to which the machine metaphor shapes our perceptions. But our language gives away our underlying assumptions. We talk of leaders "driving change," as if they were operating heavy equipment. Have you tried to "drive" a teenager lately? Machine thinking is not limited to the subject of leadership. Our organizational lexicon evokes a mechanical world of *measures, plans, programs*, and managers *in control*. In fact, as Arie de Geus has argued (*The Living Company*, 1997), society views the corporation as a machine for making money. It has *owners*. By contrast, would a living human system be owned? The corporation has designers and builders, those who create its formal *systems* and *procedures*. In contrast, a living system builds itself (this is one of the definitions of a living system in biology). The corporation's *health* is measured by how much output (money) it creates for its owners, again a perfectly reasonable criterion for judging a machine but not a living system. Lastly, of course, as a machine, a corporation cannot change on its own—this is why it needs leaders who can *drive* change.

Noncorporate organizations are no different. For example, the industrial-age school is clearly modeled after an assembly line: everyone is expected to start and end at the same time and the same age and everyone is to move at the same speed. Those that move at a slower speed are given labels like "learning-disabled" and typically pushed off the line, to make way for the "smart" kids, who move more quickly.

Thinking of leadership as an expression of a living system requires fundamental shifts. It requires a new definition and new metaphors, that is, new language. It requires new principles and new perspectives. But, interestingly, none of what is needed is really new. In fact it is quite old. The foundations for understanding leadership in a world of living organizations already exist, recollections that predate the machine age and that we have not yet entirely lost.

An Alternative Definition of Leadership

The following simple definition of leadership has proved quite helpful in change projects over the years: *the capacity of a human community— people living and working together—to bring forth new realities.*

Another way to say this is that leadership energizes. Leadership breathes life into an enterprise, without which nothing truly new can emerge. The word *inspire,* long associated with leadership, derives from the Latin *inspirare,* literally "to breathe life into."

This simple notion of human communities creating new realities unifies the extraordinarily diverse individuals whom we see as exemplary leaders—public figures like Lincoln, Gandhi, Susan B. Anthony, and Harriet Tubman; organizational leaders Thomas Watson Jr. of IBM, Theodore Vail of AT&T, labor organizer Samuel Gompers; and also leaders from the arts and sciences, from Picasso, Martha Graham, and Shakespeare to Albert Einstein and Marie Curie. Obviously, many of these people were never "bosses" at the top of an organizational hierarchy, yet all are widely regarded as leaders.

This simple definition also points to the interplay of individual and community. Each of the individuals just mentioned was a product of his or her world and in turn inspired an outpouring of new theories, ideas, and approaches that had an extraordinary influence on a given field and on the culture.

Lastly, I believe that this simple definition points to much of what we are actually seeking through greater leadership in human affairs, in organizations, in schools, and in communities. Leadership is about tapping the energy to create—especially to create something that matters deeply. Where this energy exists, we are more engaged, fulfilled, and productive. We are more alive.

Creative Tension

Leaders generate such energy through creative tension.

I recall a small executive session in 1983, led by Peter Drucker, in which a CEO asked Drucker for his definition of leadership. He answered, "Leadership is vision. There's nothing more to say." Indeed, it is hard to think about human communities bringing forth new realities or organizations shaping their future without embracing the notion of "vision." The word *vision* has almost lost its meaning over the last ten years, due to the faddishness surrounding vision and mission statements. But *vision* is not a new word. We are told in Proverbs 29:18, "Where there is no vision, the people perish." It is hard to see an idea from the Old Testament as just a management fad.

Vision, an image of the future we seek to create, is closely identified with the arts as well as the world's religions. As Picasso once expressed it, "It would be very interesting to record photographically, not the stages of a painting, but its metamorphoses. One would see perhaps by what course a mind finds its way toward the crystallization of its dream."

But the creative process is equally the domain, potentially, of all managers, all practitioners, all professionals. Ultimately, people in any setting are deeply interested in what they can make happen. Make no mistake: you can have a great theory about business, or about music or painting, but the question that matters ultimately is, *What can you produce?*

Yet I think leadership involves a force beyond vision alone, as suggested by Dr. Martin Luther King Jr.'s reflection on his own work in his "Letter from the Birmingham Jail" (1963): "Just as Socrates felt it was necessary to create a tension in the minds of men so that individuals could rise from the bondage of myths and half-truths; so must we create the kind of tension in society that will help men rise from the dark depths of prejudice and racism."

The tension that King is talking about does not come from vision alone; it comes from vision juxtaposed to current reality. King is famous for his "dream," but his core leadership strategy revolved around "dramatizing the present situation," in the mode of Gandhi, from whom King gained many of his strategic insights. This is the principle of *creative tension*. It is the essence of leadership. Leaders energize through generating and sustaining creative tension, through fostering commitment to realizing a dream and to telling the truth about what is.

Tension always seeks resolution, release. If the vision remains constant, creative tension can be resolved only when reality moves toward the vision. There are no other options. This is not mystical. It is logical.

Conversely, leadership is diminished whenever creative tension is undermined. There are two ways this can happen. One is that we do not have the will or ability to articulate our dreams. The other is that we lie about current reality, especially when we deceive ourselves that reality is closer to our vision than it actually is. The first is the path of compromise; the second the path of denial. Both are commonplace in organizations dominated by fear, stress, and powerlessness.

Operationalizing the Definition

The two poles of vision and reality demarcate the territory in which leaders work. But we also need metaphors and operating principles for leading change.

When leaders contribute to initiating and sustaining significant change, they operate more like gardeners than heavy equipment operators.

Gardeners do not entreat their seeds to grow. Can you imagine a gardener leaning over her or his seedlings and shouting "grow!"— a simple image that would be well worth managers' considering. Gardeners understand that a seed has the potential to grow and also that they do not put that potential there. If the potential to grow does not exist, there is nothing a gardener can do to cause growth. Gardeners also understand that growth occurs through an interaction between the seed and its environment or, more precisely, that the seed and the environment create a self-reinforcing growth process. The seed sends out small shoots and draws in water and nutrients. As more water and nutrients are drawn into the seed, its primitive root system extends further, drawing in still more water and nutrients, extending the roots even more. As in all of nature's growth processes, what is growing starts small, and for some time, most of the change is underground.

This is the first principle of leadership: understand the self-reinforcing processes of growth. If these do not operate, change will not generate energy, it will absorb energy. This is why so many people who take on the role of change agents find themselves having to continually push change and why they so often become burned out by the effort.

But such growth processes cannot progress unless they have conducive conditions. This is why the gardener's attention must also focus on a second set of forces: the host of limiting conditions—like inadequate water, temperature, sunlight, soil nutrients, and room for the root system to expand—that could keep the growth processes from operating. The seed's potential to grow will not be realized unless these limits are eased or removed.

All things grow in nature through the interplay of reinforcing processes that foster growth and limiting processes that constrain growth. This is why all effective leadership strategies always come down to nurturing reinforcing growth processes and relieving the limiting processes. Period. Effective leaders recognize intuitively the interplay of these forces and learn to work with them. They do not drive change; they participate in the growth processes and mitigate the constraints on change.

The Dance of Change

This leads to two key questions: What self-reinforcing processes promote significant change, and what specific limits impede change? Only by seeking to understand these forces can we see what effective leaders are actually doing and why. In fact, seeking to understand these forces and the variety of leadership strategies employed to deal with them has been a focus of ongoing research for the past several years within SoL, the Society for Organizational Learning. (To learn more, visit the SoL Web site at *http://www.SoL-NE.org*— see specifically the information on the research project "Towards an Ecology of Leadership.")

Growth Processes

To date, SoL research has identified three basic, self-reinforcing growth processes. Each of them starts with initial progress made by a "pilot group," typically in a line organization in which local managers have sufficient autonomy to try out new ideas and work practices. Pilot groups may be sales or engineering teams, manufacturing units, or even top-management teams, so long as they concentrate on changing how they operate in confronting strategic issues, rather than making speeches and "rolling out" programs. Initial adopters or creators of new innovative practices are usually guided by their personal beliefs and vision. They apply new ideas in local settings where they have some control, believing that these ideas will spread if they are effective. These people usually do not think explicitly about self-reinforcing growth processes, but they often have such processes at least intuitively in mind.

The first reinforcing growth process most leaders identify and try to establish is fueled by improved *business results*, that is, improvement in the tangible indicators that practitioners see as evidence that an innovative new practice is producing real benefit. When practitioners achieve significant improvement in business results, the credibility of their innovative ideas increases, leading to more enthusiasm and the willingness of others to commit to these ideas. This "better mousetrap" theory lies at the heart of the potential spread of any new practice or way of doing things.

But achieving significant new practical results does not happen overnight. It can take six, twelve, or twenty-four months for new capabilities and new practices to take root and produce tangible evidence of improvement. Moreover, business results are influenced by many factors in addition to an innovative way of doing things; for example, many promising innovations are thwarted because of external forces like an economic downturn or a new competitor. This is why better business results are a weak reed to rely on for change and why we have found, from deeper examination of countless real cases at SoL, two other primary growth processes at work.

The second growth process functions through enhanced personal *results*. Simply put, people become more committed over time to changes that matter to them. Specifically, people value work environments in which they experience trust, shared vision, and genuine listening to one another, and in which difficult issues are dealt with openly, rather than in private hallway conversations. When such environments develop, more people become enthusiastic and willing to commit to further change.

But people are also greatly influenced by peers, by what colleagues in other working teams are doing, and this constitutes the third self-reinforcing growth process. Why does one department head try something that has worked in another unit? Usually, it's not because the boss told her to try it; it's because she knows the people involved and considers them credible or because she sees the business results they've achieved. As more people become involved in any innovative practice, that practice reaches further into their informal networks, exposing still more people; if people are enthusiastic about the personal and business results achieved, their enthusiasm spreads through ever widening circles. Such crosscutting *communities of practice*, not formal management hierarchies, have been shown in many settings to be the primary channels through which new ideas and practices actually diffuse in large organizations.

What is important for leaders to understand is that the reinforcing effects of enhanced personal results and informal networks can develop more quickly than increased credibility through improved business metrics. All three growth processes matter, but leaders who rely on increasing credibility from measurable results may miss the leverage from personal commitment and growing networks of like-minded people.

Limiting Processes

These self-reinforcing growth processes are only half the story, however; by themselves, they would cause all new ideas with potential merit to take root, and those that proved their merit locally would then spread without limit. But this is hardly the case in today's organizations. If anything, the opposite is more likely. Most promising new ideas never get tested seriously, and most of those that do prove themselves in one local setting do not spread, especially when they challenge established assumptions and ways of operating. In fact, as business historian Art Kleiner has shown (*The Age of Heretics*, 1996), one of the most compelling features of the challenge of organizationwide change is how often good ideas not only do not spread but get their proponents into trouble. When this occurs, most change advocates "push harder," trying to overcome those resisting change. Few understand that they are encountering ubiquitous balancing or limiting processes that keep promising new ideas from getting implemented and practices that prove themselves locally from spreading.

These limiting processes are the challenges to significant change, and they fall into three broad areas.

Challenges of initiating come into play in the pilot-group setting and can prevent significant change from ever getting started or progressing very far.

Challenges of sustaining develop once significant momentum has built up; they can arise within the team or pilot group or at the interface between the pilot group and the larger organization.

Challenges of redesigning and rethinking grow out of the fundamental features of industrial age institutions that thwart significant change regardless of how it begins.

Altogether these challenges encompass ten distinct sets of balancing processes. Many of them are sufficient to limit change by themselves. Together they represent a virtually insurmountable array of forces aimed at preserving a host of balances most change agents either disregard or naively believe will not affect their aspirations (see Exhibit 7.1).

In initiating change, for instance, people must have enough flexibility to manage their own time; if they cannot invest the time and effort necessary to develop new capabilities or work processes, no growth will occur. But time to develop without help to develop can result in a waste of time, especially if the changes people are trying to achieve involve significant new capabilities. Likewise, people must understand the business case for change. They must also see that the advocates of change are willing to "walk the talk," that their values and goals are authentic.

These are the kinds of limits that managers seeking to initiate real change must attend to. They are the water, sunlight, and soil conditions that can arrest significant change before it ever gets started. In initiating change, leaders *must* deal with time, help, relevance, and walking the talk if they hope to succeed. It does little good to have brilliant innovative ideas if people have no time to pursue them or no help in implementing them or cannot connect them to their business priorities.

Exhibit 7.1. Challenges of Change.

Challenges of Initiating

- *Time flexibility.* Do people have sufficient control of their own time? If they don't, they will not have enough time for significant change initiatives.

- *Help.* Do people have the coaching support they need? If not, they will flounder in initiatives that require new skills and capabilities.

- *Relevance.* Does management make a compelling case for change? If not, people will conclude that the change initiative is not relevant.

- *Personal alignment.* Are management's values and goals perceived as authentic and aligned with its actions? If not, people will see that management is not "walking the talk."

Challenges of Sustaining

- *Fear and anxiety.* How will people deal with the personal threat of more honest, direct, and inquiry-oriented working teams? If this threat is not recognized and addressed, some in the pilot team will disengage and even work to undermine the initiative.

- *Assessment and measurement.* Do people have the patience to persist in difficult learning efforts even though significant business results might take many months or even years? What happens when some results look worse by traditional measures? If this challenge is neglected, many will view otherwise promising innovations as unsuccessful.

- *Believers and nonbelievers.* How will the organization deal with the threat posed to those outside the team by the new behaviors of team members? How does a successful pilot group avoid having its confidence turn to arrogance and the consequent siege mentality? If these issues are neglected, polarization between innovators and mainstream people can become unresolvable.

Challenges of Redesigning and Rethinking

- *Governance.* Is the enterprise able to effectively distribute legitimate power to local operations, or does management seek to maintain control? Are people capable of assuming more power in pursuing new business

---

Exhibit 7.1. Challenges of Change, cont'd.

opportunities and in managing interdependencies? Neglect of these issues leads to continual destructive power struggles between innovative pilot groups and senior management.

- *Diffusion.* Can profound change initiatives spread effectively across organizational boundaries, both internal and external? If not, people will keep reinventing the wheel.

- *Strategy and purpose.* What will it take for the organization to continually reinvent itself as its world changes? How can new ideas about purpose and strategy that emerge from innovative pilot groups influence thinking more broadly? Failure to address this challenge cuts off a source of key ideas about the future and prevents continual renewal and rediscovery of genuine purposefulness.

But leaders must also be prepared for the challenges that arise once a pilot group has begun to build some momentum. They must have strategies for dealing with the fear and anxiety that will eventually arise within the pilot group as difficult issues that have been buried in the past come to the surface (it is these issues that become the subjects of hallway conversations). Leaders must be prepared for the polarization that can occur between believers in the pilot group and nonbelievers outside. They must deal with established performance measures, even though some might be inappropriate for their efforts. Ultimately, organizationwide change requires dealing with the sources and uses of power (governance), the fragmentation caused by rigid boundaries (diffusion), and reluctance to rethink what the enterprise is all about (strategy and purpose).

If personal and collective vision lies at the heart of generating significant change, then willingness to look deeply at current reality is the key to seeing the forces that can limit change. Often this is a blind spot for passionate innovators. They behave like gardeners who believe so much in their seeds that they neglect the conditions

necessary for their growth. Some see the basic challenges of initiating as too mundane for their efforts; consequently, they have great
ideas but no significant change ever starts. Others are more successful in initiating yet systematically neglect the challenges of sustaining; finding it incomprehensible that others do not share their
zeal, they become increasingly ineffective beyond their small circle
of followers. Last, the challenges of redesigning and rethinking are
widely ignored because most people in large institutions cannot
imagine changes in such entrenched concepts as the central concentration of power or the assumed purpose of the business.

Leadership Communities

Addressing only some of the challenges of change makes the others
even more limiting. It is like being a gardener who pays attention
only to water and ignores soil nutrients. The success in providing
water makes poor nutrients a more severe limit.

This is why leadership communities are so vital. The diversity
of forces represented by the different challenges requires a diversity of leaders. So far, within the SoL community, we have found
that three types of leaders are essential: local line leaders, internal
networkers, and executive leaders. Each plays key roles, and each
needs the others.

Local line leaders are critical to initiating because by and large only
they can deal with important day-to-day matters like time, help, relevance, and walking the talk. They are also vital in dealing with the
challenges of sustaining, including challenges within the pilot team
and at the interface of the team and its larger environment. In fact,
some research suggests that a defining characteristic of a successful
team is that it is effective at managing its boundaries with the large
organization. Contrary to the myth that the hero-CEO is the primary innovator, our experience within SoL has been that local line
managers, with business accountability, operate at the heart of all

significant organizational innovation, for the simple reason that they are at the front lines, where value is generated and where new ideas can be applied, tested, and assessed.

But the strengths of talented local line leaders are also their limitations. They are often so focused on their own business or sphere of accountability and its improvement that they are isolated from other like-minded colleagues. This is one reason why *internal networkers*, people who spread new ideas and move freely across functional boundaries, are also important leaders. Internal networkers can be internal consultants, training professionals, or human resource staff; they can also be engineers or salespeople. They serve as guides, advisers, active helpers, and *accessors*, connecting people and ideas across the organization. They are vital partners to local line leaders in dealing with the challenges of initiating and sustaining, and they also contribute in unique ways to resolving challenges of diffusion, especially as critical agents in communities of practice that cross organizational boundaries.

But neither local line leaders nor internal networkers can deal with the challenges of redesigning and rethinking without the active engagement of *executive leaders*. Ultimately, executive leaders are vital for influencing the overall environment within which all innovation and learning occurs. They are designers, teachers, and stewards. They have unique responsibilities for the infrastructures of governance, measurement, and strategy. Good design will not create commitment and energy, but poor design will surely thwart them. Executive leaders also play key roles as mentors and coaches, especially in helping local line leaders face complex organizational and political responses to their efforts. Last, effective executive leaders serve as role models. By focusing their energies on the functioning of their teams, they communicate a symbolic and practical message about willingness to change. As recently retired Shell CEO Phil Carroll says, "You have to start, in the first place, with yourself. Every process of transformation is a series of individual learnings and decisions by people. It has to start with personal change. The abstraction of corporate change and so forth—that's a result, not a method" (R. Hanig, *Leadership* [video], 1997).

One thing executive leaders are not is the primary agent of change. Initiating and sustaining significant change, the operational definition of leadership, is much too complex for any one group. In re-creating industrial-age institutions for the postindustrial world, either there exists a healthy leadership ecology or there is no leadership at all.

8

DAVE ULRICH

MAXIMIZING CREATIVE COLLABORATION

Dave Ulrich is professor of business administration at the University of Michigan, a consultant to the Fortune 200, and the author of over eighty articles and book chapters. His books include Results Based Leadership, Organizational Capability, The Boundaryless Organization, *and* Human Resource Champions. *The editor of* Human Resource Management, *he has been listed by* Business Week *as one of the top ten educators in management.*

*W*hy? Too often leaders have no answer or only a feeble answer about why they do what they do. Leaders act in a certain way because other leaders have acted that way, because they have been trained to do so, or because they have always done things that way. When leaders understand why they act, and when they invest in programs that affect the actions of others, they create value. And value must always be defined by the receiver more than the giver. When I give my wife a gift, she tells me the value of the gift. I may intend the dozen roses delivered on our anniversary to communicate affection, but if she reads this act as my being out of town (again) and my minimizing our anniversary by offering a gift that only took a few minutes to order, then my gift of roses creates no value. Leaders who master "why" define the value they create by understanding who receives the benefits of their actions.

So that . . . ? A leadership action leads to value when it resolves the "so that" query. The leaders who ask "so that . . . ?" about an action must identify a receiver, must focus on what they deliver as much or more than what they do, and must be able to prioritize. As leaders face mounting demands on their time and talents, they must be ever more aware of the value they create by what they do; this knowledge comes from answering the "so that" question.

Increasingly, the answer to the "so that" question goes beyond the walls of the organization within which the leader acts and makes actions happen. It is not enough to lead so that employees are happy, committed, and productive or so that organizations are agile, innovative, and lean. In both the competitive private sector and partisan public sector, the answers to the "so that" question must connect what goes on inside the organization to what goes on outside the organization. This often focuses the "so that" query on customers and investors outside who receive value from activities inside the organization. When able to connect activities inside with results outside and demands outside with investments inside, leaders answer "why" and create value. In creating value, leaders may learn from two "so that" queries, about customers and about investors.

So That: Customers

Many leaders preach that their "employees are their most important asset" or that the company wants "to be the employer of choice." When the "so that" query is focused on customers, these mantras change to "employees are our customers' most important asset" and "we want to be the employer of choice of employees our customers would choose." The criterion by which employees are hired or trained becomes less what they know and more what they can do for customers. When working with the members of one senior executive team, I rhetorically prodded, "If the customers could hire the twenty of you as officers to run the firm, would they hire the twenty of you?" When someone answered, "How could they do that? They don't know who we are," I suggested that the executives think about this comment and that I had made my point that what goes on inside the firm may not be well enough connected to what goes on outside the firm.

Leaders should act so that if valued customers had a time log of leader behaviors, the customers would be delighted and excited. (Although this does not mean that leaders should always do what the customer wants, because customers may not fully realize what the firm offers and the excitement generated by good leadership may be offering customers services beyond expectations.) And a number of firms have begun to invest in management actions that connect the organization's programs to customers.

Customers and Staffing

An airline attempting to put more fun into flying filters résumés for flight attendants then invites finalists to "audition" in front of a customer panel, giving frequent flyers a voice in the flight attendant selection process. A restaurant selecting a chef invites target customers to taste the selections of the finalists and to offer their vote on which chef they would prefer. A consulting firm invites individuals from large accounts to interview potential members of the account team prior to joining the team. A college hiring committee observes a candidate for a teaching post teaching a class of students. A manufacturing firm invites customers to join the team that is defining the competencies for first-line supervisors. A hospital invites physicians, third-party payers, and investors to interview potential administrators. A high school involves parents in the PTA in selecting a principal.

In each of these cases, the critical staffing decision, traditionally held close by leaders, is opened to customers. The fear that the company is, in effect, letting the fox guard the henhouse or letting prisoners pick their guards may be mitigated by giving customers not *the* voice but *a* voice. And in many cases, leaders may be surprised to find that customers actually pick individuals who add value through different ways of thinking and approaches.

Customer participation in staffing increases the quality of hiring decisions, just as observing teachers teach and soliciting data from the students helps ensure the hiring of quality teachers. Asking customers to define competencies of first-line supervisors creates a dialogue about what matters most to customers and how that translates to internal managerial behaviors. Inviting customers to screen potential employees may result in better employees being hired. In addition, customer participation in staffing likely increases customer commitment to the person hired. Customers who help pick a chef for a restaurant are more likely to frequent the restaurant. When parents help select a principal, that principal may take actions knowing she has the support of those parents.

Customers and Training and Development

What percentage of the participants in training courses offered by your firm are also customers of your firm? When I ask this question, I am amazed at the number of training courses offered in which 100 percent of the participants come from inside the firm. Training represents a relatively fixed investment in space, material, faculty, and time. If a training experience involves thirty internal participants, it will not cost much more to add five or six customers to the event. The payback for this investment is often huge. Motorola University opens many of its programs to customers, particularly in emerging markets. Motorola finds that by including key customers in these programs, it is able to shape how customers think and act. By educating members of the value chain in the Motorola language, management philosophy, and decision processes, Motorola redefines the rules of engagement and succeeds quickly in new markets.

An oil service company used customer training prior to introducing a new product. In one region many potential customers for the new product were assembled with the new-product salesforce. Together, they shared the training and education about the new product, and the experience of deploying it. Another region introduced the new product in the traditional way, with internal salesforce training, marketing, and one-on-one sales to targeted customers. The region with intense customer and employee training prior to product introduction outperformed the traditional region ten to one in sales in the first six months.

Companies may begin customer involvement in training by identifying customers who would be well served by the content of a course, extending a special invitation to them to attend, and building relationships with them during the program. One company now requires that 10 percent of the openings in all courses be available for customers and encourages those who have customer contact (for example, sales and marketing employees) to include attendance at these courses as part of the customer sell. It is easy for a good sales representative to make the opportunity to attend a course a "special offer" to a valued customer.

Customer involvement may also include programs designed primarily for customers. A company that has excelled in productivity gains has prepared a productivity tool kit that it shares with its customers. This tool kit offers customers (and suppliers) the tools the firm has mastered and encourages application of these tools in the customer firm. In addition, the company finds that many of the productivity tools may be leveraged at the boundary between the firms. In one case a firm that repaired railroad cars had engaged in process improvement and cut from twenty to ten the days required to repair a railcar. The company was disappointed when it found that customers were not as delighted as they might have been about the process improvements. But then, in a customer workshop, the company learned that customers generally had the railcars out of commission about ten days on either side of the company's repair services. So the ten-day reduction cut the total time only from forty to thirty days, an improvement but not as dramatic as the company would have liked. Through a customer productivity workshop that shared technology and processes, the company was able to focus on the forty-day total time a railcar was out of production and reduce it to about fifteen days.

Customer involvement may mean the customer actually presents the information in a course. An electronics company invited a panel of three customers who had recently purchased from a competitor to attend a meeting of company officers. The panelists talked about their decision process and why they had shifted to a competitor. Collectively, these three lost customers represented a major account erosion, and officers at the seminar not only listened but committed to act. Customers have reason to improve supplier performance and are often willing to share candid observations about why they do or do not purchase. When shared within a learning environment, this information may be turned into customer-focused action.

Finally, customer involvement may include sharing talent across boundaries. In a utility firm, one talented executive had little experience in marketing. The firm then found that one of the budding executives in one of its accounts had little experience in quality systems. The two firms did a three-month executive exchange that assigned each executive to an appropriate project in the other firm. These executives learned more than concepts; they also forged relationships across boundaries.

Customers and Appraisal and Rewards

An airline sends its most frequent flyers an annual letter stating: "We know you are one of our most frequent flyers. We are committed to excellent customer service. Because you travel on our airline so often, we assume you know how to define customer service. Enclosed with this letter are ten coupons, each worth $50. When you experience exceptional service from an airline employee, ask for the employee's name, sign the coupon, send it to the company, and we will pay the employee $50." This firm sets aside a percentage of its bonus pool and asks customers to decide who gets that money. As a result, customers feel engaged, committed, and happy to share with employees their satisfaction with the service rendered.

Some hotel chains have guest surveys about check-in service, room service, and room cleanliness that provide guest feedback on specific employee behavior. A retail chain now interviews targeted customers about their satisfaction with their shopping experience and ties their scores to the employee who attended to them. Their hope is to have twenty to thirty customer responses per employee per quarter and to create a clear line of sight between customers and employees.

Customers may help design appraisal systems by defining behaviors they need to see more or less of in employees, by participating in the appraisal process, or by allocating rewards based on quality of employee service. By so doing, customers feel more committed to employees and employees to customers.

Customers and Governance and Communication

Almost every organization uses task force teams to design and deliver systems and services. Generally, membership on these teams is limited to employees inside a firm, often from multiple functions. However, when the teams are expanded to include suppliers and customers, better decision making occurs, as evidenced in the railcar example. It is not difficult to invite targeted customers to participate in teams. Often a customer has experts who are more than willing to share knowledge and experience in order to receive better service.

Communication between firms and customers has also become a connection point. Sharing newsletters, videos, and other public communications helps transfer knowledge across units. At times, involving customers in such communications results in enormous emotional appeal. A company making heart valves often has customers talk to employee groups about their gratitude for the product and the quality behind the product, stating that their ability to be present at the event is due to the firm's product. These customer testimonials help employees focus on who matters most and what matters most to them. Other companies share actual data about products and operations. When Wal-Mart sells products, the companies that supply those products know immediately. Wal-Mart's electronic check-out system is used not only for inventory control within Wal-Mart, but for letting suppliers know how well products are selling for this major customer.

Summing Up the Customer Connection

In one workshop, I asked participants to list their three largest customers on the left-hand side of a page and then write the name of their company on the right-hand side. The challenge was to then fill the page with ways to connect the company with the customers. The more lines that could be drawn between the firm and the customers, the more the customers would be committed to the organization.

So That: Investors

Some recent research by economists shows that the regression between earnings and shareholder value in the recent past (1960 through 1990) was between 75 percent and 90 percent. This meant that 75 to 90 percent of the market value of a firm (stock price multiplied by shares outstanding) could be predicted by the financial performance of the firm. However, since 1990, this percentage has dropped to about 55 percent. This means that an increasingly large portion of the market value of a firm is not directly tied to present earnings. Experts in the financial world assign this increasingly high percentage to *intangibles*, which means all things nonfinancial. Too often, intangibles is a catchword for "things we neither understand nor control."

I want to propose that a large portion of this intangible part of market value comes from quality of management. Financial results often indicate what is, not what will be. So investors seek lead indicators that seem to anticipate future success. Such indicators might be a firm's brand identity or its ability to be innovative, act quickly, or deliver what it promises. Underneath such organizational capabilities lies the firm's *quality of management*.

Although quality of management remains somewhat fuzzy as a concept and is hard to specify and measure, investors increasingly make buy-or-sell decisions on what they perceive the quality of management to be. In our work on results-based leaders, Jack Zenger, Norm Smallwood, and I have proposed some indicators of quality of management, such as the extent to which the top team faces and makes bold decisions, attracts and retains the best talent in the industry, learns from mistakes, forms relationships with key suppliers and customers, and has personal ownership in the firm. Often investor perceptions of quality of management are based only on intuition and presentations crafted for the investment community. Wise investors go beyond the stagecraft and explore actual organizational workings that reveal quality of management. Some of the questions investors could ask to investigate quality of management might reflect the practices I have described that companies use to connect with customers.

Investors and Staffing

What if the investors could vote on individuals hired and promoted in the firm? In some limited cases, investors do so through their surrogate voice, the board. But what if some of the large institutional investors participated in the interviews for senior officers? What questions would they ask? What leadership and management qualities would they look for? What types of individuals would give them confidence that the management team possessed the capacity to make correct decisions? Or alternatively, what if institutional investors reviewed the competence models used as candidate screens in the hiring process? Would the institutional investors focus on the same attributes as the traditional hiring manager? Would their interview questions be different?

These questions suggest that quality of management depends primarily on quality of hires and promotions. Using investor criteria and participation in the staffing process brings a rigor and discipline often overlooked. In addition, just as customers become more committed to firms in which they get to pick the employees, investors who participate in the selection of the management team may be more committed to that team's decisions and choices.

Investors and Training and Development

In a seminar to chief learning officers, I posed the following question: Assume a representative of the largest single investor in your firm sat through the last five-day leadership program you offered. What would be his or her investment response (buy, hold, sell) at the end of the week? This question forces officers to consider a new filter for what is taught, how it is taught, and what participants in training leave with at the end of the week. I would predict that most investors would be more positive if participants invested their training time focusing on real business issues within their firm rather than case studies of other firms, faced their competitive realities in candid conversation with thoughtful responses laid out, and left with clear and specific actions that would be taken as a result of the training experience. The ultimate impact of such training is to show investors that the leadership team knows what needs to be done, understands strategic choices, and is willing to make and implement bold decisions.

I would also predict that many of the training dollars currently spent would not lead to buy decisions because investors would not see the link between the training activities and business results. Some popular training exercises might need to be tweaked to serve investors. Outward-bound activities, for example, offer wonderful insights into how a team operates, makes decisions, and gets things done. But without skillful facilitation, the lessons learned from outward-bound exercises may not improve how work decisions are ultimately made back on the job. Investors would likely prefer that personal learnings and insights lead to business actions and results and that training investments require explicit translation of ideas into action.

Investors and Appraisal and Rewards

Many firms already tie management behaviors to investor-focused rewards. Putting a larger percentage of total compensation into stock-based incentives (grants, options, and so forth) links management actions to investors. Many claim that CEO pay relative to average employee pay is excessive. Such arguments are less tenable when CEO pay is linked to stock. When Michael Eisner, the CEO of Disney, makes a great deal of money because the price of Disney stock increases and much of his total compensation derives from that stock, few can argue, because they also had the opportunity to buy that stock. I would propose that the boundary between managers and investors is removed when managers become investors. In addition, the wider and deeper the investment mind-set throughout a firm, the more managers act and think like investors.

In the 1980s, I had the chance to work with a firm going through a leveraged buyout. The firm required that all managers invest from $100,000 to $5 million in the leveraged firm. The amount was high enough that it got the attention of the new owner-managers. And this simple act changed mind-sets and actions. Instead of flying three people to visit a customer, managers sent one. Instead of holding conferences at five-star hotels, they used company facilities. Instead of making visits to plan visits, they used phones and faxes for preliminary work. Literally thousands of decisions were made when managers shifted from being agents to being owners.

Developing investor bonds between managers and owners may go even further than making managers owners. Institutional investors might examine the firm's compensation philosophy and practices. In theory board members do this, acting on behalf of the owners, but institutional investors might become more active by reviewing standards set in performance appraisals, compensation practices used to change behavior, and feedback mechanisms used to share information. I have never seen a compensation task force include investors, but I hypothesize that the discussions of such a group might be more results focused.

Investors and Governance and Communication

Investors in publicly traded firms have traditionally been hands-off. They do not participate in teams, help develop processes, or work to set and accomplish strategy. However, when investors realize that intangibles predict shareholder value as much as financial performance does, they will begin to explore these intangibles. This means investors may help diagnose how well the organization makes decisions, allocates responsibilities, and follows up on commitments. Peter Lynch, a prominent investment adviser, has suggested that smart investors recognize firms that provide customers what they want (for example, Toys "R" Us). I would suggest that investors will increasingly explore the quality of management and governance to anticipate how well a firm will perform over time.

Communications between investors and the firm also must be candid and frequent. Investors do not like surprises, so managing their expectations becomes a critical issue. I worked for one firm where the relatively immature management team had experienced enormous success, which then led to arrogance. They claimed they knew the secrets of success within their industry and they could dictate to customers and overwhelm competitors. Their arrogance did not impress investors. When this company missed earnings projections, its stock fell dramatically. Investors quickly lost confidence in the management team because it had failed to learn and to share information openly. Other managers I work with share their firm's results openly with investors. One new CEO holds a weekly phone call with institutional investors in which he answers all questions and shares his observations. Because of the frequent and open communication and his ability to share problems early, the investors trust his judgment and make investments in his ability.

Summing Up the Investor Connection

Quality of management matters. When management practices connect with investors, the quality of management depends less on one person and more on the firm's ability to generate long-term management capability. In most firms, investors stay separate from the firm. When investors are connected to the firm more tightly through involvement in management practices, employees gain awareness of market realities, and investors develop credibility in management.

Implications

Leaders who blur the inside with the outside understand why things happen. They create value by connecting their work to both customers and investors. When they explicitly connect management practices to both customers and investors, they deliver long-term value to the firm. In the process of making these connections, they clarify the most important results for the firm (the things in which it must succeed), find ways to measure them, and build accountability for them.

9

REGINA E. HERZLINGER

CULTURE
IS THE KEY

Regina E. Herzlinger is the first Nancy R. McPherson
Professor of Business Administration at the Harvard
Business School. She has written many articles on
management control and health care, and her books
include The Four by Four Report: A Practical
Guide for Nonprofit Managers and Board Members, Conducting Your Financial Checkup, *and the*
best-selling, award-winning Market-Driven Health
Care. *Her research has been profiled in industry and*
business publications and recognized by the American
College of Healthcare Executives.

I s big beautiful?
Do economies of scale inevitably create low costs, satisfied
clients, ecstatic stakeholders?

Note: I am very grateful to Bea Bezmalinovic for her excellent research assistance
and to Kathleen Ryan and Chris Allen for their rapid and complete library research
in the preparation of this chapter. As always, I am enormously indebted to Aimée
Hamel's word-processing skills. The names in the two examples in the "Culture
Club" section of this chapter are pseudonyms.

A torrent of managerial advice would have you believe that they do. Integration is the key word in the advice, modified by various adjectives—horizontal, vertical, or in a postmodern incarnation, virtual. The vertical and horizontal integrators are traditionalists, who grow through marriage and progeny: the horizontal integrators bear many identical children, while the vertical integrators prefer arranged marriages to families that bring complementary skills to the union. In contrast, virtual integrators eschew the whole notion of marriage and family; instead, they live with different strategically selected partners, albeit in long-term relationships.

Because nonprofit organizations are typically small—only 19 percent of those filing financial information with the IRS had expenses of more than $1 million (V. A. Hodgkinson and M. S. Weitzman, *Nonprofit Almanac, 1996–1997,* 1996)—they are a tempting target for big-is-beautiful advice. In *Nonprofit Mergers and Alliances* (1998), for example, Thomas A. McLaughlin deplores the fact that small nonprofits are like "a multistory building heated entirely by a basement filled with stoves, each capable of warming no more than a room or two, instead of a single centralized heating system." Similarly, Martin W. Sandler and Deborah A. Hudson (*Beyond the Bottom Line,* 1998) argue that the key to obtaining the new resources urgently needed by nonprofits lies in "collaborations with other entities."

Is That All There Is?

Peggy Lee presented an existential view of life in her small, beautifully modulated voice when she sang the Leiber and Stoller song

> Is that all there is?
> Is that all there is?
> If that's all there is, my friend
> Then let's keep dancing
> Let's break out the booze
> and have a ball
> If that's all . . .
> There is.

So, following the great Peggy Lee's advice, if integration is the key to success, then let's close the book and have a ball. After all, integration is no big deal. All it requires is some horizontal and vertical alliances, whether real or virtual—a mere shuffle of the organizational deck. After that—it's party time!

But *is* that all there is?

What evidence do we have that big is really beautiful? That a large scale really creates economies? At one time, industrial successes provided seemingly indisputable proof. Take Andrew Carnegie, for example. His giant Homestead factory, employing four thousand men, enabled Carnegie to slash the price of steel rails from $160 a ton in 1875 to $17 in 1898 (P. Johnson, *A History of the American People*, 1998). But such big-is-beautiful economics were seemingly overturned by the more recent stunning success of steel minimills. By 1998, they accounted for 43 percent of U.S. steel production (C. Adams, "Steel Minimills," *Wall Street Journal*, Jan. 12, 1998). Although the diminutive, *mini*, is a tad misleading (these mills, whose revenues can reach billions of dollars, are hardly pocket-sized), they are nevertheless smaller than the integrated, big-is-beautiful steel firms they supplanted.

So what is a nonprofit to do? Yes, up to a point big is beautiful; but beyond that point big can be ugly, inefficient, unsustainable.

Where is the magic inflection point on the bigness curve at which the beauty is transformed into the beast?

It's the Culture, Stupid

George Bush, the forty-first president of the United States, began his reelection campaign in the warm glow of a dazzling U.S. military victory in the Persian Gulf War. He was a sure bet. After all, he was a military hero, a patrician Yale Phi Beta Kappa, a true public servant, whereas his opponent was the virtually unknown governor of one of the nation's poorest states and tarred with unsavory allegations. But Bush lost the election to his opponent, William J. Clinton.

What happened?

As James Carville, President Clinton's political adviser, gleefully pointed out in his distinctive wise-guy persona, Bush missed the obvious: "It's the economy, stupid." The U.S. economy was in the doldrums, and Americans vote for their pocketbooks above all else.

Many smart people replicate Bush's mistake: they miss the obvious. To my mind, leaders who believe that structural rearrangement of an organization—horizontal or vertical, merged or virtual—is the key to performance similarly miss the obvious. It is the culture, not only the arrangement of boxes on the organization chart, that counts.

In many organizations, culture—an attitude, a way of doing things, a set of values—is so deeply internalized that it is not readily observable. Nevertheless, it is the key to their success. When these cultured organizations become uncultured—by distancing themselves from their internalized values, attitudes, and approaches—they falter. In this chapter I argue that organizational culture is the handmaiden to beauty in bigness. In support of this view, I describe a health care organization that first grew successfully by maintaining its culture and subsequently grew unsuccessfully by neglecting it. Because the nonprofit health care sector has long been in the vanguard of the integration movement, this organization provides valuable lessons for other nonprofits.

The Culture Club

We were in a charming restaurant on the north shore of Massachusetts. The Essex River flowed gently outside. The delicious fruits of the Atlantic Ocean—lobsters, clams, scallops—graced our plates. The mood was mellow. We had all safely reached middle age: our marriages and health intact; our kids great, so far, so good; and our careers satisfying.

Nevertheless, Paul, a gentle vascular surgeon, shattered the mood. He could not help himself. He simply had to get it off his chest: "Dot, you won't believe what happened to me this week."

Dot, a pediatric endocrinologist, listened sympathetically. We all knew what was coming.

"I checked an elderly diabetic into my hospital. The guy had a lot of troubles. A great guy; but he just can't manage his diabetes. I had operated on his foot only a few weeks ago. And what do you know? As soon as he heals, he goes on a bender. His sugar goes out of control. He is in terrible shape. I checked him into the hospital because I suspected he had an aneurysm. If he tested positive, I knew I had to operate immediately, the next day. That baby could blow any minute.

"Well, this PCP [primary care physician] who is my patient's HMO gatekeeper calls me when he gets the bill. He thinks I should not have admitted the guy into the hospital for that extra day. I told him in no uncertain terms that he just does not understand medicine. He is out of his league; out of his depth."

Dot's husband, a pulmonary specialist who moonlights as a reviewer for HMOs, asked: "Did you tell the PCP that the patient was in for a test and that you felt it necessary to operate immediately if the test was positive? Did you ask for authorization?"

"No," said Paul. "Look, this was a life-or-death situation. Everybody knows I had to admit the patient. Immediately. I didn't have the time to ask for authorization. Anyway, how can that PCP possibly evaluate my management of this case? He's no vascular surgeon."

Dot nodded. "He certainly was not very collegial. How could he do that to you?"

"How should he have learned to be collegial?" I asked, my curiosity piqued.

"In the home," Dot answered, unhesitatingly. "If you don't learn how to be collegial there, you'll never learn it. Parents should bring their children up right."

The conversation resonated with me. It reminded me of many similar conversations in organizations: "How could she do that? How could she be so stupid, ignorant, assertive, or fill in the unflattering adjective?" But there was an important difference. In successful organizations, if it is frequent enough, a confrontation of this sort leads to analysis and ultimately to a corrective plan of action. For example, in this case the two principals would have met, perhaps with their manager, to clarify the source of their problem and to develop a remedy. Likely they would have agreed that their confrontation occurred because of the absence of protocols: the surgeon and the PCP lacked a clear organizational relationship and a common information set. Although they ostensibly worked for the same organization, they lacked any way to dispassionately analyze their differences.

Let's examine a similar problem in a successful organization. Jane, the Oklahoma-based technical specialist for a firm that manufactures life-support equipment is notified that the device in a Louisiana hospital is not working properly. The hospital has no backup and has tried all the usual remedies to no avail. This too is a life-or-death situation that calls for immediate action. But, unlike Paul and the PCP, Jane knows how to proceed: she e-mails a request to her superior for permission to ship a replacement device on an expensive ASAP basis, with a clear explanation of the need, and beeps for an immediate response. Permission is expeditiously granted. She also knows that if she does not receive a response within fifteen minutes, she is authorized to proceed on her own.

To my mind, the crucial difference between these two similar situations does not hinge on the existence of clear organizational protocols. They are important of course, but the key difference is that one organization had a managerial culture that led to the development of such protocols and the other did not. People in an organization whose managerial culture relies on a shared vision are positive and action oriented—"let's work this out"—rather than negative and blame oriented—"it's all your fault." Because they share a common vision of the goals and activities of the organization, they do not assume that all confrontations are clashes of personality or that people must rely on their upbringing to work together in a productive way.

Nevertheless, despite the obvious importance of a managerial culture to the success of an organization, the wisest leaders may miss that point. While they shuffle the boxes on their organizational charts—integrating horizontally or vertically or merging or franchising or forming strategic relationships—the culture dies of neglect.

The Care and Feeding of Culture

What is culture? Where does it originate? How does it sustain itself?

For one answer, let us examine the history of the Jews, a group whose culture has long survived despite its members' geographical dispersion and nomadic existence. In his wonderful book *The Gifts of the Jews* (1998), Thomas Cahill explains a unique aspect of the culture of the Jewish people: "For the ancients, the future was always a replay of the past. . . . But [for the Jews] . . . history does not repeat itself . . . it is always something new—we are not doomed, not bound to some predetermined fate; we are free." This sense of freedom denied the divinity of political leaders, like the Egyptian Pharaohs, and instead emphasized the personal moral responsibility embodied in the Ten Commandments. It enabled the Jewish culture to survive in many different environments.

This culture was forged during the forty years that Moses led the Israelites in the desert (W. Keller, *The Bible as History*, 1988). It was strengthened by successful responses to external challenges. Consider, for example, the effect of the pursuit by the Egyptians. At first, intimidated, the Israelites cry:

> Let us alone that we may serve Egypt!
> Indeed, better for us serving Egypt
> Than our dying alone in the wilderness! [Exodus 14:12]

But after Moses leads them through a sea in which the Egyptians are drowned, "the people trusted in God and in Moses his servant" (Exodus 14:31). The desert itself—parched, desolate—helped to forge the culture too, as did responses to internal challenges. When the Hebrews worshiped multiple gods in the fertility rites of Baal, for example, Moses struck hard at his own people. As the Bible approvingly recounts, one of Moses' followers thrust a javelin "through the man of Israel, and the woman through her belly" (Numbers 25:8). But this harsh life had its rewards—manna from heaven and the promise that "if you . . . keep my covenant . . . you shall be to me . . . a holy nation" (Exodus 19:5–6).

Culture does not inevitably require strong leaders. Moses, for example, felt unqualified to accept leadership responsibilities. When God commands him to lead the Israelites out of Egypt, a hesitant Moses responds:

> Please, my lord,
> No man of words am I. . . .
> For heavy of mouth and heavy of tongue am I! [Exodus 4:10]

Nevertheless, Moses is a good leader—with a steadfast vision. Born a Jew, raised as an Egyptian prince, forced to flee Egypt to maintain his Jewish identity, Moses has the clear vision of those who define themselves. He also forges some powerful alliances: with God for one; with his eloquent, weak brother Aaron for another; and with his ferocious enforcers, the sons of Levi. His ultimate ally is his successor—the clever, courageous Joshua, who leads the Israelites out of the desert.

Myth or reality? As Keller points out, considerable archeological evidence supports the major elements of the story told in Exodus; but even if the physical evidence were absent, the psychological elements of the story ring true. It seems right that cultures are formed from an unusual point of view, refined and strengthened by external and internal challenges, and led by a portfolio of people with complementary skills. Failures and hardships define a culture as much as its successes. The culture survives its immediate leaders and is passed on from one generation to the next, in part through continual repetition of the pivotal events in the formation of the culture. For this reason, the story of the exodus from Egypt permeates virtually all of the Jewish liturgy.

The Cultured Kaiser Permanente

All these elements of culture were present in the early days of the Kaiser Foundation Health Plan, the fabled California-based HMO. Indeed, by 1992, Kaiser was so widely admired that many proposed it as the model for President and Mrs. Clinton's national health care reform initiative.

Kaiser, one of the pioneers in prepaid health care, was a vertically integrated troika composed of a managed care insurer, groups of hospitals, and groups of physicians. The latter two provided their services exclusively to the insurance arm. Kaiser differed from the traditional health care system in its organization—the vertically integrated, organized physician and hospital groups as opposed to fragmented providers—and in its financing—it was paid a fixed sum to provide all the health care needs of its enrollees as opposed to collecting a fee for each service rendered.

Good evidence supported the enthusiasm for Kaiser. It was among the largest health care providers in the United States—covering more than nine million people in 1995 (Kaiser Foundation Health Plan Inc., www.Kaiserpermanente.org and http://globalbb.onesource.com/brow at Health Plan Inc.). It was rated among the country's best HMOs by popular consumer publications (See, for example, "America's Best HMOs," *Newsweek*, June 24, 1996). Kaiser's excellence was evidenced by its size: if it had been a public corporation, its 1992 revenues of $11 billion and profits of $796 million would have placed it forty-third on the list of the Fortune 500 (Martha Groves, "Ailing Health Care System May Get Kaiser-Style Care," *Los Angeles Times*, May 10, 1993).

This Kaiser was as cultured as cultured can be. It developed its culture the old-fashioned way: it earned it. Its principals, an extraordinary businessman and a physician, had a long and productive history of collaboration and the other physicians and managers who formed the organization had also spent considerable time together in its early years. Like the Jews who after forty years of wandering in the desert with Moses developed a clear, cohesive identity, these early Kaiserites literally lived together in the desert for five years in the 1930s and in geographically isolated sites during World War II. External challenges from hostile medical associations and Communist hunter U.S. Senator Joseph McCarthy and internal challenges from dissident groups strengthened the organization. Failures helped to clarify its culture nearly as much as successes.

The story begins with Sidney Garfield, an entrepreneurial physician who started his career in the Mojave Desert in 1933 by building a hospital and employing doctors to provide health care to the workers who built the Los Angeles aqueduct. Virtually from the inception of his career, Garfield insisted on prepayment for his services. His reason was purely practical: "The insurance companies held the money but they were anxious to keep it. We would treat a patient with tender loving care and, more often than not, the (insurers) would discount our bill, saying we had treated the patient too many times" (J. G. Smillie, *Can Physicians Manage the Quality and Costs of Health Care?* 1991; the following information about Kaiser's history until the 1990s rests mainly on Smillie's work). Later Garfield saw that prepayment also motivated doctors to try to correct problems that if neglected would create more expensive health care in the future. For example, to avoid the head injuries caused by loose rocks in the aqueduct, Garfield convinced the contractors to shore up areas he identified as dangerous.

As this pioneering financing mechanism indicates, Garfield was an astute businessman. At the end of the project, in 1938, he had managed to accumulate $250,000 in profits (at a time when the average annual wage was $1,350). In part the profits emerged from Garfield's tight rein on the purse strings. His frugality was legendary. For example, in the 1940s, "employees could obtain a new pencil only if they turned in a pencil stub of three inches or less. A Pencil Stub

Club rewarded those who had served the organization for 35 years with a stub-shaped lapel pin." Recalls an observer, "this period of stringent economy established a pattern of frugal allocation of resources that persisted even into more prosperous years. Formed by these early economies, the physicians and staff, as a matter of institutional culture, continued to abhor waste."

Garfield's rapport with the physicians who worked for him, some of whom he had met as fellow medical students, also enabled him to earn such substantial profits without compromising health care quality. Smillie reports for example that Garfield's physicians worked six days a week on one project, but "there was no complaining." For one thing the physicians formed a tight social group, "all liking each other—we picked people who liked each other—we felt like we were enjoying ourselves." For another, Garfield, the physicians' boss, nevertheless was one of the guys; he worked alongside the other physicians and continually sought out their advice about new ideas. Garfield understood the importance of this culture; for example, he attributed the failure to provide cost-effective health services in a Vancouver project to people who "weren't producing and they didn't care about utilization of the hospital . . . they were not interested in making our plan work."

The five-year sojourn in the desert not only laid the foundation for the prepaid group practice but also introduced Garfield to his lifelong partner, the industrialist Henry J. Kaiser. The two were complementary. Garfield, a reserved, enigmatic physician, was drawn to the ebullient, expansive Kaiser, a man who could accomplish the seemingly impossible, including the construction of the massive Hoover Dam. For his part, Kaiser, who saw himself as a benevolent employer, felt that Garfield could provide excellent health care to the workers in his various geographically isolated construction and World War II defense contract sites.

Both men were self-created. Garfield was the son of Jewish immigrants whose self-creation had even extended to picking a new surname. Kaiser, for his part, had abandoned his home and school after the eighth grade to seek his fortune. He ultimately built an empire based on his astounding organizational skills: construction, ships, steel, cement, autos, hotels—he did them all. "Rome wasn't built in a day," he bragged, "because the Romans didn't give us the contract."

The bond between the two ran very deep. Garfield always referred to Kaiser as "the boss." Eventually, he even became Kaiser's brother-in-law, despite the twenty-four-year difference in their ages, marrying the sister of Kaiser's second wife. Garfield even concurred with Kaiser's critiques of his management style. "Mr. Kaiser doesn't have any confidence in my ability to manage the program, and everyone agrees [that] . . . strong leadership hasn't emerged yet," he noted in 1953 about his stewardship of the organization he created.

After Garfield successfully provided health care to Kaiser's workers during World War II, he proposed to establish a private prepaid group practice. The true believers came with him: in Northern California, only thirteen of one hundred physicians. In 1945, the nonprofit Permanente Health Plan was formed. Garfield, who owned the physicians' group and who leased the hospitals owned by the Permanente Foundation, effectively ran the whole show, although the Henry J. Kaiser Company had formal control. Garfield's unilateral management became increasingly untenable as the organization grew. In 1948, he took six partners into his solely owned medical practice and withdrew from administration of the medical group. He noted, "I did this with complete faith—blind faith—that these changes would not alter the situation. We doctors had conceived the plan, developed it, sacrificed for it, made it work, and believed that it was going to remain in operation."

Their belief in their vision of a prepaid group health practice was strengthened by the attacks of medical societies, who saw the Kaiser physicians as economic threats and as compromisers of physician independence who permitted a nonphysician board to control them. The medical societies also presciently questioned whether prepayment would motivate physicians to provide fewer services than needed. Permanente physicians were routinely rejected for membership in these societies. However, these attacks backfired. For example, Paul de Kruif, a well-known author whose son was a Kaiser doctor, defended the organization in a series of widely read *Reader's Digest* articles, thus bringing it to the sympathetic attention of the public.

The charges of Communist ties among Kaiser physicians, which began in the late 1940s and intensified during the Senate investigations chaired by Joseph McCarthy, also strengthened the organization. When Henry Kaiser fired three physicians out of concern that the charges levied against these doctors would compromise the Kaiser Company's defense contracts, the medical group, in response to this intrusion and other issues of control, argued for increased self-governance. As one physician skeptically observed after a conciliatory country club dinner, the Kaiser higher-ups were "telling us what a good job we were doing but [that] really we ought to spend our efforts in taking care of the patients . . . and they would run the business. We had sense enough to feel this wasn't quite right. Providing medical care was itself a business."

Meanwhile, insurgent physicians also quarreled with Garfield's frugality. One left the organization in a well-publicized disagreement about what he considered Garfield's overly stringent spending for nurses, equipment, and physicians. His concerns were shared: in symbolic rebellion "everyone would break a pencil into three three-inch pieces [and turn them in] and get three full pencils back." These concerns finally led to Garfield's demotion, in 1955, to vice president of facilities and management.

Integration followed culture. The relationship among the three interdependent components of the Kaiser organization was clarified well after the culture was established. In 1957, a formal agreement about the autonomy, governmental rights, and compensation formulas for the physicians' medical group was signed. The importance of the medical group's and hospitals' practice style to the overall organization was underscored by the failure of Henry Kaiser's unilateral attempt to create a Hawaii branch. When his attempts to convert five successful fee-for-service physicians to a medical group style of practice faltered, Kaiser finally brought in the true believers, Garfield and his prepaid group practice acolytes from California. The importance of the hospital and insurer arms was emphasized when the medical group's attempt to build its own vertically integrated system in San Diego, with its own hospitals and health plan, floundered absent Kaiser's approval.

The Integrated Kaiser Permanente

The founders of the cultured Kaiser Permanente had a novel vision: prepaid health care services delivered by a vertically integrated troika of insurers, medical groups, and hospitals. The vision was formed in the desert by a group of like-minded physicians and managers. It was sharpened by attacks from within and without. The opposition by medical societies forced Kaiser to articulate its vision in a way that was widely acceptable to the general public. The opposition from within to its early leaders and the friction among its three parts forced the organization to clarify and formalize its internal governance protocols and organizational structure. At the end, this cultured organization achieved great financial and medical success. And deservedly so.

Kaiser's 1992 selection by some health care reformers as the model for the U.S. health care system seemed like its apotheosis. Instead, that year marked a period of turmoil and decline for the organization. By October 1997, Kaiser's chief financial officer announced its first-ever loss, which she estimated at $30 to $50 million. She was embarrassingly wrong. The loss for the year reported in the press turned out to be $270 million.

An organization's inability to forecast its earnings correctly is usually viewed as a serious problem, perhaps even more serious than a loss, because it frequently indicates a fundamental lack of managerial control. And indeed, there were other signs at that time that the fabled Kaiser might have lost its way. As the press noted, flip-

flops in managerial communications abounded. In 1994, the organization's chairman deplored legislation that would have required
Kaiser plans to include any provider willing to accept Kaiser's fee,
noting that it "would seriously undermine or eliminate an ability to
provide high-quality, cost-effective care" (R. Pear, "The Health
Care Debate," *New York Times*, Aug. 23, 1994). But by 1998, Kaiser
had introduced a systemwide point-of-service plan that enabled
enrollees to visit non-Kaiser doctors for additional fees and, in some
areas, Kaiser's preferred provider plans included no Kaiser doctors.
In addition, Kaiser purchased health plans from public for-profit
HMOs, like Humana, that had little ideological kinship with its
group practice basis. And although in 1993 the Kaiser chairman
claimed that efforts to build networks in areas like Texas were not
a financial drain, by 1998 he acknowledged that they were spin-off
or sale candidates because of losses such as the $50 million deficit
in Dallas–Fort Worth.

Kaiser's problems were not wholly financial. The quality of care
in its Texas plan triggered a critical report by the state insurance
department (later settled by a $1 million fine) and a malpractice
lawsuit settled for $5.3 million. In California a state inspection
found serious deficiencies in its Oakland and Richmond hospitals.
Labor problems abounded too. In April of 1996, thousands of
unionized Kaiser workers picketed the organization. A nurse at
Kaiser's Oakland facility who was not bound by gag rules noted,
"We've watched the quality of care go downhill." The California
Nurses Association successfully struck against Kaiser, in part because
of their concern that the organization was spending $60 million on
marketing while laying off nurses. Doctors were unhappy too, some
even proposing affiliations with other plans.

Kaiser's explanations for these problems follow: The loss? "We
missed the price turn in the industry" (M. Freudenheim, "Kaiser
HMO, Erring on Costs, Posts $270 Million Loss for '97," *New York
Times*, Feb. 14, 1998). Employee and quality problems? "That's a flat
lie. These are human systems . . . they don't work because there are

honest mistakes" (L. Kertesz, "Which Is the Real Kaiser? A Model of Cost-Effective Quality Care or a Greedy Medical Factory That Endangers Its Patients?" *Modern Healthcare*, Aug. 25, 1997). Problems in Texas? "The media often focus on isolated incidents that are 'unrelated to the things being done to make the organization stronger'" (Kertesz, "Which Is the Real Kaiser?"). "This was a set-up" (Freudenheim, "Kaiser HMO").

But to my mind, these problems indicate a flaw more fundamental than errors in human systems or forecasting costs: Kaiser appears to have strayed from its cultural roots. In the early 1990s, Kaiser fashioned a growth strategy to reverse scant increases in enrollment. It sought out new managers (one estimate placed 50 percent to 60 percent of its top managers as new to their positions and 20 percent to 30 percent as new to the organization) and new acquisitions and affiliations (Kertesz). These changes caused membership to soar; but at what cost? The culture-imbued physicians, the Kaiser-managed hospitals, the tense interplay among the three elements of the Kaiser system—all of these were likely diminished in a growth strategy in which Kaiser embraced physicians it did not know, hospitals it did not manage, and geographical regions whose politics and populace it did not fully understand.

Don't get me wrong. I do not question the intelligence, energy, honesty, or motives of Kaiser's management. But growth by integration is intrinsically flawed if it neglects the organization's culture. Absent the financial and quality controls internalized by the Garfield-era doctors, managers, and their progeny, losses and allegations of quality problems should come as no surprise. As Sidney Garfield wisely and prophetically noted: "If you don't have the . . . groups who have it in their hearts to make it work and who believe in prepaid practice, it won't work. This is the thing that makes me wonder about HMOs all over the country. They aren't going to work unless they get men . . . who really believe in giving service to the people" (Smillie, *Can Physicians Manage . . . ?*).

Lessons for Nonprofits

The Kaiser tale carries many important lessons for nonprofit organizations that are contemplating integration strategies:

1. *Do you have a distinct culture, a point of view widely shared by a core group of true believers?* If not, don't even think about a get-big strategy. You are likely instead to get lost.

2. *Grow a culture.* Identify what is unique about your organization's goals and activities; build a group of true believers; test and strengthen your organization against internal and external critics. Then, and only then, should you think about integration.

3. *Is big beautiful?* Answer this question before you grow. Will size provide you with economies of scale or improved quality? If not, remember: big can be ugly.

4. *If you grow, grow culturally.* Don't marry or even live with organizations that don't share your culture, unless you are convinced that you can convert them to your point of view. Growth by integration with uncultured organizations will inevitably cause problems in your organization.

10 STRATFORD SHERMAN

THE POWER
OF CHOICE

Stratford Sherman, coauthor (with Noel Tichy) of
Control Your Destiny or Someone Else Will, *is a*
globally recognized authority on management issues.
He serves as an executive coach, frequently addresses
industry groups, and is a contributing editor of Fortune
magazine.

Individual contributors have never been more crucial to organizational success—or more cynical. In this era of knowledge workers, tight job markets, and Dilbert, winning voluntary commitment to shared goals has become a central challenge for leadership. While the chiefs of the world's most advanced corporations search for answers, an obscure Philippine charity serving homeless children demonstrates the principles that work. The Tuloy sa Don Bosco Street Children Project is at once an inspiring model of effective public service and a potent example for any leader hoping to win allegiance to his or her ideas.

The ambitious mission of Tuloy sa Don Bosco is to help Filipino street children—who live almost as savages amid poverty, filth, violence, and crime—remake themselves into productive citizens. Like any organization that seeks to unlock human potential, this group builds on firm convictions. It is affiliated with a Catholic order, the Salesians of Don Bosco, which is named after its founder, Saint John Bosco, a nineteenth-century Italian saint devoted to homeless children. Tuloy's founder and head, Father Marciano Evangelista—everyone calls him Father Rocky—is an energetic, clear-thinking priest with a mystical bent. Not surprisingly, his organization is deeply grounded in faith. At the same time, one of its most potent core beliefs is in the transforming power of free choice. As Father Rocky says, "How can you trust a former street child? Only when he values his choice. He needs opportunities to choose what is good and what is right—so the institution should be permeated with opportunities for these choices. Human potential is almost unlimited, and freedom of choice is the way to bring it out. A person who chooses change will himself tear down the barriers and remove the debris of the past. It takes time. Imposing the law is a shortcut that doesn't change anything. Behavior changes only when one internalizes the spirit of the law."

The lesson here for any organization hoping to alter the behavior of its members is that people *can* change—but real change is the outcome of personal choice and voluntary commitment. Force and coercion require tremendous attention and energy yet produce limited results. Genuine transformation, lasting and self-sustaining, is the fruit of freedom. It begins with the right to say no.

The blight of child homelessness, which pervades most of the world, is painfully visible in Manila, capital city of the Philippines. At last count, in 1990, some 110,000 children lived principally on Manila's streets, congregating in parks and markets, begging, selling, and stealing. Their average age is twelve, though children as young as seven make their way onto the streets, driven from their homes by poverty, family dysfunction, violence, or exploitation ranging from sexual abuse to forced labor. Three-quarters of Filipino street children find their way to some sort of home at night. The remaining 25 percent sleep on the street, fending entirely for themselves. Five percent of street children are orphans or utterly abandoned, with no home to which they could possibly return. These boys are the most vulnerable ones, easy marks for predators of all kinds, driven with dreary predictability to drug abuse and crime. (Child homelessness is almost entirely a male phenomenon in the Philippines: girls who leave home young generally become victims of prostitution and require distinctly different social services.) By the late 1990s, as the Asian financial crisis deepened poverty in the Philippines, ever more children flowed to the streets; no one knows how many, but the 1990 data must greatly underestimate the actual numbers. Visitors to Manila see street children even in the upscale district of Makati; in the barrios and outside nightclubs the kids swarm in gangs, squalid in unwashed clothes, wary, suspicious, hungry for whatever is in your pocket.

At the time of Tuloy sa Don Bosco's founding in 1993, the typical charity serving Manila's street kids was a soup kitchen, free clothing depot, or overnight hostel. Its mission was to reduce suffering, which seemed achievable, rather than to change behavior, which seemed impossible. Enter Father Rocky. Although he had spent most of his life in the Salesian order, he says he "wanted nothing to do with street urchins" until he started Tuloy. At age thirteen, hoping to become a pilot, he had left his home in a village north of Manila to attend the Don Bosco Technical Institute, one of the country's better high schools. Thriving, he went on to study math, philosophy, and organizational development at the Don Bosco College of Philosophy in Hong Kong, then trained for the priesthood at a Don Bosco institute in Rome. Thus educated, he returned to his own country as a school official, founded an engineering college, and then became the principal of his former high school. A formidable, broad-shouldered man with black hair and gentle brown eyes, Father Rocky focused on serving his order at a high level, as an effective senior administrator. He regarded street children as a smelly distraction.

Then, in 1991, the Salesian order reassigned Father Rocky as priest of its parish church in the Makati district of Manila. With the parish came a room dedicated to street urchin programs. As it happened, the church soon burned down. When Father Rocky oversaw the plans for rebuilding, he intentionally omitted the room for the street children. Then one day the top leaders of the order decided that a new program for street children was needed, even though the church no longer had space available for it. They asked for a volunteer to lead it, and Father Rocky, astonished, found himself raising his hand—an act he attributes to divine intervention. Since then, he says with evident contentment, "What was not my cup of tea has become my daily bread."

Once committed, Father Rocky approached the task as an effective administrator. He analyzed the existing programs for street children and the needs of the children he meant to serve. Taking to the streets himself, hanging around parks and nightclubs late at night in his clerical robes, Father Rocky developed a profile of his target market. "None of the existing programs were tailored to their needs," he recalls.

> I found these kids far behind the achievement levels of children their own age at normal schools, and poor in theoretical, abstract thinking. But they are survivors, very practical and concrete, skilled at making do with what they have. What they need is a practical, work-oriented education. It must be part of a program comprehensive enough, and long-lasting enough, to enable a child to reorient his whole life, acquire new habits and skills, and achieve self-sufficiency. Just as the street was the school of these children, so our program must provide an environment designed to restore the values that have been lost. And we need links with other programs, so that we can serve as a kind of catch basin for children in need. With a problem so vast, your program must be equally big—to succeed, it must be even bigger than the problem.

The name Father Rocky gave to the program he designed, *Tuloy*, is a word in Pilipino, the national language, that means "welcome" and "to continue." The mission is to welcome street children into a healing, nurturing environment and to continue the relationship with the boys until they have transformed themselves. Father Rocky and his supporters raised $700,000 to build a new complex that includes dormitories, classrooms, and a large, cement-floored indoor gym; in this complex, Tuloy sa Don Bosco can accommodate 250 students, including 150 residents. The curriculum it offers is mostly practical: basic communication skills in English and Pilipino; basic science and math; and teachings in values, character, and moral formation. Everything else is oriented to training boys in employable skills: woodworking, electrical, welding, refrigeration, automotive repair. Boys may enter the program at any age and remain until graduation—which, given their late start in schooling, may come as late as the age of twenty.

That much of the program design seems intelligent but hardly inspiring. What makes Tuloy sa Don Bosco work is the way it draws boys into its school. Dealing with one of the most cynical, even hostile clienteles that can be imagined, the program wins the allegiance of these children by offering them a real alternative at every step.

To recruit candidates, Father Rocky and his associates hit the streets, often at night, and approach street children—a particularly challenging form of what salesmen term *cold calling*. They offer what little they have to give: food, shelter, clothing, safety, and companionship.

Children who accept the offer are admitted to the *free zone*, a plain, unfurnished room adjacent to the basketball court. Here, on the floor, the boys may sleep in safety. Explaining why he doesn't offer beds, Father Rocky says, "A street child doesn't distinguish between bed and pavement. He has become insensitive to what is soft and beautiful." Most of the kids arrive with hidden weapons: crude knives, ice picks, hammers, tongs, hunks of iron fashioned into dull, pathetic bludgeons. Many also possess drugs. As a matter of policy, Tuloy sa Don Bosco makes no attempt to confiscate the drugs or weapons. "Even if they tell you they don't have a knife," explains Father Rocky, "they have something hidden somewhere, on the roof or up a tree. You can never find them all." Rather than lose credibility by failing to enforce a prohibition, the project grants children in the free zone the right to carry whatever they want. The only rules are bans on theft and violence. The penalty for violating either rule is immediate expulsion, but in Tuloy's infinitely forgiving environment even expulsion is but a temporary reproof. Violators are always welcome back, so long as they are willing to change.

The free zone serves as a laboratory for countless small experiments in socialization. There, in a safe middle ground between the chaos of the streets and the strict order of the school, children can rest, eat, and play for as long as they want. Boys staying there may not enter the dormitory and school areas until they commit to a considerably stricter set of rules and obligations, but their residence in the free zone is potentially unlimited. Indeed, children have lived there for as long as six months. In addition to free food and clothing, children receive bus fare each morning so that they can return to their accustomed parks and street corners during the day.

The money serves as a test: children who leave in the morning darkness, before the money is distributed, presumably have broken one of the house rules; why else would an impoverished kid pass up money offered with no strings attached? Thus each boy reveals his values through his own actions. Upon his return—if he returns—the boy and a member of the program staff have a conversation designed to help him face his own behavior. Says Father Rocky:

> If they come back, we're glad, but we want to process what the child has done. We want the child to open his mind, to process every experience he has. So we say, "You ran away without pocket money, why did you do it? You don't have to tell me what you did, you can stay, but don't do it again." Maybe they just wanted to steal a pair of pants, but

that is part of the game. If I lose seven pairs of pants, that is about $50. Is it worth losing $50 if then the kid comes back? Oh yes! Am I willing to lose $100? Sure! Because we are talking about the life of a child.

Often a boy will sneak away four or five times before deciding to participate in the normal rhythms of the free zone. Many may not return, but the program strategy is not based on Darwinian self-selection. Father Rocky and his staff hope every boy will come back, and if they encounter a wayward boy on the street, they will invite him back regardless of his past behavior. Each boy is regarded as precious. The mission is to try to save every one.

A key aspect of Tuloy's design limits the population of the free zone to roughly 10 percent of the total number of resident boys. Like most people, young Filipinos are strongly inclined to model their behavior on that of older or more successful people. Tuloy consciously uses that predilection as a lever, allowing the free-zone boys to mix with the schoolboys in the gymnasium area for basketball and other games. The schoolboys, dominant by virtue of their number and privileges, embody the commitment to civilized behavior, which is what won them entry to the dormitory and school. In this way the environment itself serves to reshape the values of the free-zone boys. Over time, many of them begin to wish that they too were sleeping in beds in the dorm and learning skills at the Tuloy sa Don Bosco School.

Eventually some 35 percent of the free-zone boys choose to accept the discipline of the dormitory and the school. This compares to a 10 percent retention rate at conventional institutions serving street children. That choice, freely made, constitutes a decisive rejection of the ethos of the streets. In the dorms no drugs or weapons are allowed. Boys who may never have washed themselves in their lives now must take two or even three showers daily. They wash their own clothes instead of throwing them away, tidy their beds and lockers, and eat with clean hands. They rise at 5:30 A.M.

to begin a fully scheduled day of classes, meals, worship, and exercise. The transition is difficult for most. But as the children acquire new habits of cleanliness and discipline, they become more self-conscious; with the dawning awareness of their own state comes the desire for improvement; and from that desire, change is born. In Father Rocky's view, order itself becomes an affirmation of freedom from hopelessness and defeat.

Unlike boys in the free zone, dormitory residents who break rules face punishment. One night when the kids stampeded carelessly into the dining room, for instance, the whole group was denied dinner. This shift gets to the core of Father Rocky's philosophy: "The only way you can discipline a child who has been running his own life in the street is by making him accept discipline as a value," he says. "That will only happen when he chooses to stay in a place where discipline is a value. So even when they are in the residency, the boys know they can leave. We always repeat to them, 'You are here because of your own choice.' However, once the child begins to accept discipline as a value, I can impose sanctions on his violations." At that point, in effect, the child has begun to be a responsible member of society.

Perhaps it is premature to judge the success of Tuloy sa Don Bosco, whose first formal class will not graduate until 2000. Nevertheless, the early signs are encouraging. Before starting this venture, Father Rocky had asked economists at the University of the Philippines to calculate the return on investment if Tuloy could make productive citizens of street children. The scholars calculated that the savings in avoided property loss, reduced law enforcement expense, and the like, would produce a return of 60 percent on the program's modest cost. So far most of the boys who enter the residency either remain until completing their courses or return, reconciled, to their homes. Thus far twenty-seven older boys have informally been graduated from Tuloy sa Don Bosco after relatively short periods in residence. Despite a severe economic recession, one-third of them have found jobs, another third have returned to their families' homes, and only a third have returned to the streets. Says Father Rocky, "The fact that so many were even willing to *look* for a job represents an enormous change."

While awaiting more statistical data, it may be helpful to offer some subjective observations. When I visited Tuloy sa Don Bosco in 1998, I was deeply impressed, even moved, by the light in the boys' eyes. At work in their classes, the older boys in particular made no false effort to impress or even acknowledge their visitors; yet as they concentrated on their air conditioners and car engines and made muted comments to one another, they seemed clear-eyed and untroubled. The atmosphere in the place, which might have felt prison-like, instead was delightful, energetic, and upbeat.

Father Rocky measures success in his own way: since 1996 there have been many fights, but only one with knives. The boys' lockers no longer have locks, yet thefts are becoming rare. Perhaps more important, the boys are clean, they do their homework and learn their lessons, and when something is stolen, they side with the authorities who want the wrongdoing to cease. They are, in short, becoming civilized.

By late 1998, Tuloy sa Don Bosco was operating at full capacity. Father Rocky had begun raising $6 million to build a new facility for one thousand children, on land outside Manila provided by the government. Just as the fundraising campaign began, the Philippine economy collapsed: so far Father Rocky has raised only $200,000. But he argues that with both the Lord and return on investment on his side, his quest cannot fail.

Business managers who study this case may be less certain of divine support and economic returns, but they can still learn from Father Rocky. I have observed that most corporate efforts to impose values and transform organizational behavior end in disappointment or failure, often because of undue reliance on force. The habit of relying on power and coercion to effect change is a weakness common to ineffective leaders the world over. Although telling people what to do produces limited results, many bosses regard it as their right, even their duty. The example of Tuloy sa Don Bosco suggests a different approach, based on respect, trust, and a willingness to let individuals make choices for themselves. This leadership approach boils down to seven key ideas:

1. Start with full confidence in the potential of your people.
2. Treat each person as an individual.
3. Use every opportunity to encourage people to reflect on core values.
4. Create an environment that supports and models the values you wish to nurture.
5. Distinguish clearly between those who are committed to your values and those who are not.
6. Oblige the committed to take responsibility for what they have chosen.
7. Rely on free choice as the engine of change.

11 ELI COHEN
NOEL TICHY

LEADERSHIP BEYOND THE WALLS BEGINS WITH LEADERSHIP WITHIN

Eli Cohen is coauthor of The Leadership Engine, *named one of the ten best business books of 1997 by Business Week. In addition to his research, writing, and teaching, he consults with leaders from select clients as a founding partner of the firm Tichy Cohen Associates, and he serves on the investment team at Ziff Brothers Investments. Noel Tichy is a professor at the University of Michigan Business School, director of the award-winning Global Leadership Program, and a senior partner in Action Learning Associates. He ran GE's renowned Crotonville executive development center for two years. His books include* The Leadership Engine (*with Eli Cohen*), Every Business Is a Growth Business (*with Ram Charan*), *and* Control Your Destiny or Someone Else Will (*with Stratford Sherman*).

At General Electric's leadership development institute in Crotonville, New York, fifty pupils are busily working on a problem. It's not a case study. It's a real problem, a sourcing issue that is hampering GE's drive to six sigma quality. If these teams solve it, that answer will be worth tens of millions of dollars to the company, and these managers will have some valuable tools they'll use for the rest of their careers. The facilitators are all GE veterans—part of the company's elite six sigma black belt team. But most of the pupils don't even work for GE. They work for the company's suppliers.

In Bosnia, a young U.S. Special Forces captain in his thirties conducts a briefing in a cold, bare room. Tensions are high in this corner of the war-torn Balkans as various ethnic groups move back to their homes after years of fighting. The captain lives in a rented house, drives a private vehicle, and lives with a team of half a dozen Special Forces noncommissioned officers and their interpreter. They all wear small side arms but have never drawn them. Instead, they meet daily with local politicians, religious leaders, businesspeople, and military leaders of the local armies and the international peacekeeping force. They don't order or command, rather they persuade by brokering deals, defusing arguments, providing assurances, and issuing warnings. When they need to, these men can be fearsome warriors. On this mission they are diplomats.

In Detroit, a group of executives toils over the best way to teach manufacturing skills to young apprentices. Members of the group discuss how to give them technical knowledge, to keep their spirits up as they face the tough challenges of their work, and to increase their professional skills. But these teachers don't work for the organization running the program, and the apprentices don't work for them. The pupils are in a job-training program at Focus: Hope, an inner-city nonprofit agency in Detroit. And the executives are part of the nonprofit agency's massive 47,000-person volunteer force.

Leading Is Teaching—and Learning

In each of these examples the best leadership capabilities are used to bring about the best solution to pressing issues. Each of the organizations—General Electric, the U.S. Special Operations Forces, and Focus: Hope—understands that in order to succeed, it must have a network of people committed to its mission. Its leaders must lead suppliers, customers, partners, and volunteers.

General Electric, the U.S. Special Operations Forces, and Focus: Hope all have strong records of success in their fields because they have developed good leadership within their organizations. And they are succeeding in leading others for the same reason. If you examine the qualities and abilities of the people who are good leaders within the walls of their organizations—as we have done in the research for our book *The Leadership Engine: How Winning Organizations Build Leaders at Every Level* (1997)—and then consider what is needed to lead beyond the walls of one's organization, you will discover that there is no difference.

This is so because in strong organizations the days of command-and-compliance hierarchies are gone. The companies that are succeeding in today's highly competitive marketplaces are the ones like General Electric that have made themselves lean and agile. In doing so they have cut out layers of nonproductive management and given responsibility for making smart decisions and taking effective action to their frontline workers. They have eliminated their armies of enforcers, and as a result, their leaders have little more direct control over the everyday decisions and actions of the people in their organizations than they do over the people in partner companies such as suppliers and customers. The leaders who succeed, therefore—whether within or beyond the walls of their organizations—are the ones who lead by guiding people to assess the reality of a situation and develop a beneficial course of action, and then by motivating them to carry it out. This is true for leaders of nonprofits who must draw together a variety of community resources to address social problems and for those in business who must create value-adding supply and delivery chains.

In circumstances where they can't exert direct control, what good leaders do is teach others to be leaders. Within an organization the people on the front lines generally know more than the people at the top about the specifics of any part of the operation. Therefore the people on the front line are the ones most likely to spot challenges and opportunities first. And they are also the ones with the experience and the knowledge to come up with the best responses. The same is true of partner organizations. The people in those organization know the day-to-day details of their businesses best. So even when senior leaders happen to be on the spot and could make decisions in a timely fashion, they are generally too unfamiliar with the complexities of the situation to be likely to come up with the best decision. This means that the way these leaders can be most effective is by helping others develop the abilities and tools to come up with the best responses to the problems and opportunities they face.

Becoming such a leader-teacher requires, first, the adoption of the new mind-set that a leader is a facilitator rather than a commander. A metric of this mind-set is the leader's calendar. When leaders understand that their job is to help everyone else perform better, they allocate a large portion of their time and energies to teaching.

General Electric: The Boundaryless Company

At General Electric, CEO Jack Welch spends a full 30 percent of his time teaching in both formal and informal settings and attending to other people's development activities. At least twice a month he runs no-holds-barred, give-and-take sessions with classes at GE's Crotonville executive training center. During these sessions he challenges students to wrestle with real issues facing GE and to think about such questions as "What would you do if you were named CEO of General Electric tomorrow?" He uses the quarterly meeting of the GE Corporate Executive Council to push the leaders of the company's thirteen business units and senior staff members to broaden their horizons and to work on problems that extend beyond their own units. And he travels around the world meeting with employees, collecting best practices, sharing them with others, and motivating people to come up with solutions to their own problems.

Inherent in teaching others, rather than commanding them, is that the people the leader teaches will come up with responses different from those the leader might have come up with. But that is one of the beauties of the process, because once individuals have developed a keen ability to assess problems and evaluate responses, then they are likely among them to come up with the best response. That is assuming of course that they are willing to open their eyes and their minds and to search for smart ideas and responses that may have been initiated elsewhere. Thus leading well within an organization requires that people have not only good teaching, learning, and evaluations skills but also an openness to reaching out and searching the world for best practices.

Jack Welch has a term for this ability, this drive, to get ideas from everywhere and use them as quickly as possible: he calls it "boundarylessness." Compared with looking only inside one's own walls for solutions, boundarylessness provides a competitive advantage. "In the old system, we had boundaries within our company. Marketing would think of a product. The design engineers would develop the plans. Manufacturing waited, waited patiently, to get the plans over the walls so they could build it. We never talked to each other. And we had boundaries externally. We never called in the supplier who had designed dozens of these parts and could have had useful ideas. We never got feedback before the product hit the market," Welch explains.

Now GE does things differently. "Now we start with suppliers and customers," Welch told *Fortune* magazine in 1994. "Customers come in and play with the machine. We meet with several different vendors at once to get their ideas, because the boundary isn't there anymore." As a result, the ideas for GE's products are different from what they otherwise would be. And they are better.

GE has leaders at all levels of the company who are able to lead both within and beyond the walls of their organizations because

Welch and others have worked very hard at teaching them how to work in the larger world. As the need to lead beyond the walls has increased, these executives have begun to address the topic more directly in their teaching. But the valuable concepts and the tools are the same ones they teach for leading inside the organization. Specifically, they develop leaders by teaching them to understand the business theory underlying how the company will add value and make money and then by helping them create environments in which smart decisions can be made and effective actions can be taken to make the theory work.

Teaching the Business Theory

When Welch first began to spread the gospel of boundarylessness, he explained it as an internal business necessity by describing situations in the way we quoted earlier. GE was in the business of selling high-quality, cost-effective products that customers wanted. So it needed to tear down the barriers that kept it from finding and using good ideas.

In the past couple of years, Welch has begun teaching a new business theory for GE. Because GE has been a product-based company with a rich engineering background, the thrill for its people has always been in inventing the new turbine, or CAT scan, or locomotive. GE competed on its ability to deliver on engineering advances. But, because of the rapid pace of technological change and the ability of competitors to copy new products almost as soon as they hit the market, Welch saw that these engineering wonders would face ever shrinking prices. In a plea for change, he described the outdated mind-set to his managers this way: "Our pride comes from making a great new engine, that we have to give away."

In other words, he told them, the only way GE was going to get out of this products-as-commodities trap was to differentiate itself as a global services company rather than a global product company. GE businesses needed to come to see their product offerings not simply as pieces of equipment but as packages of goods and services that help customers run their businesses better. This also meant, Welch explained, that just as GE leaders had taught their colleagues to tear down walls, they must now teach their customers to become partners by doing the same.

GE Medical Systems (GEMS) offers a good example. With the advent of managed care, GEMS saw that its customers—hospitals and medical centers—would have tighter budgets. GEMS couldn't count on growing equipment sales to provide the steady earnings increases demanded of GE businesses. It found its answer in garnering long-term profits from customers through maintenance and management contracts. Here's how it works.

Rather than compete for business by continually shrinking its profit margins, GEMS decided to fight for customers by helping them reduce the total cost of owning its equipment. So it started to offer services and knowledge to help customers use and maintain their GE machines more efficiently. This lowers the number of machines the customers need as well as their maintenance bills. GEMS hoped to capture a greater share of customer spending on equipment and maintenance.

Then GE Medical Systems thought of offering this service not only for GE machines but for other machines as well. So it set about building an equipment management business that promises to lower the customers' cost of ownership for all equipment under GEMS care. The move was difficult for some hospitals to swallow. It required that they give up their traditional position of bargainer and instead trust GE. It required that they outsource what they viewed as one of their critical tasks. So GE had to lead these customers to take a hard look at economic realities and honestly evaluate the benefits of outsourcing.

Thanks to leadership that stressed boundarylessness within GE, the medical systems unit was able to learn about partnering with customers from another GE unit. GE Capital had been a pioneer in offering equipment management services, and GEMS was able to draw on that unit's wealth of experience. GEMS has used that learning to teach its customers the value of outsourcing and the best way to out-source not only equipment contracts but other services as well.

At the same time that GE is reaching out to its customers, it is also working more closely with its suppliers. It has launched a major six sigma project designed to "move every process that touches our customers—every product and service—toward near-perfect qual-ity" (GE Annual Report, 1997). This, however, requires that it receive "near-perfect" goods and services from its own suppliers. To achieve this, GE has had to team up with suppliers to help them improve their operations. A company the size of GE certainly has the market clout to command responsiveness from its suppliers. The real issue, however, isn't the willingness of suppliers to comply but rather their ability to do so. If GE wants to see significant improve-ment in its own results, it has to teach its suppliers what it knows about quality, agility, and efficiency. As it does with its customers, it has to persuade, lead, and teach suppliers to reassess their own busi-nesses, to let go of long-standing procedures, and to adopt new ones.

Creating a Learning Environment

One of the toughest things that leaders have to do is to wipe out the not-invented-here syndrome. Even as Welch preached bound-arylessness within GE, he began to focus on ways to open up GE people to good ideas that originated elsewhere. No organization has a monopoly on good ideas, and good leadership, even within an organization, requires learning beyond the walls. As leaders begin to expand their leadership beyond the walls, this willingness to learn becomes even more important, not only as a source of good ideas but also as a means for building trust so that partners will be open to one's own good ideas.

Welch has very specific programs to encourage people to reach for outside ideas. For example, GE has several programs that focus on benchmarking.

Every quarterly meeting of the GE Corporate Executive Coun-cil (CEC) features a different executive who offers perspectives and insights. For example, Emanuel Kampouris of American Standard addressed them on zero working capital. Welch's challenge is always the same; by the next CEC meeting, he wants to see what each business leader has done to implement the idea discussed. CEC members report that when the practice was begun in the mid-1980s, it quickly became obvious that Welch was serious. "No one wants to be the person who shows up at the next meeting and hasn't done anything with the idea," reports one CEC member.

Welch has also pushed the benchmarking effort down into the company using the same practice: give people an energizing idea and remove any barriers (including other individuals) who stop them from implementing it.

In the late 1980s, Welch introduced the CEC and every GE business to a Wal-Mart practice that Wal-Mart calls Quick Market Intelligence (QMI). QMI is Wal-Mart's practice of sending key executives out into the field to benchmark competitors against Wal-Mart's own stores. Every Friday morning these executives return and convene with many others in an ultra high-tech room at Wal-Mart headquarters in Bentonville, Arkansas. Together they debate what they heard and saw in the field, and they make real decisions right there on the spot. Welch has pushed every GE business to use QMI for a simple reason: it forces that business to look outside at the best ideas in the marketplace.

Further, Welch has mandated that GE's programs at Crotonville include an element of benchmarking. Today it is a source of pride for people at GE to "steal" ideas from anywhere. It means they are avid learners, and this is their best qualification to be avid teachers.

Finally, Welch has made the ability to learn from and to teach those who are outside the company walls a key priority for managers across the company. For example, GE has hundreds of joint ventures. The successful leading of a joint venture is a key milestone on the career path of any GE executive who wants to make it to the top. (Exhibit 11.1 can help you determine if you have a teachable point of view.)

Exhibit 11.1. Do You Have a Teachable Point of View?

Here's a new way to assess how you develop leaders and whether you have a teachable point of view. Score yourself from 1 to 5, with 1 being behavior closest to the old way and 5 being behavior closest to the new way.

	Old Way		New Way
Focus	Leadership is the combination of technical skills in strategy, finance, and so forth.	1 2 3 4 5	Leadership focuses on hard and soft issues and on personal leadership stories.
Ideas	Coaching is on day-to-day items, not rethinking the business.	1 2 3 4 5	Leaders offer their own ideas and challenge people to create their own points of view.
	Development programs are theoretical and focus on business school cases taught by professors.		Development programs are practical. Participants and program leaders work on real business issues, not cases.
Values	Values statements are for one-way communication. Values transfer consists of superficial sheep-dip programs for masses of people.	1 2 3 4 5	Leaders help people deal with having to integrate their personal values and the values of their work units. Leaders talk openly about paradoxes in conflicting values, such as individual initiative versus teamwork.
Edge	Coaching sidesteps issues having to do with decision making. Development programs focus on managing time and identifying priorities.	1 2 3 4 5	Leaders help people by asking them to tackle dilemmas such as what to do with people who perform well but don't adhere to company values.
Energy	Programs are "cotton candy," giving people a sugar high. When they return to work their enthusiasm dissipates.	1 2 3 4 5	Leaders teach underlying frameworks for motivation.
Senior Executive Role	Senior executives who "sponsor" development programs parade in and out of them periodically	1 2 3 4 5	"Player" senior executives lead all or portions of leadership development programs.

Source: Training & Development, May 1997.

The Special Operations Forces and Focus: Hope

The missions and activities of the U.S. military's Special Operations Forces and of Focus: Hope, the program that runs feeding and job-training programs in Detroit, are very different from General Electric's. But the need of these organizations to lead beyond their own walls is no less than GE's—perhaps even greater—and, like GE, they succeed because they have developed solid teaching and learning leadership within their walls.

The Special Operations Forces are made up of the Army Rangers, the Green Berets, the Navy Seals, and the rapid-response teams that support these units. Before the fall of the Berlin Wall, their primary mission was to be the nation's fiercest and most-prepared fighters. This is still an important part of their mission, but increasingly they are being called upon to deliver rapid responses in noncombat situations. And as in Bosnia, Haiti, and Somalia, their role is often to organize and lead teams of people not under their direct command.

For no one has the mind-set shift from command-and-compliance to leader-as-facilitator been greater than for the Special Forces, commonly referred to as the Green Berets. In the 1960s and 1970s, the Special Forces were best known for their efforts to topple the North Vietnamese by going behind enemy lines to fight, either by themselves or by organizing others. But driven by a ferocious determination to succeed at any task given them, the Special Forces have made the leap to a new kind of force. The military is still the military with its numerous ranks and pay levels. But when it comes to doing what it takes to achieve a mission, the leadership is solidly based in learning and teaching. As at GE, the Special Operations Command develops leaders by teaching them to quickly and realistically assess situations and then develop action plans that address all the issues and draw on all the available resources.

In the spring of 1991, the Kurdish people of Northern Iraq rose up against Saddam Hussein. When the Iraqi army crushed their rebellion, the United States provided little assistance, despite having initially encouraged the Kurdish uprising. Hundreds of thousands of Kurds headed for the mountains that border Iraq and Turkey, and a massive tragedy awaited as the refugees began freezing and starving to death.

The United States responded with Special Forces teams. Seventy men were dropped near one camp at night. Their first morning they witnessed the food distribution disintegrate into a riot that ended with seven Kurds being shot by frightened Turkish forces. One Special Forces team, twelve men, was sent into the camp of 150,000 to assess the situation. Though team members felt threatened, they knew that force was not a real option for accomplishing their mission. They brought back their diagnosis: the Turkish and Kurdish leaders were not cooperating, and the humanitarian nongovernmental organizations (NGOs), such as the Red Cross and Doctors Without Borders/Médecins Sans Frontières, were being kept on the fringes. Special Forces teams met with each group. Then they brought the groups together. They devised a food distribution system, which the Kurds themselves implemented and felt responsible for and which used the services of the Special Forces and the NGOs. The Turks were kept informed and provided security.

This group of seventy Special Forces soldiers—dropped in with virtually no briefing on how to deal with the situation—organized the camp and involved every group that was there. Within one week the camp was meeting the basic human needs of 150,000 Kurds, and fatalities plummeted. Within three months the Kurds resettled into their homes in Iraq.

For nonprofits, enlisting the support of others has always been an important part of the game, and Focus: Hope is one of the best at it. The reason is that throughout its thirty-year history, it has worked just as hard as GE and the Special Forces at developing leaders. In a sense, developing leaders is Focus: Hope's primary mission. Three of its four major programs take students from the streets of inner-city Detroit and teach them not only the technical skills to get jobs in the private sector but also the work habits to perform well in those jobs and the leadership skills to build a career. It has succeeded at this, however, because it has paid close attention to developing the leadership abilities of its staff as well.

Like Jack Welch at GE and the commanders of the Special Forces, the founders of Focus: Hope (the late Father William Cunningham and Eleanor Josaitis) coached and taught their staffers to understand the goal—the business theory—of Focus: Hope and to identify and mobilize the resources needed to achieve it. In Focus: Hope's case this has required reaching into the community, not only for financial support but also for teachers and mentors and to build networks with other social service agencies that can provide additional services needed by Focus: Hope clients.

For Focus: Hope this reaching beyond the walls has entailed leading potential partners to see how a partnership can help them as well as Focus: Hope clients. This is basically the same process GE is conducting with its customers and suppliers. For example, in return for partners' help, Focus: Hope leaders are offering to teach partners what Focus: Hope has learned over the years about running programs that empower and develop workers. The key element, however, is that Focus: Hope people lead both internally and externally by teaching.

Creating a *learning organization* has been a hot strategy for the past few years, but the real secret to successful leadership both within and beyond the walls is building a *teaching organization*: one that teaches people the importance of facing the realities of their current situation, searching everywhere for the best possible response, and mobilizing the resources to get it done—and then teaches them how to carry out these essential tasks.

Part III

THE NEW REQUIREMENTS OF LEADERSHIP

12 STEPHEN R. COVEY

THE MIND-SET AND SKILL-SET OF A LEADER

Stephen R. Covey, for twenty years a professor of business management and organizational behavior at Brigham Young University, is cochairman of the Franklin Covey Company and founder of the former Covey Leadership Center. He is the author of several best-selling books, including The Seven Habits of Highly Effective People, *which has sold more than twelve million copies in thirty-two languages.*

A new era of leadership is dawning across America. It's leadership that stretches way beyond the typical organizational boundary. It includes partnerships, alliances, and many other cross-organizational arrangements. This new model is spreading, in part due to the growing global marketplace. But there's more to it than that. Leadership in governments, educational institutions, and nonprofits is changing in the same way.

Let's focus for a moment on how the business community is reacting to this change. Several years ago I spoke at a conference that involved over half the CEOs of the Fortune 500. In one session these executives came together to discuss how to stay at the head of their craft. The tone of the meeting changed abruptly when one CEO got off the subject and started talking about what he and his organization were doing in their community. He described how they were having great difficulty in finding enough qualified people to hire. He and his company were taking responsibility and initiative by "adopting" schools and at-risk kids. This set off a literal explosion of energy among these leaders. One CEO after another began sharing with excitement what he or she was doing in the community. The whole focus of the session was transformed as the CEOs brainstormed about what could be done to help schools at risk, to help increase literacy among children, to help people get off drugs, and to help families have a father back home again. After the session concluded I spoke with one of the conference sponsors. He remarked that never in all the years he had been involved with the conference had he seen a topic ignite such passion among chief executives.

These leaders were not only being magnanimous in wanting to help society. They understood their interdependence with communities at large. Their future employees would come from these communities, these schools, these families. Investing in these other "organizations" was just like entering into a joint venture—a venture in which all parties reap tremendous rewards.

Meeting the Challenge

My goal in this chapter is to identify principles you need to be an effective leader beyond the walls. The primary challenge in becoming such a leader is directing disparate groups toward a common good. This won't be easy. Many of the players in this organizational symphony will receive their paychecks, bonuses, and recognition from outside your walls. As a result, you won't have direct control over them.

How do you lead such a gathering of internal and external participants? First and foremost you must either draw out of them a unifying vision or identify a vision yourself that taps into others' deepest and most noble motivations. This vision will supply the *extended* organization a purpose, a mission. And just as in the symbiotic relationship that exists between companies and communities, everyone wins. With mutual effort comes mutual benefit.

Second, you must strengthen the extended organization by helping it establish a value system based on timeless, universal, self-evident principles. Decisions made in the spirit of these guiding principles will keep extended organizations moving toward their goal, even during periods of adversity.

Third, you must make sure that communication lines remain wide open. Any communication barriers that arise must be quickly removed. To further improve communication, everyone must speak a common language. I'm not talking about choosing between, for example, English and Spanish. This common language ensures that when you communicate, your message is not misunderstood.

The fourth requirement is to create synergy. In order to do this, people must focus on *we* instead of *me*. That, in turn, requires abandoning the *scarcity mentality*. People are thinking in terms of scarcity when they feel they'll get a smaller piece of the pie when someone else has had the good fortune to get a larger piece. What needs to replace this type of thinking is an *abundance mentality*, in which the size of the pie can grow to meet all our needs—and our dreams.

Fifth, you must foster cooperation rather than competition, particularly among parties that are interdependent. When people are working toward a common goal, you can't reward them for competing against each other. Instead, you need systems that reward teamwork.

Sixth, you must help all participants in this grand scheme to focus on *what matters most*. There will always be more to do than there are hours in the day. The enemy of the best is the good.

The bottom line is that there are constant, unpredictable challenges in leading beyond the walls. These challenges demand both the mind-set and the skill-set of an unusual but powerful art of leadership.

The Mind-Set

Sustainable influence and leadership is built on the *mind-set of mutual benefit*. It's a deep, inner commitment toward either achieving a win-win relationship or agreeing that there's no deal. When I think win-win, I'm not satisfied until you're happy too. If I win and you lose, we've sown the seeds of a weak relationship, headed for almost certain future breakdowns. In construction terms it would be called *bad mud*. Building relationships is key to highly effective organizations—even informal ones. And to build a strong relationship, both of us have to win.

When two or more organizations work together, achieving win-win is not as hard as it sounds. By attacking a problem from several angles, a mutually beneficial solution will, more often than not, become apparent to both sides. It will be a solution that is better than either organization could find on its own.

Here, organizational as well as individual diversity will play a big role. Fresh ideas are generated by diverse groups of people and organizations. Gone are the days of the homogeneous workforce in which everyone looked, acted, and thought alike. In the future, people of all races, creeds, and nationalities will catapult extended organizations into the twenty-first century.

I remember being approached once by an organization that wanted me to join its members in their fight against a very destructive force in society. I identified very much with their cause and had always felt the same deep commitment to fighting this force as they did. Yet, as I reflected on both how they wanted to involve me and on my own situation, I concluded that I would decline their specific invitation. I explained that I was going to join in the fight in a significant but unique way—one that leveraged my own unique opportunities. I invited them to consider me an informal "partner." Unfortunately, when I declined to become involved in *their* program, they became upset, concluding that I was not truly loyal to the cause.

They had become so internally focused and consumed in their own program that their *means* of fighting this societal challenge had become the *end*. This is one of the dangers of getting involved in any good cause. Means and ends are blurred. The scarcity mentality sets in. The antidote is to constantly reconnect to the true end, to the big vision. Then seek out diversity of thinking, and cultivate an abundant, open, creative mind-set toward means to accomplishing that end. Seek out partners with strengths and approaches that are different from and that complement your own.

By celebrating the differences among people instead of stifling them, tomorrow's leader will be able to tap into a wellspring of ideas, talent, and enthusiasm.

The Skill-Set

Having the right mind-set is only the first stage. Then you and the organizations you lead must have the right skill-set—especially the skills of communication and synergy.

Seek First to Understand

Communicating effectively requires that you first understand the other party's point of view before you try to explain your own. Until you become adept at doing this, you'll often find yourself at cross-purposes with those you are dealing with. In fact I often suggest the following ground rule for increasing the effectiveness of meetings or negotiations: before a person makes his or her own point, he or she must first make the last speaker's point to that person's satisfaction.

There are at least five levels of listening—ignoring, pretend listening, selective listening, attentive listening, and empathic listening. Empathic listening is the most developed. It's done with the eyes, ears, and heart. Listening in this manner gets you inside *another's* frame of reference—with the rest of the listening levels you never get outside *your own* frame. You not only learn a lot about the other party by listening empathically. You open yourself up to a host of new ideas.

Once you understand other people's points of view, you must then get them to understand yours. If you fail to do this, the richness of your ideas will remain untapped. It's only through the *sharing* of ideas with others that the next piece of the puzzle can be put in place: synergy.

Synergize

Synergy is the second half of the skill-set equation. It's finding the *third alternative*—not *my* way and not *your* way but a third way that is better than the way either one of us could come up with independently. It's the $1 + 1 = 3$ or more solution.

Here are the steps to creating synergy:

Identify what both parties really want. Get the true end that each side has in mind very clear, then be very open and flexible on options for working out the means. Often disagreements are based purely on misconceptions and mistrust. Putting the main points on paper can sometimes clear the air. This enables both parties to get on the same side of the problem rather than on opposite sides. They become partners facing the same challenge rather than adversaries.

Create alternatives that lead to the betterment of all organizations involved. Don't let anyone's idea be ridiculed, no matter how far-fetched. Perhaps someone else can add to the idea and thereby make it viable.

Determine acceptable solutions for all parties. The people in one party may be so concerned with losing that they can't see the benefits of winning. Explaining the upside may dissipate much of their party's aversion.

Foster a spirit of mutual benefit. If people in the other party see that you are truly concerned with their well-being, there's a greater chance they will be willing to take on risk now for the prospect of future rewards.

Build relationships. Through all of the negotiations, make sure you're focusing on strengthening interpersonal ties. There's always the chance that no agreeable alternative will be found this time around. In that case, no deal will be struck. But there's always tomorrow. If you're seen as honorable today, it's much more likely that you and the other party will agree on something in the future.

The Franklin Covey Company, of which I serve as cochairman, is a living organizational laboratory for synergy. It's the product of a merger between the Covey Leadership Center and the Franklin Quest Company.

As they were "courting," both companies saw the potential for considerable synergy resulting from merging these two organizations. Franklin Quest was the leader in time management, geared primarily to individuals. Covey Leadership Center was a rapidly growing leadership training company with a strong organizational following. The combined company is now the largest training organization in the United States. Its mission: inspiring change by igniting the power of proven principles so that people and organizations achieve what matters most.

There are tremendous challenges and difficulties involved in merging two strong and different organizational cultures. But that's natural. Those of us working on this know it takes patience, persistence, and a powerful commitment to always seeking third alternatives. We constantly find ourselves needing to come back to the mission, vision, and values that we share.

Whatever the organization, when differences are faced, people have to ask each other: Are you willing to work together with me until we're both satisfied with the solution? Are you willing to communicate with me until I completely understand your viewpoint?

Leading Beyond the Walls

In addition to developing the mind-set and skill-set of a leader, you can take these steps to increase your ability to lead beyond the walls:

Foster the taking of responsibility. The organization and its people must be responsible for meeting the organization's overall mission. But if you try to govern *how* people accomplish the goal, you won't be able to hold them accountable for the results. Let them decide the how. Then measure the success together.

Help the extended organization focus on service to the world. In other words, make sure there's a social as well as an economic imperative driving the organization forward. That will make motivating individuals easier. Today people demand more than just a bigger paycheck. They want to benefit mankind.

To illustrate, I remember working once with the faculty and administrators of a college in Canada. They were dealing with some very divisive issues and were totally caught up in scarcity thinking. They were trying to develop a shared mission and vision for the college, yet the conversation and atmosphere was inundated with smallness, pettiness, and accusation. Then at one point the whole spirit of the endeavor changed. Someone said, "What if we become a mentoring educational college for our entire province?" As they discussed it, they all decided that they wanted to be an organization that cares about other colleges and organizations and mentors them in becoming principle centered. As faculty and administrators came to that decision, the smallness and pettiness evaporated. These people became energized by something more important, by a transcendent purpose that made their little problems irrelevant. The desire to contribute outside themselves enabled them to subordinate individual concerns.

Lead by example or modeling. Walk the talk. You can't expect individuals and organizations to follow your lead if you don't live up to your own vision and values.

Become a mentor yourself and build a mentoring organization. More experienced workers should help the less experienced. Mature individuals should help the younger ones. Mentoring strengthens organizations, fosters trust, and builds relationships.

Empower individuals within the extended organization. There's no longer enough time to send all decisions up the organizational ladder. Most must be made locally. The problem gets even worse when decisions involve crossing organizational boundaries. In order to empower workers successfully, you must first specify purpose and guiding principles. Workers can then make decisions based on these principles.

Build trust. Empowerment requires trust. But how do you create trust? By first being trustworthy yourself—by being a person of both character and competence. Becoming trustworthy requires making commitments and then keeping them. The loyalty that you earn in return is worth far more than the conditional loyalty money can buy.

A compelling story about Alexander the Great illustrates the importance of trust. Lying near death, Alexander was being treated for his illness by a physician who was also his friend when he received word that this friend would attempt to kill him. The friend prepared a potion for Alexander to drink. Only after he finished the potion did Alexander tell his friend about the accusation. The potion saved Alexander's life rather than taking it. Now that's trust!

Working Together

It makes no difference if we're talking about individual or organizational leadership. The principles are universal, not situation specific. Whether we're leading in governments, companies, or nonprofits, the message is clear: we have to work together in order to achieve the greater good. We live in an interdependent reality.

Just think of the family unit. It's the most basic form of organizational structure. Yet it's the model for all types of organizations.

A man and a woman get married. Prior to the ceremony they're two separate individuals with unique wants and needs.

Upon entering into the marriage they sublimate some of these wants and needs in order to strengthen the family bond. Before entering the marriage, for example, the husband-to-be may have gone out with his friends several times a week. Once married he may voluntarily give up some of these nights out.

When children eventually come along, another level of change takes place. Perhaps the man gives up additional nights out. And romantic dinners for two may become food fights for three.

The challenges don't end with the rearing of children, however. Financial problems, strained relationships, and loss of loved ones are but a few of the difficulties that await most of us. When such problems arise, it's easy for a family to get so enmeshed in its own problems that it retreats inward, forsaking others who are also in pain.

I am convinced that the deepest fundamental challenge we face in society lies in the fundamental unit of society—the family. But I'm also convinced that the family is also our greatest source of hope. Henry David Thoreau once said that for every thousand hacking at the branches of evil, there is one striking at the root. Strengthening the family strikes at the root.

As families and individuals, we must reach out:

Help kids at risk. "Adopt" your children's friends who are struggling—let them feel welcome in your home. Affirm them. Let them feel that someone believes in them and in their potential.

Identify families that are undergoing their own strife and alleviate some of their pain. It will certainly make their burden a bit lighter. But it will also help you and your family. This is family-to-family community service.

Finally, volunteer. Nothing is more strengthening and unifying to a family than its members' giving their time and energy to those in need. There's so much to be done. Become a doer, not a spectator. Your reward? First, simply helping others, but then also receiving the satisfaction of a day, of a life, well spent—of knowing you've used your unique talents and opportunities to leave an enduring legacy.

13 MARSHALL GOLDSMITH
CATHY WALT

NEW COMPETENCIES FOR TOMORROW'S GLOBAL LEADER

Marshall Goldsmith is a founding director of Keilty, Goldsmith and Company (KGC) (a key provider of customized leadership development), a cofounder of the Learning Network, and a member of the Drucker Foundation board of governors. His work has received national recognition from the Institute for Management Studies, the American Management Association, the American Society for Training and Development, and the Human Resource Planning Society. He has been ranked as one of the "Top 10" consultants in the field of executive development by the Wall Street Journal. Cathy Walt is the change management managing partner of Andersen Consulting's Global New Business Models Team, partner in charge of the Executive Leadership Theme Team at the Institute for Strategic Change, a frequent keynote speaker, and an author. With an interdisciplinary doctorate in the behavioral sciences, she focuses on the successful management and integration of business strategy, process, technology, and leadership.

Andersen Consulting is currently engaged in a multicountry research project aimed at helping global organizations understand the most important characteristics of the leader of the future. As part of this research, leading companies have been asked to identify future leaders, those who have the potential to be the CEO of a global organization. Then, rather than employing the usual process of asking *today's* leaders to describe the future of leadership (when they are unlikely to be the ones who must practice it), we decided to ask the people identified as *tomorrow's* leaders. We have received input from these future leaders through focus groups, interviews, and surveys. To date we have received the views of over one hundred future leaders who were nominated in over fifty major companies around the world.

In comparing the desired characteristics of the leader of the future with the desired characteristics of the leader of the past, we found both consistent themes and emerging trends. Many qualities of effective leadership are seen as being important for yesterday, today, and tomorrow. Characteristics such as communicating vision, demonstrating integrity, focusing on results, and ensuring customer satisfaction were described as vital in the past as well as the future.

In addition, five key factors have emerged that are seen as clearly more important in the future than they were in the past: thinking globally, appreciating cultural diversity, demonstrating technological savvy, building partnerships, and sharing leadership.

In this chapter we cannot address each of these factors in detail, but we will briefly describe some of our key learnings for each factor. (For a full report, contact Cathy Walt at Andersen Consulting, 215-241-8360.)

Thinking Globally

Globalization is a trend that will have a major impact on the leaders of the future. In the past a major company could focus on its own region (or even its own country) and still prosper. Those days are soon going to be over. At the time of this writing, a financial crisis that began in Thailand and spread to Southeast Asia is beginning to dramatically influence the rest of the world. The trend toward globally connected markets is likely to become even stronger in the future. The participants in our interviews mentioned that not only will leaders need to understand the economic implications of globalization, they will also have to understand the cultural, legal, and political ramifications. Leaders in every arena will need to see themselves as citizens of the world with a greatly expanded field of vision and values.

Two factors that are seen as making global thinking a key variable for the future are the dramatic projected increases in global trade and integrated global technology such as e-commerce. Robert Reich, former U.S. secretary of labor, in a speech at a 1998 *Insights* conference in San Diego, joked that he had difficulty trying to buy an "American" car because it was almost impossible to determine what percentage of each car was actually made in America. In our research, participants from around the world predicted that the value of global trade would grow. Several suggested that future leaders might need to spend time working in multiple countries and in virtual networks to help them understand how multicountry trade could help their organizations achieve a competitive advantage. In an environment where competitive pressures are rapidly increasing, producers will have to learn how to manage global production, marketing, and sales teams both actually and virtually.

New technology is another factor that is going to make global thinking a requirement for future leaders. With the use of new technology it will be feasible to export white-collar work around the world. Computer programmers in India will communicate with designers in Italy to help develop products that are manufactured in Indonesia and sold in Brazil. Technology can help break down barriers to global business that seemed insurmountable in the past. Leaders who are mired in local thinking and hands-on micromanagement will be hard-pressed to compete in a global marketplace. Leaders who can make globalization work in their organization's favor will have a huge competitive advantage.

Appreciating Cultural Diversity

As the importance of globalization increases, future leaders will also need to appreciate cultural diversity, defined as diversity of leadership style, industry style, individual behaviors and values, race, and sex. They will have to understand not only the economic and legal differences but also the social and motivational differences that are part of working around the world. Our research is consistent with research from the Center for Creative Leadership, which showed that "respect for differences in people" is one of the most important qualities of a successful global leader (J. Alexander and M. Wilson, "Leading Across Cultures," in F. Hesselbein, M. Goldsmith, R. Beckhard, Editors, *The Organization of the Future*, 1997). The high-potential leaders we interviewed believe that developing an understanding of other cultures is not just a good business practice—it is a key to being able to compete successfully in the future.

An appreciation of cultural diversity will need to include both the big things and the small things that form a unique culture. For example, few Europeans or Americans who work in the Middle East today have taken the time to read (much less understand) the Koran. Yet it is clear that religion is one of the most important variables that affects behavior in the region. Smaller issues, such as the meaning of gifts, personal greetings, or timeliness, will also need to be better understood.

Participants noted that the ability to motivate people in different cultures will become increasingly important. Motivational strategies that are effective in one culture may actually be offensive in another culture. The same public recognition that could be a source of pride to a salesperson in the United States could be a source of embarrassment to a scientist in the U.K. Leaders who can effectively understand, appreciate, and motivate colleagues in multiple cultures will become an increasingly valued resource in the future.

Demonstrating Technological Savvy

High-potential leaders from around the world consistently expressed the view that technological savvy will be a key competency for the global leader of the future. One trend connected with this issue was clear—the *younger* the participant, the greater the emphasis on the importance of technological savvy. Many future leaders have been raised with technology and view it as an integrated part of their life. Many present leaders still view technological savvy as important for staff people and operations but not for the line officers who run the "real" business.

As we have commented elsewhere ("Developing Technological Savvy," *Leader to Leader*, Winter 1999):

> Developing technological savvy will be largely up to the individual. That does not mean that we all need to become gifted technicians or computer scientists. It does mean that we need to:
>
> - Understand how the intelligent use of new technology can help our organizations
> - Recruit, develop, and maintain a network of technically competent people
> - Know how to make and manage investments in new technology
> - Be positive role models in leading the use of new technology

Almost all of the younger participants believed that new technology would become a critical variable that would significantly affect their organizations' *core* businesses. They expressed little sympathy for executives who thought they were either too busy or too important to learn the power of new tools. The clear consensus was that organizations that have technologically savvy leaders will have a competitive advantage over organizations that do not. Without technological savvy, the future of integrated global partnerships and networks would be impossible.

Building Partnerships

Building partnerships and alliances of all kinds was viewed as far more important for the future than the past. Many organizations that seldom formed alliances in the past are regularly forming alliances today. This trend will be even more dramatic in the future. A recent *Forbes* article cited Andersen Consulting as a major example of such a partnership and IBM as "still old school."

Reengineering, restructuring, and downsizing are leading to a world where outsourcing of all but core activities may become the norm. The ability to negotiate complex alliances and manage complex networks of relationships is viewed as becoming increasingly important. Our leaders identified joint leadership of new business models as an element vital to a successful global venture.

The changing role of customers, suppliers, and partners has deep implications for leaders. In the past it was clear who your friends were and who your enemies were. In the future these roles will become more blurred. In fields as diverse as energy, telecommunications, and pharmaceuticals the same organization may be a customer, supplier, partner, and competitor. In this new world, building positive, long-term, win-win relationships with many organizations becomes critical. Defeating an enemy who then turns out to also be a potential customer can prove a short-term victory.

Sharing Leadership

In a world where leading across a fluid network may become more important than leading from the top of a fixed hierarchy, being able to effectively *share* leadership is a requirement, not an option. In an alliance structure, telling partners what to do and how to do it may quickly lead to having no partners. All parties will have to be able to work together to achieve the common good.

Not only did our participants believe that the leader of the future will be different from the leader of the past, they also believe that the *employee* of the future will be different. Many of the future leaders saw that the management of knowledge workers is going to be a key factor in their success. Peter Drucker has noted that knowledge workers are people who know more about what they are doing than their managers do. In dealing with knowledge workers, old models of leadership will not work. Telling people what to do and how to do it becomes ridiculous. The leader will operate in a mode of asking for input and sharing information. Knowledge workers of the future may well be difficult to keep. They will probably have little organizational loyalty and view themselves as professional free agents who will work for the leader who provides the most developmental challenge and opportunity. Skills in hiring and retaining key talent will be a valuable commodity for the leader of the future (see M. Goldsmith, "Retaining High-Impact Performers," *Leader to Leader*, Summer 1996). Sharing leadership may be one way to help demonstrate this skill. Sharing leadership was viewed as also requiring new values of cooperation and rotational leadership—knowing when a strength or a weakness needed balancing.

Implications

The high-potential future leaders we interviewed believe new times will require new skills. Unfortunately, many of today's leaders have not been trained in these skills or even encouraged to believe that these skills are important. Thinking globally, appreciating cultural diversity, demonstrating technological savvy, building partnerships, and sharing leadership are competencies that many present leaders do not have or do not even realize are important. They are also skills that most future leaders will need and must recognize as essential to the success of development programs.

To prepare successfully for the next millennium, tomorrow's organizations will have to change the mind-set of many leaders or change their employment status. For leaders who are near retirement, this may not be an issue. For midcareer leaders who lack the needed new skills, this may be a challenge. They will have to learn why the new skills are important. They will have to understand what they need to learn and be shown how they can best learn it. The organization's reward and human performance reinforcement systems will need to be augmented to reflect the importance of new competencies.

The bad news is that many existing leaders do not see the value of these new competencies—most likely a consequence of not being measured by them. The good news is that most high-potential future leaders do see the value of these new competencies and believe our human performance system should incorporate them. Historically, present leaders have been expected to help mentor and develop future leaders. Although this will still be true in the future, there may be a major addition to the process—*future* leaders may also be recruited to help mentor and develop *present* leaders. If future leaders have the wisdom to learn from the experience of present leaders *and* if present leaders have the wisdom to learn new competencies from future leaders, they both can share leadership in a way that can benefit their organization.

14 ROBERT PORTER LYNCH

HOW TO FOSTER CHAMPIONS

Robert Porter Lynch is president of the Warren Company, which helps companies build alliances throughout the globe in a wide variety of industries. He is the author of the award-winning Practical Guide to Joint Ventures and Corporate Alliances *(1989), the best-selling* Business Alliances: The Hidden Competitive Weapon *(1993), and the forthcoming* Breakthroughs in Cooperation. *He has been recognized for his groundbreaking work in creating alliance architecture and the alliance industry's first benchmarking studies.*

Courage enlarges and cowardice diminishes resources. In dangerous straits, the fears of the timid aggravate the dangers that imperil the brave.

Eighteenth-century philosopher

Champions are probably the most influential factor in creating a synergistic relationship that achieves a mighty purpose. Without at least one accomplished champion, the chance of successfully sustaining, nurturing, and transforming an alliance is virtually nil.

(The unique characteristics of alliance champions, as described by a survey of several hundred champions and their alliance associates, are described in Exhibit 14.1.)

Cooperation beyond the walls is in many companies considered an unnatural act; alliances are therefore often perceived as foreign entities. Alliances are essentially start-up companies and must be led by champions who are at the same time entrepreneurs, risk takers, visionaries, and results-oriented managers. Unless an energetic, visionary leader is in place, the parent corporation's immune rejection response will kick out the alliance before it has had a chance to become established.

Champions exist in a perpetual state of enlightened dissatisfaction, always looking for a new idea that will improve on the current state of affairs. Typically, they have a long history of pursuing new ideas, attempting breakthroughs, and challenging the accepted.

Champions cannot command because their authority is not positional. Their authority comes from their vision, their energy,

---

Exhibit 14.1. Characteristics of Champions.

- Visionary
- Energetic, confident, optimistic, with a can-do attitude
- Results-oriented, with demonstrated leadership and a track record of success
- Passionate or charismatic, a crusader with powerful belief systems
- Credible and knowledgeable in the field of endeavor
- Tenacious, persevering
- Able to focus the team on initiating things for the greater good
- Team-spirited and persuasive with team members
- Adventurous, regarding adversity as opportunity and eager to rise to a challenge
- Entrepreneurial, a risk taker
- Demanding, working on the edge
- Innovative and creative

and their ability to touch the hearts of those who believe their vision is the reality the organization must achieve for more than its future survival, that vision contains the organization's *thrival*.

To be effective, the champion needs a track record of success. Yet down deep most champions are idealists; therefore, they often tend to become overly optimistic. Thus it is not ironic that the hallmark of real champions is not how many successes they have had, and they will have had many, but rather how they have dealt with failure. Failures should be the learning experiences that temper their idealism sufficiently to make them effective. Often the best champions will have at their side a seasoned realist or skeptic, to provide balance and practicality to their idealistic vision.

Not surprisingly, many champions are entrepreneurial at heart, which enables them to excel with broken tools and inadequate resources, under adverse conditions, and with minimal organizational support.

Their extraordinary results come from a blended potion of vision, persistence, ability to learn from mistakes, a willingness to take risks and possibly fail, and an abiding commitment to the greater good of all.

Breakthroughs are the way of life for champions, whose challenge of the status quo is often regarded as unreasonable, who are interested in creating new pathways and love to discover what others have overlooked. Gary Horning, an alliance champion at NCR, advocates, "The champion must be very reasonable, recognize the realities of the future, and see issues and solutions from diverse perspectives." Yet more conservative managers are often blind to the verities of the champion's vision and new operating scheme, thereby branding the alliance champion as unrealistic—or worse.

When operating in the truest sense, champions are the passionate pioneers, the discoverers, the true learners, the ones who will never accept mediocrity and are even willing to destroy what they've built in order to build something greater.

Champions are omnidirectional in that they know the necessity of navigating the halls of power and at the same time are willing to jump the chain of command or network the bowels of the organization. Although champions think of organizations as networks, not hierarchies, they also somewhat grudgingly but patiently acknowledge the realities of the corporate ladder, without giving it their blessing.

What is often perceived as their neglect of protocol causes champions to be slightly off-center from corporate norms and to have offended traditional corporate sensibilities more than a few times in the pursuit of a worthy cause.

Typically an alliance champion is not initially anointed from above. Instead, he or she seizes the high ground and then asks for support. The motto of the champion is "Tis better to ask forgiveness after the fact than permission before." Pat Bryant, an alliance champion at EKA Chemicals, states, "I almost never have to ask for forgiveness. It just amazes me that others ever ask for permission."

Because champions operate on the organizational fringe, they are often isolated and neglected. However, wise corporations with a heavy investment in alliances learn to nurture their champions and to empower them once they emerge independently. Top managers create more successful alliances when they *recognize* champions than when they *select* them.

Further, career rotational cycles of alliance champions need to be carefully planned to diminish any destabilizing impact they might have on the alliance. Honeywell shifted its champions' rotational cycles from eighteen months to five years and found that trust levels, which had been decreasing, were reestablished and the success rates of Honeywell alliances doubled. Brian Ferrar, alliance champion at Compaq, points out that "there needs to be a sufficient reward for the five-year plan," for without such rewards, the champion can become isolated and deprived of career advancement.

When describing their competencies, champions express the uniqueness of their function in their organizations in a variety of ways (see Exhibit 14.2).

**Exhibit 14.2. Things Alliance Champions
Do Extremely Well.**

- Build great teams that bring out the best in everyone
- Articulate a powerful vision embraced by all
- Maintain their own integrity and self-discipline
- Relate to and communicate well with people
- Build trust, keep their commitments, and treat people justly and fairly
- Have the courage of their convictions
- Take action; don't wallow in platitudes and complaints
- Are great partners in times of adversity
- Have heart and compassion
- Face reality and then change it
- Commit to win-win arrangements for both partners

How Champions Become Successful

Seven particular issues reflect how champions become successful, and the leader of the future must understand them to manage alliance champions effectively. They are as follows:

1. Building trust
2. Maintaining resiliency
3. Working for cocreative change
4. Building alliance teams
5. Problem solving and negotiating
6. Practicing transformational leadership
7. Gaining top-rank support

Building Trust

Trust is the foundation of all cooperative enterprise, and integrity is the basis of all trust. Alliance managers see integrity as the ability and commitment to honor one's word, especially during times of adversity and often regardless of personal cost.

For Gerry Dehkes, an alliance champion at Lucent Technologies:

> Integrity includes setting expectations and consistently meeting them. Doing both is important. Making sure that your counterparts will know (and be able to trust) that you will act in a certain way in a given situation. Then meet or beat that expectation consistently. This extends beyond the individual to the rest of the people in the alliance partner's organization. Or better, [to use] an old Minnesota expression: "Underpromise; overdeliver." View problems or barriers, especially early on, as opportunities to show your trustworthiness, meeting the expectations you've set with your partners. These have strong impact beyond the decision of the moment. They engender trust that later on you will indeed act that way, thus inviting reciprocal actions.

Alliance champions are the principals who set the tone for building the trust that forms the chemistry and culture of the transorganizational interaction.

Every experienced alliance leader will comment on how trust is an essential ingredient of cooperation. Without it the venture will crumble, disputes will go unresolved, and passion will wane. Outsiders tend to describe trust as *great chemistry*; others see it as *honesty*. But champions tend to know that the trust they create, often internationally across wide cultural chasms, is based more on integrity than any other factor.

When trust collapses, communication is either halted or turns to threats, blaming, and accusations and at the same time decision making becomes focused on protection and defense, not on innovation and creativity. Forward progress slows to a snail's pace, or worse, reverses.

The champion who builds trust has a powerful advantage, because, when analyzed in detail, that trust is shown to be simultaneously the *glue* that holds teams together during times of crisis and the *grease* that smooths over rough interactions when cultures clash. Brian Ferrar, alliance champion at Compaq, recognizes how this bonding affects the relationship between champions: "An alliance manager and his [or her] counterpart at the partner company are often closer than each may be to many of their coworkers because of the trust it takes to form the alliance." However, this bonding across organizational boundaries can be quite disconcerting to many insiders, who see this as a serious breach of loyalty (as we shall see later in this chapter).

Inevitably, "trust also demands win-win scenarios and reciprocity for each other's pet projects and investments," comments Gary Horning, alliance champion from NCR.

How does the alliance champion build this trust? Exhibit 14.3 presents some lessons from the field that exemplify not only how such trust is created but also how it can be destroyed.

Building trust starts and is maintained at the highest leadership positions. If leaders do not forge the bond of trust, it is highly unlikely to be found within the middle echelons. Coincidentally, there is a very high correlation between *trust, relationships,* and *control.* As trust and relationships increase, the needs for command and control diminish, replaced by coordinative interaction. This matters to leaders as they face today's compression of time and increase in speed, which force faster decision making, and today's complex interrelationships, which force slower decision making. Knowing how to manage this dilemma and balance these forces requires adroitness and a deep level of trust.

Is the creation of high trust worth the effort? Successful alliances provide very strong evidence that high trust is the catalyst of very high performance, greater innovation, creativity, synergy, expansion of possibilities, enhanced problem resolution, faster action and implementation, lower litigation costs, and lower transaction costs.

Exhibit 14.3. Leaders' Trust Destroyers and Trust Creators.

Trust Destroyers		Trust Creators	
Behavior	Percentage in Agreement	Behavior	Percentage in Agreement
Act inconsistently in what they say and do	69	Maintain integrity	58
Seek personal gain above shared gain	41	Openly communicate vision and values	51
Withhold information	34	Show respect as equal partners	47
Lie or tell half-truths	33	Focus on shared goals not personal agendas	38
Be closed-minded	29	Do the right thing regardless of personal risk	36
Be disrespectful to employees	28	Listen with an open mind	33
Withhold support	16	Demonstrate caring compassion	22
Break promises	14		
Betray confidences	13	Maintain confidences	15

Source: Manchester Inc., 1997 survey of executives at 215 companies. Used with permission.

Because trust factors dramatically improve financial performance, corporations cannot afford to forsake the champions' role in developing trust across organizational boundaries.

Maintaining Resiliency

But how does the champion reconcile the seeming conflict between maintaining trust and integrity and working in a world that is constantly changing and requires frequent repositioning of the alliance and all its attendant relationships? How does the champion maintain integrity when the conditions that triggered the birth of the alliance are no longer valid? The answer lies in the champion's tendency to be resilient.

Resiliency is like a spring: the more it is tensioned, the more powerful it becomes. Champions can bounce back into shape because their spring-steel inner core of values and principles is not altered by circumstances. However, this inner core is surrounded by a flexible outer core of practicality, which provides them the freedom to shift with changing circumstances, to be influenced by the insight and wisdom of others, and to avoid rigid thinking and obsolete paradigms.

Tenacity and persistence are always associated with successful champions. One champion in our focus groups said it quite well: "You cannot cut out too early, you must follow your instincts. When you get knocked down, you must get back up again. It takes more than ego to get back up—it's beliefs, knowing you are right, it's an intuition that what you are doing is worthwhile. Doing this takes an innate ability to deal with uncertainty and risk."

Champions often see their falterings in life as opportunity. They experience adversity as the door opener for regeneration. They see life as not about *perfection* but about *perfecting,* losing your spirit and gaining it back again. The losing of spirit becomes the breakdown that creates the opportunity for a breakthrough, the possibility to regain spirit at a higher level. Living in the status quo is to live too safely, without challenge and opportunity to achieve a dream. Therefore, the true champion experiences adversity with a quiet smile, as a hidden treasure from which he or she can obtain new levels of experience, awareness, and energy. Seasoned champions have failed enough times to know that failure is only temporary; they tend not to let their personal identity be strongly influenced by their experience.

One of our focus group champions, when asked to what he attributed his resiliency, stated, "I never take myself too seriously, and find my failures are an opportunity to refine my sense of humor." Adds Brian Ferrar: "I find humor absolutely necessary—both as an icebreaker and bonding agent and as a stress reliever."

Working for Co-creative Change

Creativity is the most effective response to rapid change, and all breakthroughs rely heavily on creativity. However, champions are not independent, isolated creators. Instead, champions bond with their counterparts in the alliance as kindred spirits in co-creation; that is, they are typically co-creative synthesizers, linking new ideas and innovations together, building bridges with other creative individuals whose voices have not previously been heard. Champions typically do not require full credit for an idea to satisfy their egos, because they know that the idea itself is less than 10 percent of the game.

Paradigm shifts come not from incremental thinking but from fundamentally new ideas, typically originating from outside the mainstream of accepted thought. Carl Gustav Jung foresaw an alliance's greatest strategic potential when he commented that the greater the contrast, the greater the potential and that great energy only comes from a correspondingly great tension between opposites.

Alliances create breakthroughs out of differentials in thinking. Inherent in the differences between two alliance partners lies the champion's unique opportunity to initiate the creative tension that can generate the essential shift in perception and thinking that underpins all true innovation. Managing this synergy of compatible differences through the process of co-creation is a fundamental attitude and skill of the best champions.

Champions see that the real value in an alliance lies in the diversity of thinking across the boundaries of different organizational cultures, perspectives, and thinking. Fundamentally, champions honor the dignity of diverse thinking, a point of view that can often evoke strong negative emotions from conservative traditionalists bound to the status quo within the alliance's parent organization.

Building Alliance Teams

Champions play a vital role in building alliance teams. By their nature, alliances are populated with diverse perspectives. Unless the champion integrates and converges partners' energies on a focused mission and objective, the alliance will tend to crack, as divergent interests pull in nonsynergistic directions.

Unfortunately, experience has shown that just putting highly creative people on a team neither generates breakthroughs nor drives convergence. All too often the creative people are too individualistic to be great team players or too competitive with each other, or their creativity escalates, generating even more creativity with no grounding in reality, or they think their cultures are too different for them to be co-creative with others.

Effective champions pull together diverse alliance teams, developing a very healthy balance, like that of yin and yang, which enables members to experience the *synergy of compatible differences—* that very elusive chemistry that characterizes powerfully successful alliances. At many companies, such as Compaq, the alliance "core team" is well defined and a time-honored tradition drawing from several types of people:

Champion. The champion fills the critical leadership role that keeps the team focused on the ultimate, long-term objective and maintains its spiritual center of effort. Champions will never be satisfied unless there is some connection to real action, and they may not have the patience or discipline to engage in a detailed analysis of all the operational components necessary to make a plan a raging success. Further, the champion must not fall into the trap of "ruling" the teams.

Facilitator-integrator. This person coordinates the group and brings together the key individuals who will have to buy into the plan. As facilitator this individual keeps people emotionally engaged, making the best use of team resources, maximizing each member's potential, and monitoring members' personal needs and focusing their minds on the ultimate objective. As integrator this individual acts as liaison between diverse groups, often translating one corporate culture's needs into terms understood by the other culture. Facilitator-integrators tend to have excellent listening skills and are highly tuned to the personal needs and sensitivities of team members, thus contributing enormously to the building of a consensus. Often they will search for resources and ideas from outside their team by accessing, leveraging, and building other external networks.

Creative introverts and creative synthesizers. The creative introverts are those inward, reflective thinkers who often seem withdrawn and distant, almost to the extent of being considered antisocial. The creative synthesizers are far more interactive and do most of their creating in teams, bouncing ideas off others, playing a friendly tug of war to see whether an idea is sound enough to fly. The synthesizers will pick up on ideas from very diverse sources, sometimes adapting, sometimes splicing, and sometimes being very original themselves. Both these roles are vital for innovators seeking to break new ground.

Helpful skeptics and analyzers. The skeptics and analyzers are constantly evaluating, judging, and testing to see whether what may seem like hare-brained ideas from the creative types and the champions can really be implemented and address the problems at hand. They will confront new ideas with such questions as: Can you show me where this has been done before? Do we have the resources? Who will actually make the sales calls? and so on. They will invariably focus on the details overlooked by most champions. A senior manager with extensive experience who commands respect in the corporate hierarchy is usually most effective in this role of prudent oversight. Do not confuse the helpful skeptic with the critical cynic or contrarian, whose negative attitude and unhealthy analysis will destroy the energy of the team and contradict even the champion's positive energy.

Process and task managers. These highly organized and procedurally disciplined individuals turn visions into corporate goals and are necessary to carry out the details of the plan, determining roles, responsibilities, decision-making procedures, functional interactions, contingency plans, measures, and rewards. These individuals direct the manner in which the alliance team's effort is applied, focusing on objectives, structure, and task completion. Often they have good project management experience.

It typically falls into the champion's hands to build this team, this mix of players in which no one is more or less important. Moreover, too many or too few of one type will defeat the chemistry of the mix. Gerry Dehkes, alliance champion at Lucent Technologies, notes, "Each of these roles is crucial to a high-performance team. Team members may and often do play multiple roles. They may also play different roles at different times and on different teams. Champions must recognize these roles and ensure that each role is filled by team members." However, Richard Marrs of BHP cautions, "A problem can occur when the champion has to wear multiple hats, playing the roles of process manager and facilitator, which are often quite different from the champion role he or she must play. It can become too much, stretching the champion's capabilities to the limit."

The champion must be acutely aware of the shifting nature of the team roles. Dehkes observes:

> Leadership roles and individual enthusiasms shift, depending on where in the alliance process or project life cycle you are. In the early brainstorming phase, the creative, flexible-minded person energetically takes the lead. As the need for a clear vision becomes important, the big-picture, decisive person moves to the fore. Then the detail-oriented organizer puts the action-plan flesh on the vision bones. Finally, the flexible but task-oriented implementers adapt the plan to reality. Champions recognize this process along with the differing strengths and interests of team members, helping each make the strongest contribution at the appropriate time. Alliance leaders know how to move their teams quickly through the life cycle to the high-performing stage and know when to end a team, too.

This is the type of team that is capable of designing break-throughs and operating at a high level of performance. However, because high-performance teams are likely to have a higher inci-dence of breakdowns than other teams and because alliance teams are particularly vulnerable with their intensity of cross-corporate, cross-cultural, and cross-functional diversity, the role of the cham-pion in alliance teams becomes increasingly important, and his or her co-creative problem solving and negotiation skills are essential.

Problem Solving and Negotiating

Because the driving forces that underpin alliances are always in a state of flux, all cooperative ventures between companies must be continually repositioned in the strategic environment to retain competitive advantage. This is the work of the alliance champion. Therefore, champions must be excellent negotiators.

Gary Horning of NCR is clear that "great champions drive to create plans that reflect win-win scenarios. Champions must put themselves in the place of both their own company and their part-ners. Without reciprocal commitments from both parties, the rela-tionship will fail." John Mazur of Siemens believes that "alliance champions should always be on the lookout for the win-win and breakthrough value propositions because these are the right bait to attract the attention and support of senior management on both sides of the alliance."

Yet this approach is not shared by less experienced transactional negotiators, as Gary Dehkes of Lucent Technologies comments: "I know some people who think a win-win situation means 'We kick their butts twice!' They are not successful alliance champions, how-ever, just challenges for the rest of us." And Brian Ferrar of Com-paq points out, "The difficulty regarding win-win negotiations is often that companies are generally not truly equal. Some are bureau-cratic when their partner is entrepreneurial; some are rich when their partner is poor. This imbalance can make negotiations quite difficult."

Champions will seldom engage in win-lose negotiations because they know these efforts may quickly degenerate to lose-lose games. It's more than likely that they will chose a synergistic style of negotiating (which to the hard-nosed win-lose negotiator may look soft, overly trusting, and prone to giving away too much too fast). Champions entering into alliance negotiations don't see the process as a tug-of-war between "sides" but rather as an interactive process of designing the future, then reverse-engineering that future back to the present. This synergistic negotiation style focuses on co-creation and expansion of possibilities rather than on win-lose bargaining or a win-win solution in which the parties simply accommodate each other's interests.

Champions know that win-lose situations freeze people in their positions, thus freezing both time and thinking. Once time and thinking freezes on both sides, the result is all too often a lose-lose game, which will blow the alliance apart and bring a tragic end to everyone's dream. Gary Horning at NCR observes that "many uninitiated alliance champions are not so 'enlightened,' do not care about win-win, do see the tug-of-war, and this then becomes a central issue that must be addressed and overcome."

Synergistic, co-creative negotiations enable a rapid building of trust and avoid the unproductive behaviors that come from meaningless conflict.

Nevertheless, there will be conflict. Conflict is the inevitable by-product of all change, and any proposition of new ideas will generate some amount of conflict. The objective is to prevent the conflict from degenerating into blind fear and inflexible rigidity. As one champion in our focus groups articulated it: "Without conflict there will probably be no buy-in. I just have to be careful we do not take conflict personally as an attack on myself. Conflict is just a tool to get people talking and debating an issue from one side or another. It promotes the kind of understanding necessary to be successful in this business." Here again, the power of the champion's vision, credibility, trust, and integrity plays a preeminent role in transforming conflict into a productive commitment to the future.

The champion will not be a great compromiser between the diverse elements, however, unless every other avenue has been explored. A compromise is usually seen as a poor second choice, the forsaking of a dream. Forging a new unity from seemingly diverse values and thinking will be the champion's first choice. This unity becomes a new order of interaction, better than the original, thereby creating a "superordinate" culture for the alliance.

Practicing Transformational Leadership

It is quite common to find champions functioning as transformational leaders, attempting to use an alliance as a mechanism to introduce new ideas, new values, and a new culture into their parent organizations. In a survey of several hundred champions, they reported that 85 to 90 percent of all organizational change is driven by a crisis or some outside force, such as a competitive maneuver, a market shift, or government regulation. Champions will often try to shift that proportion, making *vision* a far larger causal factor for change. Gary Dehkes, when playing the role of champion, states: "The way to cause change and to help an organization reach for a vision is to raise the perception of dissatisfaction with the present and simultaneously lower the perceived cost of changing toward the desired vision. People don't jump the fence for greener pastures unless they are unhappy enough with the side of the fence they're on and the fence isn't too high to jump!"

Transformational champions are trying to change the order of the future; therefore, the process of change itself triggers deep fears and insecurities and thus resistance in their parent companies. The daring champion, unknowingly, is likely to polarize an organization, often evoking both love and hate, but seldom neglect and apathy.

Gaining Top-Rank Support

In this organizational effort, top-rank support is indispensable. Champions must often confront other top executives strongly yet diplomatically when the corporate castle walls seem impenetrable and resistance to new ideas becomes overwhelming. Therefore, to be properly anointed, the champion must have the support of the organization's high priests. Top-level sponsorship is often referred to as the "godfather" role.

When the venture has widespread organizational impact, established power structures and political relationships will be disrupted. The presence of the godfather validates the strategic value of the venture and helps shield it from the onslaught of naysaying cynics and those threatened by the alliance's very existence. Brian Ferrar notes that the godfather role requires far more than mere support— he sees it as a "protector providing air cover." Another champion from our focus groups commented, "We need a godfather to protect us. But often the godfathers get clobbered themselves by the empire builders and fiefdom creators, who feel threatened by us because, in their view, the alliance diminishes their power."

The seemingly innocent activity of getting autonomous business units to work together is fraught with danger. Business unit executives with profit-and-loss responsibility often see the alliance as a threat to their power and authority and even a drain on their resources, thereby diminishing their unit's profitability. All of this is fodder for political infighting. According to John Mazur at Siemens, "Alliance champions are usually unpopular within their organizations and are challenged by the powerful empire builders, who believe they can do it better than the alliance partner, or by individuals who view the alliance partner as the enemy merely because of its high visibility." In fact, many alliance champions report that it is easier to form an alliance with a competitor than with another division of their own company.

The godfather's support of the champion becomes increasingly evident once an alliance begins operations. In Gary Horning's view, "One can have an excellent executive relationship, a terrific engineering relationship, and even a great cooperative marketing effort, but the rubber hits the road in the local field engagement process. Unfortunately, it is here that the champion, who can be little more than a cheerleader or educator, requires the support of the sales VPs and staff to engage with the partner." Without a strong godfather to influence the corporate rewards system, the real benefits of the alliance may be lost. Understanding how champions use their leverage on the organization's leadership is essential according to Lucent Technologies' Gerry Dehkes: "Champions need to differentiate among targets (people who must change their behavior), sponsors (people who can cause targets to change their behavior), and advocates (people like themselves who have a vision but little power to change targets directly). Champions, in their advocacy role, must spend their time working the sponsors, not the targets. Finally, sponsors need to care as much about the alliance as the alliance champion."

The godfather must have access to the other side of the alliance as well. John Mazur adds: "Senior executives also need to make themselves available to their partner's alliance champions, something many don't think about or do."

Paradoxical Qualities

Champions are not superheroes; they suffer the pains of defeat and the quandaries of leadership just like other leaders. Many are torn between two worlds, thus living a paradox

> Between the patient need to nurture relationships and the impatient, compelling desire for achievement, knowing that personal relationships, trust, and sensitivity to people's personal needs and feelings are essential to building a successful team but being driven by the desire to see results, to make a difference, to translate ideas into action. One side of the dilemma makes the champion want to lead by consensus, the other by command.

> Between forcing the trauma of disruptive change and enduring the pain of inertial stability. Champions know people are not happy about change, but they can't understand why everyone

needs so much coddling and why resistance to a glorious future is so heavy. They see a new future as inevitable, like an unstoppable railroad train barreling down the tracks.

Between the visionary's denial of reality and the realist's acceptance of reality. This seemingly profane balancing act acknowledges that we must pursue a dream if we are to reach the holy land (because it will mean the renewal of our organization—a true new beginning), yet we must accept the reality that the dream is very difficult to achieve and quite risky (the organization might fail; individuals might be hurt; the champion might get fired).

Such paradoxes often leave the champion mired in dilemmas, sometimes seemingly paralyzed in procrastination. Ultimately, however, the champion awakens from being a prisoner of paradox, with a passionately bold move toward the real vision.

Achilles' Heels

Champions have several other traits that can create difficulties. In addition to being overoptimistic, the typical champion is overcommitted, unable to say no to another request even if it entails stepping aside from the perceived pathway of highest and best destiny. Only after seasoning do champions begin to learn their limits.

Administrative duties and routines are boring, and the details of project management are usually sacrificed by the champion for the larger strategic and visionary tasks. Comments Pat Bryant, alliance champion at EKA Chemicals, "I'm no good with the details. It's the ideas, the presentation—that's what I'm good at. People often think that I'm going to be a detail person because I have a Ph.D. in chemical engineering. However, my Ph.D. was for me only a mountain to climb that made me focus on details to succeed. I hate details: it takes great focus for me to work on details."

If the champion has not already acknowledged these weaknesses, it is wise to be sure he or she is matched with a good administrative team to balance them out.

Qualities and Characteristics That Evoke Resistance

The insecure and the egocentric often confuse the champion's passion and enthusiasm with egocentric behavior. However, *enthusiasm*, in its most noble definition in ancient Greek, signified the god within; similarly, a champion's missionary zeal is born of the commitment to a greater good. Excellence is never born from a disengaged heart.

In essence, the true champion begins to live the vision he or she beholds. Among those who have never embraced this type of life, becoming a vision is anathema to many and misunderstood by more. It looks like ego drive, but it is not. The champion's courage is obtained from a commitment to a vision far larger than his or her fears. The champion's willingness to make powerful commitments is based on belief, not evidence, which to many looks like the behavior of an unbridled zealot.

The champion's ability to navigate the halls of power makes him or her look like a politician, which the champion is not. Champions often remark how they dislike the lobbying role, but acknowledge that they have to do it if they are to compete for executive airtime.

And the champion's frequent disregard for the organizational hierarchy gives credence to the criticism that champions are sacrilegious, which they are not. In fact, many alliance champions have referred to the art and architecture of cooperation as a spiritual experience, fulfilling an inner personal need to do something valuable for their organization, which the champions regard as their own community.

Most people see organizations as they are drawn on organizational charts, as hierarchical structures with functional silos composed of somewhat isolated departments. Champions never describe organizations that way. Instead they see organizations as networks, and navigate the networks like a honeybee on a summer's day: in a zigzag pattern. Naturally, this drives the traditional organization man absolutely insane. Champions see the other management team as extensions of themselves, as an integral part of the alliance itself. In this way, the borders of the organizations become transparent to the champion.

Champions march to the tune of a different drumbeat—faster, more futuristic.

Their tolerance for ambiguity and uncertainty is higher than that of most logical linear managers like to handle.

Slightly off-center from corporate norms, champions are often regarded as somewhat eccentric but not defiantly deviant or rebellious. Because champions are often trying to address problems that others frequently do not recognize as problems at all, they are often unfairly perceived as unreasonable, undisciplined, and unrealistic, as outside the mainstream, as agitators, troublemakers, and professional irritants.

Understand and Support the Unique Role of the Champion

Many champions comment that they are deeply misunderstood and often rejected by members of their own organization. Ironically, often the more successful the champion is with an alliance, the deeper the rejection. To fulfill the commitment to a win-win position for the alliance (and sometimes to avoid isolation), the champion often bonds tightly with his or her counterpart in the other organization. States Compaq's Brian Ferrar: "Your partner must see you as his or her company's advocate, never having any doubt that you're helping their cause forward. This also helps keep the inevitable conflicts from escalating." However, such a powerful commitment to the other company's cause often simply serves as evidence to confirm the suspicion that the champion is disloyal.

Not only do champions have a tendency to bond powerfully with the champions of the alliance partner, but they also bond with their mission and with the cooperative venture itself, thus evoking scorn and often rejection from traditional organizationalists. Cautions NCR's Gary Horning, "Champions cannot succeed in an environment where they are rejected or not supported by the executive members of their own organization. Champions must bond with both their partners and their own company, and they must coordinate compromises with their own organization for the ultimate good of the big-picture relationship."

Having a deep understanding of the personalities and roles of the champion can help organizations ensure champions' success and prevent champions from having to fight needless rear-guard battles with their own troops, enabling them to focus their energies and spirit more rightfully on their mission.

Give champions the support and resources they need to be successful. Tolerate them even when they don't play by the rules. Give them clear boundaries, but let them range broadly within these boundaries. Make them catalysts for change. Push them to behold a breakthrough value proposition powerful enough to break the stranglehold of the inertial resistance that stifles most organizations. And always remember: they will ask forgiveness after the fact rather than ask permission before the fact.

When venturing beyond the hallowed walls of the corporate castle, consider—

A true champion without a cause is entrapped energy.
A great cause without a champion is but an elusive dream.
But a great cause with a true champion is the realization of a vision!

15 JIM BELASCO

CREATING SUCCESS FOR OTHERS

Jim Belasco, a professor of management at San Diego State University, is a rigorous and dynamic visionary who helps organizations reinvent themselves and the author of Teaching the Elephant to Dance: Empowering Change in Your Organization; Flight of the Buffalo: Soaring to Excellence, Learning to Let Employees Lead *(with Ralph Stayer); and most recently,* Soaring with the Phoenix: Renewing the Vision, Reviving the Spirit, Re-Creating the Success of Your Company *(with Jerre L. Stead).*

Three key threads form the design of the tapestry of leadership in the twenty-first century. They are interconnectedness, interdependency, and creating success for others—both for all those leaders serve and all those who contribute to leaders' success. These characteristics make it possible for everyone to be a leader in the twenty-first century.

Interconnectedness:
Everything and Everyone Is Connected
to Everything and Everyone Else

"De knee bone connected to de thigh bone, de thigh bone connected to de hip bone, de hip bone connected to de back bone, . . . I hear de word of de Lord," the old spiritual went. That's also the word of today's leader, looking over the landscape of the globe and seeing a mosaic of interconnected people and institutions.

Interconnectedness Produces Power

NCR implemented a new organizational concept, Customer Focused Teams (CFTs). These cross-functional teams from sales, finance, marketing, and professional services were organized around specific customers. The new model changed everything, not only within NCR but also with all its interconnected customers and suppliers.

In dealing with Wal-Mart, for instance, many things changed. Members of the CFT for Wal-Mart spent many hours working side by side with Wal-Mart employees at store locations across the country, solving installation problems, training store personnel, and actually operating the system during *crunch times*. "I thought they were on our payroll. I even issued them an employee badge," a store manager said about her NCR CFT members.

The shift to CFTs changed the interconnected systems within NCR as well. For example, the human resource senior vice president decentralized much of the HR function out of headquarters, placing staff geographically closer to the CFTs. He gained significant productivity improvement by focusing the objectives, measures, and rewards for all HR associates around creating success for client CFTs.

The CFT model also redefined NCR's relationships with its interconnected suppliers. For example, members of a CFT held monthly videoconferences with people from Intel, a key supplier of chips. As a result of those meetings Intel sped up its development of the high-performance chips NCR needed for the massively parallel processing equipment it sold to Wal-Mart.

Here's the bottom line: change one institutional characteristic—in this case, how the field organization is structured—and you affect every other interconnected institution both internally and externally. The NCR story is a good-news story. NCR grew its revenues more than 20 percent during the next twelve months, the largest increase at NCR in many years.

Interconnectedness Gives *Every Person* Power

When one is part of a vast array of interconnected people and institutions, it is easy to feel overwhelmed and powerless. That feeling was expressed by a machinist we know who said, "Hey, I'm just one person. How much of an impact can I really have?"

Actually, as a direct result of interconnectedness, any single person can have far-reaching impact. A shipping supervisor at a Square D factory in South Carolina was one person who made a big difference. One weekend the company received an emergency call from a nuclear power plant on the East Coast. The plant needed a critical part immediately. The supervisor took it upon herself to use her personal credit card to fly the part to the Boston area. The part solved the problem, and the plant continued to operate. Square D kept the customer that contributed to keeping a two-thousand-person plant operating. Two million people kept their lights on. One person took a small action that made a big difference.

Business Week (July 29, 1996) once reported the work of James C. Bulin, another person who made a big difference. He lived his working life buried in the bowels of the Ford Motor Company. His offbeat ideas were often ignored or laughed at. Imagine his surprise when he was singled out for his contribution to the success of Ford's best-selling F-150 truck. Rather than beginning with the traditional benchmarking of other successful cars, midlevel designer Bulin focused on customer desires. He identified six generational groups and their values and tastes. Virtually every detail of the F-150 was redesigned using Bulin's generational value groups data. Bulin's ideas produced the next category-killer automobile for Ford and more than $1 billion in net earnings. Not bad results from one small idea.

Each of us can indeed have a significant impact, like that shipping supervisor at Square D keeping the lights on for two million people. In short, the kneebone is connected to the thighbone, and every other bone as well. Interconnectedness offers many people the opportunity to act like leaders and make a big difference in the lives of others.

Interdependencies: Leaders Unleash Chute-Packer Power

I heard a story told by a former Navy pilot that illustrates the power of interdependency.

> I flew thirty-seven successful missions off the deck of the carrier in Vietnam. Then I was shot down, captured, and spent five years as a POW before being released at the end of the war. Several years later a man approached me in a hotel lobby. "Hi, Commander, how have you been?" he asked. Seems we served on the same carrier in the Gulf.
>
> After exchanging pleasantries I asked, "What did you do, sailor?"
>
> "Packed chutes," he said.
>
> We chatted for a while about old times and said good by. On the way home that evening I realized that I owed my life to that man. He likely packed my parachute that opened perfectly that fateful morning—and enabled me to land safely. I owed my life to that man, and I never even knew him or thanked him.
>
> Then I realized that my life is filled with people who "pack my chute"—my occupational chute, my career chute, my emotional chute, my financial chute, my community chute, my family chute. From that day forward I

promised to identify and acknowledge all the "chute packers" in my life.

There are many chute packers in the life of each of us, and we need them all. No one lives in isolation. Successful leaders figure out ways to help people pack each other's chutes.

Whenever Two or More
Are Gathered in His Name . . .

Pastor Michael Slaughter is an excellent leader, unleashing chute-packer power. He leads the Ginghamsburg United Methodist Church. Once a small steepled country church in a rural countryside, Ginghamsburg is now a sprawling, bustling community worship, activities, and counseling center. It includes a resale clothing store, women's counseling center, food pantry, community-crisis outreach program, furniture warehouse, three children's clubhouses, and many other critical support services. The church holds four worship services each weekend—with attendance averaging more than three thousand.

In his book *Spiritual Entrepreneurs: Six Principles for Risking Renewal*, Slaughter underscores the importance of small groups of interdependent parishioners as catalysts for meaningful spiritual experiences. These small groups "have the power to break addictions, overcome codependent tendencies, and restore broken relationships." Slaughter organized these groups of interdependent parishioners and leveraged their power to grow both the spiritual lives of his followers and the success of his church.

Interdependencies Give Rise to a Roman Empire

From the Prato region of Italy, between Florence and Pistoia, the *Strategy and Leadership* journal (July–Aug. 1996) reported another example of chute-packer power. Massimo Menichetti exploded a large textile organization into small chunks and created a hugely successful interdependent network of chute packers.

He broke up all the departments into specialized small companies, separating finishing from spinning from weaving, letting each excel in its own speciality. Menichetti sold half of each small companies' stock to employees. These small firms were forced to work together because they depended on each other to succeed. The disaggregation helped them see their mutual interdependency and helped them work together more effectively. Menichetti's program worked, in spades. Today there are more than fifteen thousand interdependent firms with five or fewer employees. Their textile products produce millions in revenues—and twenty thousand area jobs.

Michael Slaughter and Massimo Menichetti are excellent examples of the thousands of twenty-first-century leaders who use the power of interdependency to create success for everyone they touch: parishioners, investors, employees, and community members.

Create Success for Others: The Mentality That Establishes Leadership

Given interdependency and interconnectedness it's clear that we need each other. Hands need bodies. A healthy hand depends on a healthy body. A healthy body depends on a healthy community, a healthy nation, and a healthy planet. My health depends on your health. My success depends on your success. Therefore, I must be as committed to helping you succeed as I am to helping me to succeed. Isn't that logical? Of course it is—and that simple, logical conclusion shapes leadership behavior in the twenty-first century.

The leader of tomorrow recognizes and leverages her or his interconnected interdependencies to create success for all those with whom she or he is connected. Unfortunately, too many people are focused on their own little piece of the elephant, believing that it is the whole animal. Individuals often act as though every other interconnected or interdependent person or organization is an interference on the set of *their* big movie. They don't see their own critical interconnections and interdependencies. Their narrow view is like a puzzle missing several large pieces. In fact, it isn't really a puzzle at all—because the picture of the big picture just isn't in the picture!

Each and every one of us owns the responsibility to hold that picture of the big picture high enough that others can see it. Given the complexity of our world, life today is like bowling blindfolded. Each of us is responsible for providing the eyes for others so they can know where and how to roll the ball and how many pins they knocked down. We are more than our brother's keeper: we are his eyes—and that's an essential leadership mentality in the twenty-first century.

Just what others must we create success for? The answer is almost too easy. They are family, friends, people we work with, and people we directly supply. In short we must create success for all those we serve and all those who contribute to our own success.

It's easy to follow the business trail of people for whom we create success. Imagine: Brian builds massively parallel processor servers in California. A network services provider in New Jersey buys one of his computers. This server then enables connections across the globe, as countless people use it to access the Internet. A cologne designer in Paris uses the Internet to gather data about designing a new fragrance that will be produced in a company's New Jersey plant. The fragrance is sold in Sydney, Australia, and sparks a romantic relationship in Singapore. Brian has lots of other people for whom his quality work creates success.

Good capitalists must look beyond their shareholders and be concerned about the health and success of employees and community members. James Gwarty, Robert Lawson, and Walter Bark of the Cato Institute point out that free market activities exist within a democratic context. On the most macro level, democracy fosters a market economy that in turn creates prosperity. Political democracy in a community, then, is the driving force that enables economic prosperity for any given organization within that community. Successful U.S. business organizations today can thank the framers of the Constitution two hundred years ago for their success. To ensure their future success, those same organizations (and their leaders) must work today to strengthen future political freedom and the long-term viability of the market economy.

Family members are also important recipients of the results of the injunction to create success for others. We've all sometimes misread a family member's needs. For instance, the English grades of one of our sons dropped. We pushed him hard to improve, spending hours each night reviewing his work. He resented the increased pressure, and our relationship soured. Then we went to his school and saw the problem. His teacher was new and ineffective. Every student in that class was struggling. There were many great teachers in his school. This teacher wasn't yet one of them. We arranged to transfer our son to another class. His grades improved, so we stopped hassling him about studying harder. Our relationship with him improved, and we all went to a ball game together. Before that, we had been failing to create success for one of the important people we serve: our son.

The injunction for personal leadership success in the twenty-first century is clear: create success for all your interconnected inter-dependencies. The "success equation" shown in Figure 15.1 should be a lighthouse beacon for the twenty-first-century leader.

Figure 15.1. Success Equation.

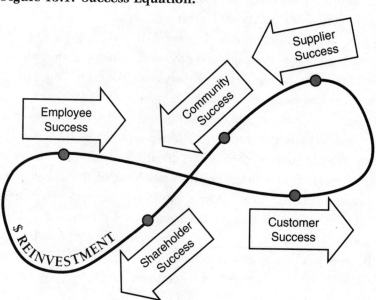

Finally, take the need to create success for others to a more personal level. Teaching is the best way to learn. Medical training, for example, is based on the *see one, do one, teach one* philosophy, according to which the doctor in training sees a procedure done, does the procedure, and then, to reinforce the knowledge, teaches the procedure to the next group of doctors-to-be. I've learned a lot about life teaching scouting to our kids. My wife has learned a lot about faith teaching Sunday school. Helping others learn helps the teacher learn. I guess that's why I teach. What a win-win deal—and a great example of how the create-success-for-others philosophy helps create success for you.

Summary: Fellowship and Leadership

The twenty-first-century leader creates success for others—those she or he serves and those who contribute to her or his success. A commitment to that result causes the leader to continually ask whether she or he can answer yes to this question: Does this action, policy, strategy, plan contribute to success for our interconnected and interdependent employees, end-user customers, suppliers, communities, and shareholders? The twenty-first-century leader proceeds with only those actions that pass the yes test.

Twenty-first-century leaders are both fellows and leaders in their interconnected, interdependent relationships. People who see themselves as part of a fellowship with others accept the responsibility to cooperate with others, helping them achieve their goals. Leaders go further, taking responsibility for creating success for all those with whom they are interconnected and interdependent. In the twenty-first century everyone is a leader, as everyone is a fellow.

16 CHRISTOPHER CAPPY
ROBERT ANTHONY

LEADING SUCCESSFUL CHANGE INITIATIVES

Christopher Cappy is president of Pilot Consulting Corporation, a firm specializing in the implementation of strategic objectives for corporations worldwide. He has extensive experience at General Electric with its Work-Out process and Management Development Institute, and at IBM with its ACT change initiative. His work is grounded in action learning methodologies and high-performance team protocols. Robert Anthony is a management consultant associated with Pilot Consulting. He has extensive experience improving operations using GE Work-Out and the Pacific Gas & Electric Action Forum processes. He has led business reengineering, continuous improvement, and organizational change initiatives for clients spanning the globe. He holds an M.B.A. from the Harvard Business School and an A.B. in philosophy from Occidental College.

In the speed-hungry world of business, the ability to accelerate significant measurable change across a large, complex organization has become more prized than ever. In every industry sector, the most competitive and most innovative organizations have created aggressive "processes of engagement" and incorporated them into their leadership systems. Though the form may vary, these processes drive large groups of the right people to confront and resolve the most challenging issues. The best simultaneously get results, drive cultural change, and build internal capability. For the most successful, the change process becomes a tool, a reusable asset spread throughout the organization, at last delivering on the often made but underfulfilled promise that "better, faster" ways will win in the marketplace.

Central to advancing on the business challenge du jour is the ability to resolve conflict at organizational boundaries. Resolving conflicts between work groups or functions, on the one hand, and management levels, on the other, has long been recognized as a special challenge for corporate managers and organization development professionals. Over the past decade we have seen the focus of this challenge shift away from attempts to build smoother working relationships and decrease the cost of transactions between groups to much bolder and more systemic initiatives that fundamentally change work processes and structures. This trend is driven primarily by competitive demands for relentlessly better productivity, innovation, and performance improvements. In many cases corporatewide initiatives attempt to bridge the gulf between a company's ambitious goals and its current management processes and capabilities. Some notable successes, described later in more detail, have espoused and aggressively pursued the "breaking down of boundaries" as a primary tactic of their initiatives. Also, the examples support increasing evidence that corporatewide efforts to improve competitiveness need not always be patient and incremental, that in effect business, behavioral, and organizational change can occur simultaneously from the common experience in engaging the toughest business challenges.

Change Initiatives and Change Acceleration

Corporatewide change initiatives have certain characteristics in common. Usually, an initiative provides an umbrella under which a variety of change-related activities, such as reengineering, quality improvement, continuous improvement (incremental problem solving), or accelerated problem solving, will occur. Typically rolled out with much hope and fanfare, the initiative addresses some pressing problem that dictates a need for change, a vision for the anticipated results of the change process, and some degree of specification about what the change activities should look like. Initiatives of this sort have sprung up across the corporate landscape, often beginning as an important priority for the companies who take them on.

These change initiatives, in our experience, are subject to some predictable pitfalls. Initiatives aimed at "doing things differently" can be swamped by short-term performance pressures. Often leaders are unprepared to do the many things required of them to execute the desired vision successfully. Also, an initiative may be greeted with cynicism due to failure of previous attempts at change or lack of follow-up on once promising change activities. Few change initiatives live up to their intended promises.

One reason is that change initiatives are being attempted in contexts where the boundaries between groups in an organization have become rigid, bureaucratic, and ineffective, characterized by unhelpful stereotypes. The organization may place too much emphasis on individual and functional goals and too little on marketplace realities; it may have employees who lack an understanding of how their work fits in with the work of the company or corporate cultures that favor dictatorial management styles, paternalism, or entitlements. It is precisely where these conditions exist, along with their inevitable outcomes, that "boundary busting" becomes a crucial goal that should pervade every aspect of a change initiative. In such cases aggressive approaches using accelerated problem solving are most effective.

Accelerated problem solving is a highly focused approach for creating and implementing in a matter of months needed changes that might ordinarily take years to accomplish or might never take place at all. The approach marries both the human and technical aspects of improving performance in the context of a corporatewide initiative. The umbrella framework, we have learned, is important because interdependence in most business systems mandates that all parts of the system need to be brought along at once. Similarly, leaders and managers in organizations will typically change the way they operate only when they are confident that other people are changing too. Thus one part of the trick in accelerating change is fashioning an overall initiative that is powerful enough to survive competing forces and can take root throughout a large organization. With this comes an overarching message about the "new way" that is behaviorally descriptive, simple, and purposeful. The other part is making sure that the right things consistently get done.

At a most practical level, doing the "right" things means taking on a company's thorniest, most pressing problems in a quick, collaborative manner, tapping its best internal resources. It means addressing problems of strategic and tactical importance with strong, dynamic cross-functional teams, providing resources almost instantly to implement high-stakes action plans over a short time period, and relentlessly monitoring the process and its results in terms of real time and money. Although accelerating change requires workshop-oriented "events," real change occurs through implementation of a series of projects commonly defined by stretch goals, thoroughly documented action plans, and designated accountability for results. The immediate benefit of this approach is that positive movement occurs on the issues under scrutiny.

The focus and speed delivered via this approach typically translates into significant business results. The collateral prize is that the participating organizations gain valuable experience in working across boundaries, which helps set the tone for all other work, thus substantially demonstrating "new ways of working together." This is in fact behavioral change.

The kinds of issues attacked in this way range widely. Although the change acceleration methodology is not overly complex (this is one of its strengths), implementing it well takes courage, discipline, and skill. It is a very powerful tool when correctly targeted and supported because it unleashes the full force of an organization against its most important challenges.

Propositions for Accelerating Change

A number of propositions underpin much of our work in the area of change acceleration and are key assumptions of the examples we shall cite.

Proposition 1: Nothing produces change like change.

All too often, change initiatives are long on talk and short on action. Although the pace of change can seldom be adequately prescribed or predicted, the best way to make change occur is to set stretch goals and work to make them happen. Exhortations from management, training in the use of change tools, and analysis of problems as they exist do more to reinforce the status quo than to produce organizational renewal and different business outcomes. True change requires an imagination of what is possible that extends beyond the firsthand experience of many in an organization. Active experimentation with new formulas can turn new possibilities into realities. Where successful, a bias for action breeds confidence and momentum, which stimulates further action. Even if actions are unsuccessful, lessons learned can become the foundation for future success.

Proposition 2: Speed is key.

Change to strategies, structures, processes, and behaviors needs to happen fast in corporate environments characterized by inertia between levels and functions, if it is to happen at all.

People in an organization lose interest in a change effort that is talked about but not fully implemented after about ninety days. If a problem is so large that significant action to solve it cannot be taken within this time frame, it should be left until a time when the change initiative has begun to take effect and the organization has a greater reserve of problem-solving skills to fall back on.

To achieve speed consistently, organizations need to enhance their tolerance for solutions that are less than comprehensive, and they need to learn to reduce the time required to move from concept to decision to action. Both of these skills are counterintuitive in most organizations, which strive always to "get it right," and they tend to stimulate quite a bit of healthy discomfort. Change acceleration initiatives need to incorporate the "80 percent solution" as a rule that counteracts natural tendencies to overrefine plans that are fraught with uncertainty. They also need to force the hands of decision makers by confronting them with proposals that have the support and conviction of their most trusted people and by taking away the safety net of closed-door reviews and private resolutions.

Proposition 3: Successful change is driven from many directions at once.

There is much debate about whether change is best driven from the top down or from the bottom up. In our view, all levels of an organization have a role to play, and the roles need to be played on a stage that all can see and understand. The people at the top must demand change, provide real resources and critical decisions that shape the pace and direction of change, and become role models for the company's stated vision. In our experience, however, the top cannot become exclusively accountable for change, or nothing will actually get done. Most change agendas are in fact shaped and implemented in middle and supervisory management. People at these levels often assume that they have less authority than they actually do and that the top is in more control of operations than it is. Unfortunately, statements to the contrary cannot alter this misperception. The best remedy we know of that consistently works to "mobilize the middle" comes about when the change process provides no alternative but for the middle to use its power. We advocate finding ways to spotlight and support the role of the middle and to design a change process that requires the exercise of its authority and influence.

Proposition 4: Lack of leadership, not resistance, is most likely to derail sustained change.

Understanding the nature of resistance and planning to over-come it are important topics to consider when designing a change initiative. The strategy of creating "wins" that demonstrate that change is possible has the dual advantage of isolating cynics and skeptics in an organization and creating a situation where small breakthroughs can be exploited into bigger successes. However, overcoming resistance, real though it may be, is less of an issue in situations that are truly ripe for change. What is more difficult is finding people who are ready to step up to the challenge of mobi-lizing an organization for change. Over time, a critical mass of such people is required at various levels in an organization if changes are to be sustained. It is for this reason that we advocate priming the pump for change leaders with special roles and training built into the change initiative itself.

Proposition 5: Boundaries make work transactional; transactions can be taken to a higher plane.

Most large, complex organizations are cauldrons of competing interests. Boundaries between groups in organizations exist naturally because the various subunits, by definition, pursue different goals and tasks. This means that relationships between work groups are trans-actional, based more or less on leadership and cultural factors. In our experience, it is impractical to expect people to act as if these bound-aries did not exist. Rather, we advocate that transactions between groups be taken to a higher plane by infusing them with a common understanding of the big picture, that improvement goals be designed with enhanced accountability for outcomes, and that the process enable groups to learn about one another in a practical way.

Proposition 6: The most substantial change is often unseen by the people experiencing it.

Both business results and behavioral gains are necessary for a company to renew and sustain its competitive position. In our experience, the behavioral capabilities and disciplines gained by way of the change process are often imperceptible to the people directly participating, especially at the beginning. Most eyes are consistently focused on the quantitative results, which keep people from appreciating other equally important behavioral changes. Such changes in a large, complex system can remain subtle until a pattern begins to establish itself via repetition and demonstrated success. Among them are

- An improved ability at all levels to think strategically about business problems, which we refer to as "business literacy"

- A widespread attitude that every problem has a solution, every solution has an action, and every action includes accountability for someone

- An understanding throughout the organization of the many people and interests that have to be aligned to achieve certain outcomes and creation of the relationships to make the alignment possible

- A willingness among leaders, based on positive experience, to make firm decisions publicly, trust the organization across its boundaries, and enable positive change

Cases of Successful Accelerated Change: GE Work-Out and IBM ACT

A number of well-known companies have successfully implemented change acceleration initiatives that are based on propositions like ours. Two major initiatives are General Electric's much-heralded Work-Out process and IBM's less publicized but equally sweeping initiative labeled ACT ("Accelerate Change Together").

GE Work-Out

GE's flagship change initiative spawned the vibrant movement toward change acceleration methodologies. Introduced in 1989 and used on a wide scale for many years, Work-Out was conceived and implemented as a bold and ambitious stroke to transform the behemoth conglomerate into a lean and agile growth machine.

GE's visionary and inspirational new leader, Jack Welch, had taken steps to restructure what he called the "hardware" of the company by shuffling its portfolio of businesses, and he needed an equally ambitious approach to rewire the "software." Welch became quickly aware that the company's engineering-driven culture was often awash in bureaucratic red tape and hence slower to act and react than he desired. Welch's mantra, and the focus of Work-Out, became "speed, simplicity, and self-confidence." The goal was to create a corporation that could consistently "get there faster, get there first" by simplifying processes in a manner that also engendered strength and confidence in its employees.

Work-Out started small. Each of GE's thirteen business units at the time was encouraged to pilot the process, which was funded centrally at the outset. The early sessions were styled after New England town meetings, with a focus on cutting red tape—consolidating reports, streamlining approvals, eliminating meetings, simplifying procedures. In the Work-Out "town meetings" employees would make suggestions for changes, commit to implementing the changes, and receive decisions on the spot from the senior managers. Although most proposed changes were fairly small in scale, the effect of employee input and implementation and rapid decision making was quite dramatic. Work-Out effectively pulled the rug out from under actions that often bog down improvement initiatives—analysis paralysis, "suggest now, decide later," lack of management accountability, and the like. The program was broadly credited, inside and outside GE, as a major catalyst for the company's now legendary performance-driven culture.

Work-Out went in a variety of directions at GE. In some businesses it became a tool for higher-impact problem solving and a centerpiece for major cost, quality, service, and cycle time initiatives. In other businesses it went nowhere at all—either the process simply didn't take or it was thought to conflict with other initiatives. After a critical mass of GE had been exposed to Work-Out concepts and the organization had become more fluid across boundaries, Work-Out gave way to other tools, such as the formal Change Acceleration Program and the current Six Sigma quality process.

IBM's ACT

ACT is a Lou Gerstner–sponsored initiative deliberately adapted from Work-Out. When Gerstner joined IBM in late 1993, one of his first moves was to leverage the company's scale, reach, and brand strength by creating a global business process with a customer focus. What followed was a sea change in the way the company was organized, how it positioned itself, and how it operated. However, because the company had earlier emphasized a decentralized organizing model, it was unequipped to achieve the kind of integration and change Gerstner's global strategy demanded.

ACT was designed in 1994 to promote "better, faster execution" across the newly conceptualized organization by providing the tools necessary for simultaneous process and behavior change. It became a process for executing against known business challenges, emphasizing aggressive goals, promoting rapid cross-organizational communication and collaboration, offering on-the-spot decision making, and documenting relentless accountability for actions. ACT has developed by fits and starts through a variety of phases marked by funding shifts, executive emphasis, and internal leadership of the process. Although IBM's sustained focus on change activities can be credited to many factors, most important to the company has been designing an overarching initiative that consistently promotes real business wins and sustains momentum for change.

The cornerstone of ACT has been an intense, highly structured, and dynamic series of "ACT business meetings," evolved from the more refined variants of Work-Out's town meetings. During business meetings, high-level global problem-solving teams grapple with the most pressing problems facing the company, often launching multimillion-dollar change projects. The track record in implementation has been good thanks to the structured nature of the follow-up. As a consequence of more than three hundred ACT business meetings, documented benefits in incremental revenues, cost savings, and savings from cycle time reductions exceeded $6 billion in ACT's first four years. Equally important, the process has been a catalyst for enhanced collaboration and coordination across a complex global business. Evaluations have repeatedly shown that participants recognize the value of ACT in bringing about a more responsive and competitive IBM.

Making Change Acceleration Initiatives Work

Work-Out, ACT, and similar programs consistently incorporate, at various points, the attitudes and guidelines regarding change acceleration we have described. They also illustrate several principles for the design and implementation of large-scale change acceleration initiatives. As with all good principles, application of each will vary on a company-by-company basis.

Initiative Design

Principle 1: Establish a loose and organic process that has a central, consistent message.

Whatever path corporate leaders pursue, nothing will work unless a critical mass of people in the organization has accepted and mobilized around the change process. This implies, especially at the outset, that the people responsible for guiding the effort must be attentive to anyone who suggests a direction that might work. It also suggests that the right approach is often to experiment with ideas and tools, such as a particular workshop design or training strategy. At GE, for example, Work-Out, despite some common objectives and principles, looked quite different in the various business units that adopted the process. Even the town meeting took many forms in different organizations.

What is important is that a change process be credible and drive desired business and behavioral outcomes. Less important are the goals serving as the major point of departure for the process, where the process starts and with whom, what issues are taken on, how the process is positioned, and other such considerations. Of course, business leaders and their advisers may have views that are highly relevant to these issues. But if those ideas are forced on other people or if interplay in rolling out an initiative is lacking, the change process is doomed to failure.

Principle 2: Establish a results-driven framework.

There may be a natural tendency to measure progress in a change initiative by counting how many people have been involved, how many workshops have been held, or how many issues have been addressed. After all, getting any project going is difficult, and indications that an initiative is up and running can provide comfort to the parties responsible for its success. However, it is ultimately the results that come from change activities—*and only the results*—that will sustain an initiative for any period of time. Business results will earn line management acceptance and commitment, and busy schedules throughout the organization will be cleared to make time to participate in the changes. In other words, results-driven change initiatives hold the promise of specific results, and every intervention occurs only when specific results have been framed and committed to. Progress is then tracked and measured, and future work occurs only when the goals of ongoing activities are being met. For example, IBM maintains an extensive Lotus Notes database to track the results from every ACT business meeting.

Principle 3: Actively demonstrate commitment at the very top.

Corporate change initiatives need to be sponsored and driven by the CEO and ultimately by the entire executive management team. This is partly an offensive strategy for change and partly a defensive strategy. Only the CEO has the credibility to provide the kind of vision and urgency that large-scale change initiatives require. As in the cases of GE and IBM, it is often also the CEO's direct encouragement, and later review, that gets change activities rolling. Change initiatives launched without the full or active support of the CEO almost invariably fail to get off the ground and often end up sacrificed on the altar of the CEO's priorities.

Initiative Rollout and Ongoing Management

Principle 4: Use a "pull" strategy, but carefully orchestrate it for success.

Whether change initiatives are best mandated from the top or rolled out subject to demand in an organization is a subject of much debate. The obvious risk of the first strategy is compliance without commitment; the risk of the second is an ebb and flow of activities based on the vagaries of political factors and perceived business conditions. We believe that change initiatives should be able to stand on their own, although their architects need to take several steps both to prime the pump and to keep the water flowing, as it were. GE and IBM implemented the following actions:

- Conduct multiple pilots of the process in the most promising areas, using handpicked volunteers from the executive ranks as sponsors. At least one early pilot should address a difficult high-profile business problem. Choose exemplary and supportive leaders first.

- Broadly publicize "wins" from the pilots within the organization, emphasizing real changes that occurred. Publicity should make use of the full range of communication tools and resources available.

- Maintain peer pressure in the executive and management ranks to encourage future sponsorship. The CEO and top-level executives can send the message "Use this tool; we're watching."

- Establish corporate funding for initial efforts. Moreover, since the goals of change acceleration initiatives extend beyond local business results, some level of corporate funding should always be available for innovation and unanticipated opportunities.

- Promote activity by educating managers about the change initiative through scheduled staff-meeting-type reviews.

- Carefully build a "brand" for the change process that lets people know exactly what to expect when they sign up to use the tools of the process. Protect the brand's integrity.

- Integrate with other change initiatives already in place. Seek synergy wherever possible.

Principle 5: Create a credible clearinghouse within the organization to promote the initiative and broker its use.

A great deal of coordination is required to make a change initiative work. Suitable targets for change need screening; inside and outside resources need to connect; activities need to be scheduled, tracked, and paid for; and overall learning from the process needs to be harvested, built into future development, and communicated to the initiative's sponsors. The only way to ensure that these critical activities are performed satisfactorily is to formalize responsibility for them. At GE, for example, a full-time project management staff coordinated Work-Out centrally, and each business unit established its own representatives. Similarly, IBM coordinates all change activity through the mechanism of a formal project office. When an initiative's clearinghouse is credible in terms of change ambassadorship and business competence, its very existence becomes a meaningful force for change.

Also, the remarkable utility of information technology tools to support "virtual teaming" and accountability management cannot be overemphasized. IBM's use of products such as Lotus Notes for project management and Team Room for electronic group meetings have significantly enhanced the linking of people at sites around the globe to ensure that rapid response and execution occur.

Intervention Success Factors

Principle 6: Make every intervention work.

Achieving true change is difficult, and people in an organization are generally very quick to judge whether a change initiative has the stuff it needs to meet its goals. It takes strong positive testimony from people who participate in a change process, along with demonstrated results, to move it along. Many wins are required to establish a secure foothold in an organization; a single misstep can cause long-lasting damage. For this reason, each intervention in a change initiative needs to be approached with great determination and care. These steps, simple to describe but challenging to accomplish, are required to make an accelerated change initiative work.

- Work on the right issues. Only problems that are central to the major thrusts of the organization should be considered, to avoid any perceived gap between the rhetoric and reality of the initiative. Other criteria include these:

> Addressable issues must touch a number of levels and departments in an organization.
>
> Positive effects should be achieved within a short time period.
>
> Sponsors of the activity must be able to access the resources needed to resolve the problem, and participants must have the authority needed to carry out the agreed-to action.
>
> The challenge represented in the issue must be generally exciting to people. Excitement might exist because the problem has been around a long time, because it is a major impediment or frustration, or because it is on the critical path toward success in the marketplace and personal rewards in the organization

- Involve the right people. Typically, a tough business issue demands that the best and brightest in an organization be involved. It is also wise to involve skeptics—not cynics—to challenge the process and become credible champions of the initiative, once they have been won over.

- Structure the intervention for success. Change acceleration initiatives invariably engage people in activities to which they are unaccustomed, at a pace that is challenging and demands a high standard of performance. This will be uncomfortable for some. All major constituents must be given the coaching they need to succeed, and the process as a whole needs bounds so as to limit surprises and ensure that everyone plays the proper role.

A Closing Thought

Reflecting on what we've written, what comes to mind is Gregory Bateson's observation that "the map is not the territory." Our map of propositions and principles is designed to help you identify a particular vehicle for crossing the terrain and determine that vehicle's performance parameters. It is not a map of the particular territory in which you may wish to effect change, which is of course far more complex, intricate, and messy, inhabited by all sorts of very different people. So keep in mind that the work of accelerating change is as much about heart as about principles and propositions.

17 ARUN GANDHI

THE FOUR CARDINAL PRINCIPLES OF LEADERSHIP

*Arun Gandhi is the founder director of the
M. K. Gandhi Institute for Nonviolence at the
Christian Brothers University, Memphis, Tennessee.
Born in South Africa in 1934 to Manilal, the second
of Mohandas Gandhi's four sons, he learned and
experienced the principle of nonviolence at home
from his parents and grandparents.*

When Mohandas Karamchand Gandhi suffered the ignominy of race and color prejudice in South Africa in 1893, he was inspired to find a "civilized" way of seeking justice. The idea of nonviolent action dawned on him, and with it came the understanding that the success of nonviolence depends substantially on creating a more inclusive life and work ethic based on the ancient philosophy of Oneness, which quite simply means developing the ability to see ourselves in others and others in ourselves, to appreciate that every action we perform has a corresponding reaction in others. Thus exclusivity in life and in work is really a divisive force.

Nonviolence, Gandhi recognized, provides the best bridge across the barriers that we encounter in our lives and work. The first barrier that Gandhi sought to span was the one that divides humanity so inexorably even today—religion. Instead of uniting us in our pursuit of truth or salvation, religion has caused unparalleled violence, hate, and destruction in human history. In his attempt to bridge the barriers that divide religions of the world Gandhi did not seek unification or a melting down among religions but greater respect for each other among people. He sought a relationship based on *respect, understanding, acceptance,* and *appreciation*—the four cardinal principles for relationships at all levels.

When he was convinced of the righteousness of a cause, Gandhi put into practice what he believed to be the truth. His twice-daily prayer services included hymns from Christianity, Islam, Hinduism, Buddhism, Judaism, and other major religions and beliefs of the world. He impressed upon everyone that a "friendly study of all scriptures is the sacred duty of every individual." He made that friendly study himself and incorporated into his life all that he found to be useful. Gandhi lived what he wanted others to learn.

He used analogies to define and emphasize his theory of religion and spirituality. The two that are most relevant today compare religion with a mountain and spirituality with electricity. In the first analogy he said that if we visualize religion as a tall mountain with just one summit and if all of us are striving to reach that single summit, why should it matter to anyone which side of the mountain we chose to climb to get to the top? In the second he said that just as electricity is generated from various sources like water, coal, wind, and the atom, so is spirituality derived from all the different religions. Then, just as we connect ourselves to the main electrical grid and draw from it as much power as we need to enlighten our surroundings, so too each of us must enjoy the freedom to connect to the main source of spirituality and draw from it the power that we need.

These analogies bring into question a whole new line of thought. They raise among other things this vexing dilemma: As individuals can we consider ourselves totally independent? Can we look at our actions or inactions and say what we do is our business and of no concern to others? Can we live for ourselves with no respect or concern for others and their rights and privileges? The Gandhian answer to all these questions is emphatically no, no, no.

Individually and collectively, we are interdependent rather than independent. What happens to one today, ultimately happens to all tomorrow and vice versa. Capitalism, however, derives its strength from the opposite myth of self-centered, rugged individualism. From grade school onward, we teach children to become go-getters. They must strive to reach the top by any means possible.

Mohandas Karamchand Gandhi was very closely connected to Western culture for more than twenty-five years and observed Western individuals' penchant for *independence* and *individualism*—wonderful concepts in theory but much abused in practice. A society, if it is to be cohesive and united, cannot be built on selfish or self-centered foundations. Independence cannot mean solely the right to do what one pleases. Rights in a democracy flow, in exact proportion, out of responsibilities shouldered. To be free it is not enough that we exercise our franchise when called on to do so.

The ancient Eastern philosophical concepts of independence and freedom were referred to by Gandhi as *swaraj*, a word that means much more than the English words mean. It is not just political freedom but also spiritual freedom. *Swaraj* is centered on the self, not on being selfish. The word is derived from two Sanskrit words: *swa*, meaning "self," and *raj*, meaning "*rule*." In the political sense it means freedom to rule or govern, and in the spiritual sense it means freedom from desires, temptations, and possessions. True *swaraj* gives one the ability to look at oneself as just a speck on a large canvas, not in a self-deprecating way but with genuine humility.

Gandhi taught us to look at society as a gigantic machine made up of all kinds of parts—big, small, long, short, round, and flat. Assembled properly they function efficiently and make the machine work. No part in the machine can function on its own, nor can any part be discarded. Society too can function efficiently and unitedly only if all citizens consider themselves parts of the gigantic machine that must work in unison.

It was in pursuit of this theory that Gandhi evolved the philosophy of *trusteeship*. We are trustees of the talent we inherit or acquire through education, not owners. We should not, therefore, exploit the power that we have for our own aggrandizement. If we learn to share our power and possessions with those less fortunate than us, we could create a society of relative peace and harmony.

One might argue that sharing is what we do through charitable institutions, but we need to understand the difference between acting out of pity and acting out of compassion. The line that divides the two is so thin that it is easy to mistake one for the other, yet the essential difference between pity and compassion is easy to understand. In most cases when we hand out doles to the hungry and the homeless, we are acting out of pity. Giving handouts or hand-downs sends two messages—first, that we don't like the receiver and, second, that we want that person to take this and get out of our sight. We don't wish to get involved with other people's miseries because that is not our business.

Conversely, acting out of compassion requires our direct participation and involvement. If there is a hungry person in our neighborhood we must find out why there is hunger, how many are affected, and how can we harness their strengths and abilities so that they can fend for themselves. It is easy to condemn the poor as lazy, unwilling, and degenerate people. The fact is that generations of poverty, destitution, and deprivation have reduced them to a sense of hopelessness. Their self-esteem is shattered, and they have come to believe, as society does, that they are truly unworthy and incapable. Our pity will only exacerbate their condition, and they will sink deeper into the hole.

The objective of a true Gandhian trustee should be to help the hungry and the homeless rebuild their self-respect and self-confidence by developing their ability to resolve their problems. It is essential that such a trustee approach these people with utmost humility. When we have a self-centered attitude, it makes us arrogant. We claim to know their problem and the solution. The reality is just the opposite. We don't know what it means to be hungry; we don't know what it means to be destitute and sleep on the streets; we don't know what it means to be dehumanized. We haven't been in their shoes or seen what they have experienced, so how can we fully understand their problem?

The truly compassionate have greater love for people than for profit. In the world of today, making a profit, even at the expense of others, is of prime importance. Our attitude is that the public is gullible, let's learn how to cheat them. The consequences do not concern us. More than half the products in the market today would not be manufactured if we had a conscience. The world would be much better off.

If we are to work beyond the walls, we must look beyond the self. We must be willing to submerge our identity and individuality in order to heed the needs of others. We must learn to build individual and corporate relationships not on selfish motives, as we do today, nor on the principle of tolerance, as we are taught in a rapidly acculturating society. Meaningful and lasting relationships can be built, Gandhi said, only on the principles of respect, understanding, acceptance, and appreciation.

We must learn to respect ourselves, respect others, and, importantly, respect our connection to all of creation. It requires humility to accept that on the canvas of creation we, individual humans, are just tiny specks. It is only collectively that we make a significant impact on the canvas. A drop of water taken from the ocean quickly evaporates, but every drop that falls into the ocean adds to the power of that mighty sea.

When we learn to submerge the self for the sake of the many, then the meaning of respect becomes clear. At this stage we begin to understand who we are, what the purpose of life is, and how we can attain it. The average individual may think we humans are simply products of someone's sexual desires. This is only partially true. Rain does not fall simply because clouds have gathered. The interrelatedness within nature (which human beings seek always to destroy) ensures that all elements play their role. The sun draws water from the ocean, the water condenses into clouds, the wind carries the clouds over land, and we have rain.

This cycle embodies the essence of life on earth. If wind, water, and sun did not perform their designated tasks there would be no life. Sex is part of human regeneration. Although sex is an act of immense pleasure, it is not the only purpose of human life. We have abused the sanctity of sex to such an extent that we have made it despicable.

A deeper understanding of our purpose in life comes when we realize that there is more to life than sensual pleasures. In fact, it is only when we transcend the physical pleasures after enjoying them that we find the true spiritual meaning of life. Until then we flounder in the pond like tadpoles. It is only when a tadpole matures into a frog that the frog ventures out of the water to explore what lies beyond the pond. A tadpole's vision of life is just water and wetness everywhere.

From an understanding of who we are we reach an appreciation of our differences. We are all same and yet we are all different. The sameness in individuals is mostly internal, whereas the minuscule differences are very visible and create animosity and prejudice in human society because we live in ignorance, plagued by illusions.

Ignorance is a result of our self-centeredness. We are so immersed in ourselves that we have no time to learn about others. This ignorance leads to illusions and fear of the unknown. A story from the Upanishad illustrates the fear and illusions that beset modern society.

A man needed some papers from his workroom late one night in a home without electricity. When he entered the dark room his eyes fell on an object dangling from the ceiling. He ran out, convinced the object was a cobra.

Because he had to get the papers rather urgently, he ventured into the room when there was a little more light. He peered cautiously in the corner, saw the object was still where it had been, and now he was unsure whether it was what he thought it was or something else. However, he was too scared to go closer and check it out. So he left the room and returned when there was daylight only to find the object that resembled a cobra in the dark was nothing but a rope hanging from the ceiling. We conjure up demons in our minds because of ignorance, but the demons disappear when there is enlightenment.

When we learn to accept the differences among us, we appreciate our humanity and transcend the illusions that create dissension. We cease to focus on differences and begin to recognize each other as human beings, not as black, white, brown, or red people or as possessing the many religious, class, and gender labels that we put on ourselves.

The walls that we have built to divide us and the blinkers that we have put on our eyes are a shocking example of the disintegration of the human society. My grandfather always told me: "*Your mind should be like a room with many open windows. Let the breeze flow in from all of them but refuse to be blown away by any one.*"

A woman graduate of the University of Chicago once made the startling confession that she had rejected all morals and ethics because she could not decide "whose morals and ethics I should follow." What she was unknowingly referring to were the *labels* that we have put on morals and ethics—Hindu, Muslim, Christian, Jewish, Catholic, and so on. She was right to reject these labels. When we dispassionately look into those morals, ethics, and values, we will find no important difference between those practiced by Christians, Hindus, or Muslims. Any differences are as insignificant as the differences between two human beings.

When I suggested to this young lady that morals and ethics were nothing more than a definition of right and wrong and that we should have the intelligence and moral strength to know the difference between the two, she was shocked. The idea that parochial labels for moral systems are meaningful had been inexorably impressed on her, as it has been on others; in the final analysis this labeling of morals does more harm to the propagation of our beliefs than good.

In the work for peace and nonviolence, one encounters the same type of constraints. Religious labels like Baptist Peace, Hindu Peace, Catholic Peace, and so on imply that each is different from the other. Yet in reality peace and nonviolence are universal and like morals and ethics do not belong to any particular group. The assumption that only Christians or only Hindus or only Muslims can lead us to peace and harmony in the world is absurd. Awareness of this absurdity can come only when we agree to break down the collective prejudices that hamper our understanding of each other.

When I made this observation at a conference in St. Louis, another young lady, representing the Pax Christi organization, said it will always be so because "we Christians work for Christ." Her remark revealed the depth and width of the chasm that divides humanity even as we approach the twenty-first century and a new millennium. The irony is that as we preach tolerance, respect, understanding, and love toward all, we still punctuate our message with divisive language, still implying that one person is better than another.

Is there any hope for unification and mutual respect? Of course there is hope. The key is this: Are we prepared to be "the change we wish to see"?

Part IV

LEADING
THE LARGER
COMMUNITY

---

18 IAIN SOMERVILLE
D. QUINN MILLS

LEADING IN
A LEADERLESS
WORLD

*Iain Somerville is a partner in Andersen Consulting,
where he founded and led the Organization Strategy practice and the Institute for Strategic Change—the firm's
global business "think tank." As a top management consultant and educator, he has for more than two decades
served the world's leading private, public, and social sector
organizations. D. Quinn Mills is Alfred J. Weatherhead
Jr. Professor at the Harvard Business School and previously taught at MIT's Sloan School of Management. He
consults to major corporations and is author of numerous
articles and eleven books, including* Broken Promises:
An Unconventional View of What Went Wrong at
IBM *and* Rebirth of the Corporation.

W ith the extraordinary amounts of time, money, and effort
invested in developing leaders in business and civic institutions, we might expect a greater degree of leadership in the world.

Note: Bruce Friesen of Andersen Consulting assisted with the preparation of this
chapter.

Yet, paradoxically, we seem to have less leadership, not more. The shortage of leaders is deeply tied to a phenomenon that causes both hope and fear in society—the rise of the global economy.

The growth of the global economy and the interdependence of all nations and organizations within it have been restricting the power of the nation-state and enhancing that of the business enterprise. People looking for effective responses to such social concerns as reducing poverty, enhancing education, promoting economic development, and improving public health have found today's politicians less able to help than yesterday's and have turned to business leaders. Often, business leaders have focused on increasing shareholder value, to the betterment of overall economic health but often to the detriment of social well-being.

When government officials are increasingly powerless and leaders of global businesses are increasingly preoccupied, who will provide leadership in the next century? A possible solution comes from a new kind of partnership at the local and regional level between private businesses, social institutions, and government officials.

The Rise of a Global Economy

For years observers have written about the rise of the multinational corporation, but its real growth is only now apparent. International economic activity has grown rapidly in the past two decades. World economic output has roughly doubled since 1975, the bulk of this growth led not by the industrialized nations but by those catching up to them.

World trade has risen about threefold over the same period. Faster still has been the growth of foreign direct investment (investment by citizens and businesses of one country in another), which has risen sevenfold. Yet this growth pales beside that of capital market activity. Foreign exchange trading has increased by five times, international bank lending by fourteen times, and cross-border securities market transactions by thirty-two times (see Figure 18.1).

Figure 18.1. Growth in Product and Capital Markets.

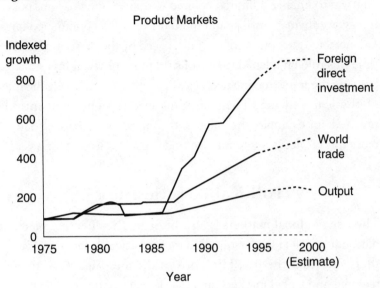

Product Markets

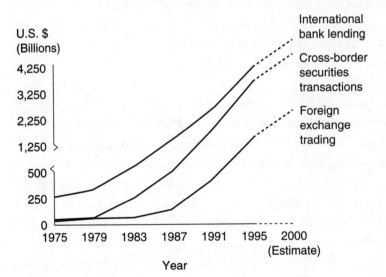

Capital Markets

It's easy to forget that the original role of international capital flow was to finance a limited volume of trade among nations pursuing avowedly mercantilist and mutually hostile economic policies. Financial transactions were the tail wagged by the dog of trade. Over time this role broadened to one of sustaining physical investments, building the infrastructure necessary to support trade. Today the roles of physical trade and financial transactions seem to be entirely reversed: for example, the value of the currency exchanged daily is more than is necessary to finance trade and investment for a year.

Political Powerlessness

The rise of global markets is also limiting the effective reach of national political leadership. Whereas political leaders once were sheltered from the discipline of world capital markets, today's regional and global markets undercut leaders' policymaking power. Countries throughout Asia, for instance, cannot currently pursue desired infrastructure projects because of the collapse of their currencies on foreign exchange markets. Programs to improve public health, advance education, and reduce unemployment are held hostage to budget stringencies enforced either by the markets themselves or by international agencies such as the International Monetary Fund.

As a result politicians are confronting new realities. For years commentators have deplored what they describe as the eclipse of the nation-state by the multinational corporation in the exercise of economic power. But the multinational corporation is not the cause itself, merely the agent of the cause. It is not the multinational corporation that is making the nation-state obsolete but the global economy, especially global capital markets and their enabler, information technology.

As Bell Atlantic president and CEO Ivan Seidenberg has said, the confluence of economics and technology makes for not just a global society but a "global *information* society." Despite continuing attempts, governments cannot control the flow of information across borders nor contain its influence on economics, education, expression, and entertainment.

What is a politician to do? Even those committed to the betterment of less advantaged constituents are constrained by the global market forces. Perhaps this is why politicians of the day seem so ineffectual. Yet being ineffectual, they try harder to appear caring. Their position brings to mind a comment attributed to François Mitterrand by a former aide. When asked what was the most important quality for success in a modern politician, the Socialist president of France replied, "I wish that I could say honesty, or caring. But in reality, it is merely indifference."

Why indifference? Because there is so little room left for policy initiatives that political leaders become unaffected by the suffering of others. The global economy cannot help the weak, the poorly educated, or the disadvantaged unless national leaders are willing to adopt policies in tune with global economic realities. The citizen is equally frustrated but cannot afford to be indifferent. "I can elect my government," thinks the citizen, "but it can do less and less for me."

Politics is local; power is now global—and the disconnect is explosive.

The beneficent state is gone, forced aside by demands for increasing entitlements and consequent budgetary strictures and by the global capital markets, which punish the currency and credit of too generous welfare states.

Opponents of globalization ascribe to it a welter of misfortunes. Wherever local competitiveness lags, transitory unemployment and declining wages may result. People in the developed world look at the spotty environmental records, fraying social safety nets, and limited workplace safeguards in the developing world and clamor for protection from globalization. People in the Third World look at the economic competitiveness of developed nations (provided by centuries of capital accumulation) and likewise demand protection.

Yet evidence suggests that in countries that have most insulated themselves from the global economy, economic growth has been the weakest. Indeed, globalization has contributed to the growth of less developed countries and has hastened the formation of a middle class in societies that never before had one.

Hence it is less the reality of globalization that is resented abroad than the powerlessness it seems to engender. Even where growth is welcomed, people feel that their leaders are unable to address pressing problems and that their future seems at the mercy of the largely remote and impersonal global marketplace.

Executives as Alternatives to Political Leaders

With the political process enfeebled there are pleas for the corporation to assume much of the social welfare role being abdicated by the state. Will corporate executives accept the leadership mantle being thrust upon them?

Although some will, most will not. Roberto C. Goizueta, late CEO of Coca-Cola, indirectly addressed this issue when he observed that "businesses are created to meet economic needs. . . . When institutions try to broaden their scope beyond their natural realms, when they try to become all things to all people, they fail. . . . We have one job: to generate a fair return for our owners. . . . We must remain focused on our core duty: creating value over time."

Did Goizueta speak for his peers in global business? Probably so. The notion that business meets its public obligations by making profits for its shareholders now has a powerful grip on the thinking of many executives. Gone is the model of business so dear to European hearts—that of executives who see themselves as responsible to stakeholders of whom one is the shareholder and the others are the employee, the customer, the supplier, and the community. Business executives can no longer freely respond to the sometimes competing demands of these various constituencies. The shareholder value movement has deprived them of that discretion; sharehold-

ers increasingly demand sole fealty and despise the efforts of executives to take a broader view. And what was once seen as a narrow
American definition of the role of corporations is spreading around
the world, impelled by unforgiving global capital markets.

This is perhaps one of history's great and unfortunate ironies:
just as globalization thrusts the mantle of world leadership onto the
shoulders of business executives, most are committed to a self-view
that prohibits them from accepting the challenge.

New Sources of Leadership

It's no longer enough for government and business each to do their
own thing well, for neither has the power to resolve pressing common problems. When no one player calls the tune, all must impro-
vise collectively.

But that is not possible when business, government, and nonprofit organizations preserve arm's-length relationships. Historically,
these three sectors have tended to act individually, with little coordination or accountability, then react, then act again. The nation-
state tries to operate methodically, but the global economy thwarts
it. The global enterprise pursues its own objectives without careful
regard for popular concerns. The social sector works to address critical needs but depends on others for essential resources and operational guidelines.

Rather than retreating in the face of new roles and realities, each
sector needs to support new partnerships. Perhaps what leaders are
unable to do alone at the national level, they might be able to do
together, as partners, at the local and regional level.

Globalization is necessary for economic growth and fiscal responsibility; localism is necessary for community, efficiency, and
belonging. The challenge is to create effective mechanisms at the
local end as well as the global.

There can be effective leadership in a leaderless world. Leadership doesn't have to come from the official leaders; it can come from
unexpected places. The leaderless world begets a different kind of

leadership, one that is likely to be situational and dynamic. It is determined to resolve the controversies that stymie progress in a leaderless world.

The best prospect for such resolution is partnership at local and regional levels of the business, government, and social sectors. Partnering makes local people free to act. But too often gaps of motive and suspicion separate the partners.

Business, government, and social sectors hold negative stereotypes of each other that make cooperation difficult: for example, that governments are bureaucratic, inefficient, and fail to deliver results; that businesses are interested only in short-term financial gain; that nonprofit leaders lack decisiveness and impact.

In this environment it's a mistake to ask: When will government lead? When will business lead? The right questions seek the nature of key controversies in the leaderless world and ways to overcome them.

Understand Controversies

The sectors need to find common ground and learn to respect their differences if they are to work together effectively. To do so they must resolve several recurrent controversies that thwart cooperation.

Long-term vision versus short-term opportunism: How do people decide between a short-term opportunity and a long-term vision when the opportunity is not consistent with the vision?

Inclusion versus exclusion: Does exclusion imply elitism and risk losing the necessary support of the broader community? Or does inclusiveness so dilute those who hold the vision that action drifts aimlessly?

Exploration versus goal orientation: Should partners deliberate their vision and proposed methods, or should they adopt clear goals and move aggressively toward them? If they move aggressively, are they overlooking the unintended negative consequences of action?

Collaboration versus competition: Should a partnership involve only collaboration among its various elements, or is there room for competition as well? If competition is permitted, will it undermine cooperation?

Attainment versus compassion: Is it more important to complete the project or to care for those who might be harmed by progress? Does advancing the goals of a project mean that the partners are without compassion for those whose interests might be harmed?

Self-interest versus wider interests: Is a project that furthers the interests of members of the government-business-social sectors team morally compromised? Or is self-interest a necessary motivation in any project of significance, as long as wider interests are also served?

Each of these controversies can stall effective action in a partnership. Yet they can sometimes be overcome with the help of a few operating guidelines and a set of shared values. These controversies reflect dimensions of diversity among the partners, and the challenge, in the midst of the dynamic change of an ongoing project, is determining where to strike a balance.

Start with Shared Values

The resolution of controversies begins when individuals and organizations embrace shared values—commitments or beliefs that drive behavior. Commonly held values may lead to operating guidelines that create in turn a process for resolving controversies. A set of values embedded in the way people work permits cooperation and leadership across sectoral, cultural, and organizational chasms.

Successful cross-sector partnerships around the world have suggested just such a value set. Its four essential values have bound together networks of political leaders, business executives, professionals, and religious leaders around the world:

- A *commitment to constant change:* a recognition that traditional economic and social systems cannot be maintained and that change can be consistent with the needs of various peoples and nations.

- A *recognition that financial values are not all that matters:* a way of rejecting exploitation and of trying to promote meaningful non-pecuniary aspects of life.

- An *acceptance of personal responsibility for outcomes:* an insistence that people be truly engaged in attempting to bring about meaningful change.

- A *bias for action:* an insistence that more be done than talk.

None of these values conflicts with the more sophisticated versions of most of the world's religions and cultures. They are not American values projected onto the global stage where they are challenged by values of other civilizations. Instead, they have emerged out of the confluence of European, African, Asian, and American cultures. They are among the best business values, yet applicable far beyond the business sector.

These values may not seem special in places where they are largely accepted. But many people do not accept them at all, and others merely give them lip service. Honestly embraced, these values provide a basis for new leadership among people who are neither heads of state nor chief executives of global corporations. They become the basis for partnerships among local government, business, and professional leaders. They permit economic and social advance even when national entities are caught up in rivalries and resentments.

Alternatively, when not even these four values are held in common, cooperation may still be possible if one particular behavior is shared: the ability to hold what appear to be mutually contradictory values at the same time. Collaboration can then occur even in the face of diversity of beliefs.

New leadership springs from a dynamic network of committed people, not from political or corporate structures. At the top you often find posturing and frustration; in the network you may find accomplishment. The resolution of contradictions makes accomplishments possible. Effective partnership is not about structure but about process—the process by which people come together to cooperate. The issue isn't to develop a new set of organizational choices for firms but a world of choices about interaction—that is, about what's going on in the spaces between structural elements, not about the hierarchical order of the elements themselves.

We used to organize around government agencies, business units, and social organizations; these units determined the flow of action. Now we organize around interactions of people, with formal affiliations being incidental. We build not institutions but networks.

As society evolves we have different perspectives and incentives. To work together we agree to look past the incentives and perspectives that our sectors impose. To accomplish meaningful results we seek a purpose-based network bound by shared values. At least in part, we also seek cooperation on a local scale. Economic development projects in Melbourne and Glasgow, for instance, worked because people could identify fully with the requirements of their city.

With common values and purposes, individuals can break through stereotypes so that real cooperation is possible among social partners.

Create Partnership Opportunities

Applying shared values to a change effort requires both commitment and capability. Sometimes commitment is easier to build than capability, as when people are desperate for a change of circumstances but lack the means to achieve it; sometimes, however, capability is easier to build than commitment, as when business and government have the resources to effect change but are mired in complacency or mutual distrust. In a leaderless world those people who can provide both the vision that builds commitment and the resources to develop capabilities will emerge as real leaders.

New forms of leadership are taking shape throughout the world. Often these models grow from the fertile ground of high technology, through business, government, and community partnerships. Done well, such efforts can resolve controversies through principled action. For instance, Glasgow in the early 1980s was a run-down city whose manufacturing base was deserting it. There was little or no will on the part of national government to stem the tide and little or no local government capability to do so. A public-private partnership was the only hope. Local business took the lead with the support of local government and developed the vision of a new, vibrant economy based on high technology, education, and services. Proponents of the revitalization plan sought wide participation but insisted that all participants commit to a shared vision. They recognized that the path to success would be long and challenging and that commitment to a vision would provide staying power.

The key to implementation was to support a series of projects rather than a master plan. Sponsoring individual projects—addressing issues such as city center revitalization, headquarters activity retention, and exportable services development—gave partners the flexibility to respond to changing circumstances and the ability to build a record of tangible success. Each small success helped resolve the recurrent controversies that can so easily derail a partnership. By the 1990s, a new economic mix based on information technology had indeed revived the fortunes of Glasgow and accelerated the development of the surrounding region, now known as "Silicon Glen."

To resolve the natural tension between long-term goals and short-term opportunities, Glasgow's leaders defined their purpose expansively as promoting broad, sustainable prosperity. They exploited events people had not previously seen as opportunities (such as Glasgow's international festivals and conferences) by encouraging complementary efforts. Although these efforts might have seemed like detours at first, they instilled confidence, built credibility, and created a foundation of relevant successes. To provide balance between the temptations of exclusion and the hard work of inclusion, project leaders sought wide participation but insisted on a commitment to the common vision. To maintain both an exploratory and a goal orientation, they avoided the straightjacket of a master plan. And, taking a lesson from Silicon Valley, project leaders embraced both collaboration *and* competition by preserving autonomy as they built a sense of collective identity and coherence.

Stick to Your Principles

This and other successful ventures suggest eight operating principles of partnerships. Some are strategic and values-based, such as favoring inclusion over exclusion. Others are more tactical and self-evident, such as celebrating success. Taken together, these principles offer a set of tools for resolving recurrent dilemmas and for getting results.

1. *Define a compelling purpose:* a shared mission and vision should be so compelling that the higher common goals of the parties involved override diverging interests.
2. *Include all stakeholders:* a process must be established that involves people, even those appearing to be in opposition, as early as possible in order to build commitment, and to reconcile ends and means.
3. *Show trust and respect:* partners must behave in ways that recognize diversity of ideas and philosophies, as well as backgrounds.
4. *Take personal responsibility:* commitments must be honored and promises delivered on; each partner takes responsibility for the whole.
5. *Focus on results:* the end must be kept in mind so that partners can be appropriately entrepreneurial, seizing opportunities that lead to productive outcomes.

6. *Celebrate successes:* results must be constantly spotlighted in order to increase credibility, build commitment to the shared effort, and point the way for further success.

7. *Learn and adapt:* to be effective, partners must learn quickly to do what works, drop what doesn't work, and develop their skills and others' along the way.

8. *Establish common horizons:* people must reach early agreement on the scope, pace, and sequencing of a project or a partnership so that they have a useful road map for decision making and conflict resolution.

Foundations for New Leadership

Variations on Glasgow's approach have achieved results around the world. In Australia, the Committee for Melbourne—a network of more than one hundred fifty concerned and eminent citizens drawn from business, science, trade unions, government, academia, and the arts—forged a vision for the city, to reverse thirty years of industrial and urban decay, and regain its former glory as a "great international city." Their results-focused strategy, which involved cross-sectoral consensus building, business-led infrastructure projects, and government-led policymaking, revitalized the waterfront, upgraded the transportation system, secured world-class tourist attractions, and revived the local economy. In North Bay, Ontario, a small community imperiled by the loss of its largest employer, built a modern telecommunications infrastructure to attract new businesses— with the help of its departing employer, Nortel. In Maryland, former governor William Donald Schaefer responded to slowing economic growth and dwindling government resources by creating a state board of business and community leaders to help educational, commercial, and medical institutions take better advantage of new technology.

Opportunities for partnership are everywhere. Similar private-public partnerships to create technology centers in Finland, Estonia,

Israel, Malaysia, and India have developed communications, educational, and industrial sites whose benefits extend throughout those countries. These efforts show the importance of engaging all stakeholders, preferably from the start, to gain commitment through involvement. They allow each partner to do what it can do distinctively well. In business-led, government-enabled initiatives, government should not try to do what business does better—deliver results; business should not try to do what government does better—make policy.

Inaction by national political leaders and global business leaders on fundamental human concerns creates a need for partnerships that reach across all sectors. Such partnerships can bridge a gulf of mistrust and resolve controversies that paralyze action. Examples from around the world demonstrate that new forms of cooperation at the local level allow individuals and organizations to attain meaningful results.

The provident state is gone; the provident corporation is not to be. It is now up to us to create a new kind of partnership, which provides for ourselves and for one another.

19 PATRICK J. WAIDE JR.

PRINCIPLES
OF EFFECTIVE
COLLABORATION

Patrick J. Waide Jr. is former president and CEO of the Peter F. Drucker Foundation for Nonprofit Management. He also served seven years as the chief financial and administrative officer of the Bessemer Group and Bessemer Securities Corporation, as a senior partner with Deloitte Haskins & Sells, and as a board member and an officer of many nonprofits.

Despite five years of impressive economic growth that has produced over 3.4 million millionaires and a twenty-four-year low in the unemployment rate, one child of every five in the United States—14.5 million in all—still lives in poverty. Overall, 13.7 percent of the U.S. population lives in poverty, an increase from the 11.1 percent rate of a generation ago. And the poverty rate among different segments of the population remains at 29.4 percent for Hispanics, 28.4 percent for blacks, 14.5 percent for Asians, and 11.2 percent for whites. This is an environment in which every day there are more people to serve, more societal problems to solve, and fewer resources with which to work.

Today we have a greater understanding that the challenges ahead in saving the society are awesome. Forward-looking social sector leaders and board members also have an increased awareness that they cannot fulfill their mission by going it alone. They will have to build alliances, networks, partnerships, and other types of collaborative relationships. Each organization will have to look anew at its leadership roles and the related competencies required to achieve its mission, as well as at how it measures results, if it is to achieve the necessary level of performance for ongoing funder support. For example, it must periodically assess its organizational structure and its management practices and policies for the delivery of service to its primary and supporting customers. And its leaders and staff must receive training that will keep them ahead of the curve in addressing the new ways of work, particularly during a period of devolution of government-funded social programs.

Learning how to use collaboration and outsourcing partnerships to leverage the quality and efficiency of staff performance will be a continual management challenge for the leader and senior staff. Integral to this process will be developing the internal organizational guidelines that will be the basis for entering into effective collaborations, both within the social sector and across the three sectors of private enterprise, governmental organizations, and nonprofit organizations. An overview of the Drucker Foundation's approach to this challenge and the lessons learned in that process may be helpful in broadening others' understanding of how to make diverse partnerships work for the organization.

Partnering Through Core Values

The founders of the Peter F. Drucker Foundation for Nonprofit Management determined that it would serve its customers, the leaders of nonprofit and social sector organizations, by providing them with educational opportunities and resources that would help them in changing lives and building community. It was not to be a grant-making foundation.

The foundation's founding president, Frances Hesselbein, and its board of governors decided that this mission could best be accomplished by working in alliances with corporations, other foundations, individuals, government agencies, and thought leaders to hold conferences and conduct special projects in which all would be equal partners. Some of the partners would be *financial partners*, underwriting the foundation's work; some would be *project partners* for the leadership conferences and projects, providing expertise and personnel resources; and some would be *thought partners*, contributing their time and intellectual talent through pro bono participation in conferences or by contributing essays for foundation publications. Of course there are wonderful occasions when the boundaries of these partner distinctions overlap, as when financial partners contribute personnel resources in addition to monetary support or when thought partners also make monetary contributions to the foundation's operating budget.

Early on, in seeking partnerships with others, the Drucker Foundation was not unmindful of the goodwill that immediately accrued to its efforts from being named for Peter F. Drucker, the widely acknowledged founder of modern management theory. The foundation also benefited in its early years from the 1990 publication of Peter Drucker's book *Managing the Nonprofit Organization*. Nevertheless, foundation staff operated from a core value that foundation work itself must always reflect excellence in performance worthy of the acclaim associated with the writings and consulting of the foundation's honorary chairman, Peter Drucker. Moreover, leading social sector organizations toward excellence in performance also required this high standard of excellence as a Drucker Foundation core value.

The foundation reinforced this core value of excellence in its partnerships with other organizations by ensuring that both its board members and senior staff had strong visibility and program involvement in foundation conferences and publications. This guiding principle enhanced the ability of the foundation to develop collaborations with organizations and individuals with a similar standard for excellence that truly made a difference. Preserving the core value of excellence has also caused the Drucker Foundation to avoid endorsing products or groups; franchising domestic and international affiliates; entering into licensing arrangements with non-partner third parties for publications, videos, or training materials; and taking part in other indirect financial opportunities.

This core value approach to partnering has been the soul of the foundation's success to date as it has both enhanced the scope and assured the overall quality of the foundation's conferences and leadership projects. And, most important, it has immeasurably leveraged the effectiveness of foundation staff.

Establishing Guiding Beacons

Understanding an organization's core values and therefore what can not change in entering into partnerships with others is of pivotal importance. Core values define an organization; they are its guiding principles, stating what it will do and how it will operate or be. These core values must be consistently reflected in everything the organization represents and does if its employees, the customers it serves, and its funders are to have confidence in its ability to further its mission and provide a meaningful service. Accordingly, *preserving the organization's core values* is the foremost guideline for success when entering into partnerships with other organizations to carry forward a mission or find new or more effective ways of serving primary customers.

The Drucker Foundation's experience of partnering as its modus operandi during the past nine years also suggests the following guidelines or benchmarks for organizations to consider as they seek optimum effectiveness in their social sector and cross-sector collaborations:

Maintain absolute integrity in the internal and external operations of your organization. This operative character is crucial if an organization is to be an attractive partner for others. In most situations attractiveness means more than just preserving core values; it is evidenced more positively by the way the organization maintains high standards of civility and ethical behavior in all of its relationships.

Enter partnerships only with organizations that have comparable credibility. An important part of the partnership process is establishing the criteria for partner selection. In effective partnerships each member must be an equal partner, having the capability to influence the end objective or expected outcome. Keep in mind that in today's litigious environment, you frequently do not get what you deserve; you get only what you negotiate. It is therefore important that what is expected as the contribution or work product of each partner be well defined in the memorandum of understanding or partnership agreement, along with the timing of the expected outcomes on which collaborative actions are based.

Enter partnerships only with organizations whose values and mission are similar to yours. Commonality of purpose is most important in maintaining performance quality and in achieving the desired results. There are lots of things that would be nice to do and an organization's association with a prestigious partner might attract useful attention. However, serving effectively the organization's principal and supporting customers goes to the core of its reason to be.

Understand that people relationships are crucial for the effectiveness of collaborative endeavors. Managers involved in partnerships should be both diplomatic and astute. One party or group of participants cannot dominate the others. Each must approach the effort with a learning perspective, each must be influenceable, and each must be open to gaining additional insights.

Avoid alliances in which the social sector contribution is not a critical value for a partner. Social sector partners generally should be independent of government or private sector control and able to cultivate potential partners across all three sectors. They should be highly cooperative with all partnering candidates as they also maintain their own independence. In a word, remain pragmatic in terms of long-term strategy for each particular partner.

Collaborate only with social sector organizations with staff, volunteer, or board relationships comparable to yours. Staff-directed organizations rarely work effectively with volunteer-led organizations. Collaborations rarely are successful when governance issues are not clear, particularly in regard to proper board and staff responsibilities.

Understand clearly what makes the critical difference for each partner's mission and organizational effectiveness. Identify the objectives, goals, and functions that reflect the heart of each organization; identify the functions that are candidates for outsourcing or that would benefit from other alliances. The ability of an organization to identify and outsource functions not critical to its mission frequently correlates with the scope and quality of overall performance that can be achieved.

Commit adequate time to plan for and build the collaborative effort. Top management support and commitment is vital for any joint venture or partnership activity and particularly for developing interpersonal relations and effective communications among the parties. Trust is a crucial factor for a successful partnership, and trust can be easily destroyed by surprises. Techniques leaders can use to build trust and greater openness in participant dialogues include rotating meeting discussion leaders, holding informal social functions, and conducting joint staff presentations to the partnership principals.

Fix responsibility and financial accountability. Ineffective leadership makes coordination difficult and expensive. It is essential that the right people are asked to transfer detailed knowledge to a shared resource activity. Accordingly, responsibility also should be fixed for any contributed resources, operating budgets, expected outcomes, and the respective timing thereof.

Understand that networking, both internally and externally, is an important leadership function in new collaborations. Key people, on whose success the alliance or venture will depend, should have the opportunity to have their views heard and to participate fully in the planning process. They should also be the communicators of the strategy and vision that underpin the newly launched activities. Effectively communicating their passionate commitment to the collaboration is often a crucial factor in building internal and external support for the alliance.

Determine what the new partnership has to offer that meets funders' needs. Keep in mind that collaborating with other nonprofits presents a new opportunity to impress funders with the impact their financial support can make. For example, potential donors may be more willing to respond to a joint venture funding request than a single one.

Engage in contingency planning to ensure that the alliance is structured in a way that will continue to serve partners' interests. Consider early on in the negotiations the means of resolving disputes between partners. And partners must not be afraid to adapt their overall objectives to meet changing circumstances. Formal abandonment of the collaboration may become appropriate or alternative partners may be sought who can more clearly help your organization meet its desired objectives.

Building Bridges

A healthy society requires three vital sectors: a public sector of effective governments; a private sector of effective businesses; and a social sector of effective community organizations. The mission of social sector organizations to change lives is too great to be addressed by the social sector alone. Bridges of cooperation and collaboration must be built both across the three sectors and among organizations within the social sector.

Clearly, the partnership relationships that the Drucker Foundation pursued during the past nine years were crucial for the significant results achieved and the high standard of performance attained. However, the foundation has also experienced situations in which partnering with a particular organization appeared desirable but in the end was not effected. Some of the reasons the foundation abandoned these efforts were that the proposed partner's culture or style appeared too different, the proposed structure for the partnership seemed unacceptable, the ways of work were too dissimilar, and the time commitment required to achieve alliance objectives did not seem the best use of the foundation's time given other desirable opportunities. Each of the perceived obstacles, or red flags, would have detracted from the foundation's core value of excellence in performance.

As noted earlier, every organization will have several opportunities to do noteworthy activities or be associated with prestigious funders or partners. The paramount question in evaluating these opportunities is, Will this collaboration make a substantive difference in serving the organization's primary customers? As an organization examines its partnership opportunities and works through the partnership process, the guiding beacons outlined here can illustrate both the *way to be* and *how to build* for teaming up in the next millennium.

20 RITA HARMON
MEL TOOMEY

CREATING A FUTURE WE WISH TO INHABIT

*Rita Harmon is president and CEO of LEADERSHIP
AMERICA, Inc., a national organization that edu-
cates and connects women to increase their impact.
Her diverse experience in business, government, and
the nonprofit sector has included serving as communications director for the Los Angeles office of Governor
Edmund G. Brown Jr. and managing a wide range of
initiative campaigns. She is a cofounder of the leadership
forum Global Leadership Initiative. Mel Toomey is a
cofounder of Generative Leadership Group. He coaches
and trains senior executives and also trains leaders in
consulting and program delivery. He has served as a
bank board chairman, helped formulate the concept of
mortgage-backed securities, and created widely accepted
accounting system designs. He is also a cofounder of the
leadership forum Global Leadership Initiative.*

Mounting economic, political, and social problems are challenging leaders at every level of our organizations, both public and private. Faced with citizens' demands for an increased role
in solving problems and also with issues that need attention from

multiple institutions (both public and private), governments are losing their ability to solve both domestic and international public issues.
At the same time, growing participation by other institutions—
including businesses, nongovernmental organizations (NGOs), and
citizens groups—is creating new models of cooperation to solve these
public problems. This newly emerging cooperation of multiple sectors
creates the possibility of promoting further cooperation and training
leaders to initiate and manage it.

Why We Must Expand Our Leadership Model

The issues of leading beyond the walls, for leaders of all institutions,
begin with leaders' ability to exercise leadership and serve the public interest outside their domains without compromising the interests within their domains. Leaders need to be able to organize other
leaders in a variety of domains to promote redefinition of the
responsibilities of governments and private actors for the public
business and public interest and to redesign institutions, organizations, and policies to support that redefinition.

Domestically, governments and private institutions are both
concerned about such social problems as education, housing, poverty, and substance abuse. There is a growing recognition that governments cannot solve these problems alone but need help from
citizens in business, in nongovernmental organizations, and as individuals. In reality, all successful social service programs—from the
self-governing educational system developed in Harlem District
Four to tenant management of public housing to San Francisco's
Delancey Street Foundation's drug rehabilitation program—feature
strong elements of citizen participation and shared responsibility
with governments.

Enormous progress could be accomplished by encouraging
increased cross-domain citizen participation, creating institutions
that would encourage replication of successful social programs and
issue-resolution strategies, and training leaders who could work

comfortably across the domains of governments, businesses, and NGOs.

In international relations, foreign policy experts and policy-makers are concerned about the decline in governments' ability to address effectively, and without resorting to armed conflict, the growing numbers of economic, social, and political problems that have appeared since the end of the Cold War. These problems include ethnic conflict, terrorism, nuclear proliferation, economic disruption, and political crisis. Nongovernmental organizations, in contrast, have shown extraordinary abilities to address many of these problems that require working across national boundaries.

Private business also has an obvious, important role to play in coping with these issues, but the development of leaders' skills and understandings for managing multidomain (public and private) participation in addressing problems and the training of leaders for operating outside their own domains are sorely lacking in today's leadership climate.

The need for multidomain problem resolution for a variety of public issues raises serious questions and issues for leaders. For leaders in government, the questions derive from government's ultimate responsibility for public business—whether domestically, in public education and other economic and social issues, or internationally, in foreign policy. To facilitate participation by citizens, businesses, and NGOs in foreign policy and to achieve multidomain, public-private cooperation, regulatory structures and spending policies would need to be reformed. This would require training leaders to provide leadership across the domains that give rise to their leadership and encouraging citizens to embrace new public responsibilities.

These leadership challenges create new possibilities for training leaders, arming them with tools and distinctions to promote and implement institutional change and to produce a true democratization of participation in the public interest. In this democratization, private institutions and individual citizens would share responsibility with governments for both domestic and international public business.

Concern about leadership in every domain is reflected in the large and growing numbers of leadership training programs sponsored by governments, universities, associations, and other institutions. But despite the economic, social, and political changes that are altering leadership challenges, many leadership programs continue to focus most of their attention on management of single domains. Each domain needs and depends on cooperation with others to accomplish its objectives and replicate its successes. Institutional leaders therefore have a substantial stake in working outside their domains. And yet the opportunities to become proficient with the distinctions of cross-domain leadership are sorely limited.

Throughout history we have honored and memorialized the individual leader. Books and songs have been written about the great deeds of presidents and kings, freedom fighters and scientists. Portraits of famous political leaders hang in the White House and the Capitol, and the walls of corporate headquarters commemorate and the covers of popular business publications herald the accomplishments of business giants.

In each instance we have been left with what great leaders did, what they knew, and what they created. Their brilliance has inspired us to greatness, helped us bring forth our best, and allowed us to understand what living to a high standard can accomplish. But for the multitudes of modern-day leaders, who go to work each day at all levels in government, industry, and NGOs, this information gives them no access to their own leadership brilliance and contributions or at best leaves them with brief glimpses of greatness, which fade over time into cherished memory.

The traditional view of leadership as a character-driven, individual phenomenon does not account for the unacknowledged contribution that countless leaders make in their organizations and communities of interest. In a context where results produced are the only register of value, the difference people make at work has no place to be recorded, and the vast difference individuals make in businesses, governments, and NGOs slips silently away, leaving in its wake resignation and dissatisfaction.

The current model for leadership takes into account the personal but not the systemic or organizational level or the commitments people bring to their work at those levels. A senior executive in the oil industry recently suggested that perhaps no more than 20 to 30 percent of what people come prepared to contribute to the organization is ever used, and employees languish, often unwilling to make known their commitment to their organization.

But circumstances require more expression of organizations' talent. More than ever we need the contributions of leaders throughout organizations. As we deal with the fundamental challenge of leading beyond the walls—of working across domains for the resolution of intractable problems—we find that the charismatic personal leadership of the past is still needed yet it is insufficient. Therefore, we must reach beyond a leadership model based on position, authority, and influence combined with a dose of charisma and ability to find a new pattern for leadership.

The demands of leading beyond the walls require that we shift our fundamental understanding of leadership—our sense of where it comes from and how it is distinguished—without negating our earlier understanding. We must consider the possibility that leadership is a field phenomenon, not a personal ability. What if the presence of what we have called leadership occurs only within some form of organization among people (whether formal or informal, large or small)? What if leadership is not something that an individual can provide but is available only through co-creation, that is, in concert with others—and not always others of like mind?

New structures for leading beyond the walls, in environments that cross domains, will bring to the table not only leaders from governments, businesses, and NGOs but also leaders from diverse communities of interest and leaders who have often been excluded but whose representation is essential if solutions to problems are to be lasting and representative of everyone's commitments and concerns. New distinctions about leading in such environments must be articulated, and leaders must be trained to use these distinctions and the relevant skills and to transfer them to others. And leading must occur at all levels, across all domains.

Current leadership thinking tends to emphasize tools and processes that produce incremental improvement in situations, but many of the issues and challenges of leading beyond the walls require managing discontinuous change and innovation.

Leadership preparation for the future will have to center on helping leaders become proficient in creating a context of inquiry, exploration, and possibility; in including all interests; and in operating on multiple scales. Training leaders in this way will allow them to work on behalf of the public interest without compromising their domains of interest and to produce sustainable systemic solutions and innovations.

Characteristics of the New Leaders

Here are five specific characteristics, or abilities, needed by leaders beyond the walls.

The Ability to Design Powerful Relationships

Many contributing factors—competing strategies and views, diverse participants and cultures, and disparate and unresolved or compromised interests, among others—affect a leader's probability of success in developing powerful relationships. Diversity can make it difficult to create or sustain cross-domain relationships.

Successful, powerful relationships require the creation of a new culture and sustainable structures unique to the needs of the relationship. Moreover, these structures must work without compromising diversity. Powerful relationships bring together the best of the respective domains represented, and design support structures that expedite the early results that will sustain the relationship. The challenge of working with people of diverse organizational histories, structures, cultures, styles, and communication approaches is that in addition to sustaining the new, all that has gone before must be appreciated for what it provided.

The Ability to Create Systemic Change

Today's leaders, at all levels in organizations, often experience working harder and producing fewer results. Over time this deepens their resignation and creates resistance to change. They often have an overriding sense that they get their jobs done *in spite of* the systems within which they work.

Leaders in the future must therefore be able to envision and lead systemic change. An entire system may be changed through work in well-chosen even though relatively small areas of the whole system. Leading beyond the walls will require of leaders the ability to build foundations for sharing, so that contribution of what is uncommon is as important as experiencing what is common among the parties. Leaders will have to establish shared expectations and set clear priorities for performance and results.

The Ability to Distinguish and Work with Preservative, Creative, and Development Systems

Leading beyond the walls requires leaders to be able to distinguish between preservative, creative, and development systems.

Preservative systems are designed to maintain the current state in ever improving form. These are the systems of stewards and managers. They are designed to foster reliability, predictability, and certainty and are judged successful to the degree that they do not require fundamental structural changes.

Creative systems bring new futures into existence—often futures that are outside anything comprehensible inside preservative systems. These are the systems for co-creation, for new possibilities, and their formulation can be awkward and messy. Creative systems are judged successful when they produce outcomes not predictable from past performance. However, they always produce results they are not designed to deal with and, because of these outcomes, require ongoing fundamental changes to their structures.

Development systems are the "midwife" systems. They move a new possibility along a spectrum, from its early intimations of feasibility until it is fully fledged and flight tested and the preservative systems can take it take over.

Leading beyond the walls will require of leaders the ability to distinguish these systems and to communicate the distinctions to their organizations in a way that inspires understanding and reduces confusion and cross-purposes.

The Ability to Develop
Comfort with Risk While Building Trust

Within the domain of leadership the relationship between risk and trust is inverse. There is no better way to reduce risk than to build trust. In today's world, risk will always be present; but when trust is sufficient, risk becomes acceptable. Leading beyond the walls will require learning new rules of trust, stepping out beyond our old concept of earned trust. Earned trust is built over time and based on performance. It is important but insufficient to the challenges we face today. Leaders must learn to generate *granted trust*—the trust individuals need to create with others and to obtain early action and results while establishing earned trust over time.

The Ability to Value Diversity
as the Source of Contribution

In order for diversity to become the source of contribution, leaders must do more than establish common ground among individuals. They must also establish *uncommon ground*—the ground of diversity. It is not sufficient to *tolerate* diversity; we must learn to *employ* what is uncommon among us, on behalf of the commitments we hold in common. What is common among us provides the fulcrum; what is uncommon provides the leverage for action and accomplishment in unpredictable ways. Leaders must come to understand and master the design of common and uncommon ground and the balance between them.

Conclusion

In the recent book *Dialogues* (Berkeley Hills Books, 1998), edited by former California governor Jerry Brown, Helena Norberg-Hodge writes, "Roughly half of the human population still lives in rural villages. When you bring that up to people in the West, immediately they call you a romantic, unrealistic. . . . In fact, it is we in the West who have become unrealistic, because we ignore the reality of what's going on in the world."

When we couple this reality with the fact that of the world's hundred largest economies, fifty are corporations, we begin to see the extent to which the problems we face in our world are lived out across a wide chasm of cultural and economic difference and diversity.

David Korten, president of the People-Centered Development Forum, observes in *Dialogues* that "part of the sickness of our society is that we've given up so many of the non-financial relationships, the things that we used to do for each other in the family and as members of the community purely out of love and affection. So much of that has broken down; we've lost the balance between monetized activities and what we might call 'the economy of affection.'" Leading beyond the walls will require a new marriage of thought and heart, an ability to bring the spirit of family and community to bear on intractable problems that require both caring and thinking. It is only through prepared leaders and an involved public in all domains that the future we wish to inhabit will be created.

21 ROXANNE SPILLETT

STRATEGIES FOR WIN-WIN ALLIANCES

*Roxanne Spillett is president of Boys & Girls Clubs
of America, the nation's fastest-growing youth development organization, serving some three million girls
and boys. She has developed and implemented innovative programs in education, career exploration,
drug prevention, literacy, and conflict resolution; she
serves on the boards of the National Assembly and
American Humanics; and she is vice chair of the
America's Promise Advisory Committee on Safe
Spaces.*

A nonprofit organization's success in today's environment is
dependent to a large degree on strategic partnerships.

The days of command and control—the days in which chief executives and their senior managers got results by controlling their
environment; their employees; their constituents; and their facilities, programs, and partners—are over. Attempting to control an
organization's every action can control that organization right out
of business. Instead of enforcing a strategy that ultimately restrains
the actions of an organization, today's challenge is *unleashing* organizational potential.

Likewise the philosophy of going it alone, of attempting to be all things to all people, will get your organization nowhere fast. To survive and thrive in today's environment, to maximize impact and satisfy the customer, strategic partnerships are a must. From the corporate boardroom to Capitol Hill, from public housing to public schools, strategic partnerships have been the name of the game. These partnerships have been the key to the recent success of Boys & Girls Clubs of America.

The Public Sector

In 1987, Boys & Girls Clubs of America launched a new strategic plan that called for aggressive growth to reach the unserved and underserved young people in America, especially those in disadvantaged circumstances. The organization initiated a discussion with the secretary of the Department of Housing and Urban Development; this effort led to a strategic partnership between Boys & Girls Clubs of America and HUD that significantly helped the organization achieve its growth goals. The plan was to establish 100 Boys & Girls Clubs in public housing. The actual result was the establishment of 350 Boys & Girls Clubs in public housing, providing a safe place to learn and grow for well over 150,000 young people.

At each local site, the housing authority contributes the facility, the maintenance, and even cash grants. The local Boys & Girls Club provides tested, proven programs, and trained professional staff. Residents of the public housing community serve on a club advisory board along with community leaders from outside the public housing development. Together they guide the overall program. The partnership with HUD certainly helped to further the growth goals of the organization and at the same time provided much needed youth development programs and opportunities for some of the most needy children in America. This was the first Boys & Girls Club large-scale partnership, and it required that both parties stick to their core competencies and give up some control in exchange for a much greater gain. This paved the way for other partnerships.

Next was a strategic relationship with the Department of Defense that not only furthered the organization's growth goals but also provided a much needed service to children at a time of national crisis. During the Gulf War, thousands of military personnel from the reserve and the National Guard were deployed. The Boys & Girls Clubs' role was to provide free club memberships for the children of the men and women who were deployed during Desert Storm, most of them living off base. That project led to an ongoing relationship with the military and the establishment of over 150 Boys & Girls Clubs on military installations in the United States and abroad. The military contributes the facility and the personnel. Boys & Girls Clubs of America provides nationally developed and tested programs, and training and professional development opportunities for the military personnel who staff the youth centers. Once again each party brought its core competencies to the table, giving up some control in exchange for a much greater gain.

In the Boys & Girls Clubs' most recent strategic planning process, improved race relations and the appreciation of cultural differences emerged as a key strategic priority. The Anti-Defamation League, well known for its successful curriculum "A World of Difference," became a likely strategic partner. In the partnership that has developed, the Anti-Defamation League is working with Boys & Girls Clubs of America to provide the materials and training for the individual clubs. The result: the Anti-Defamation League furthers its mission and Boys & Girls Clubs of America furthers its mission and addresses an important strategic priority.

The Corporate Connection

The public sector is not the only arena for establishing strategic partnerships. In the last three years, Boys & Girls Clubs of America has developed multimillion-dollar strategic partnerships with some of the largest and best-known companies in the United States, including Coca-Cola, Nike, Taco Bell, Turner Broadcasting System (TBS), and Major League Baseball (MLB). The financial commitment made by these corporations alone exceeds $100 million. Then there are the spin-offs—the advertising, the in-kind contributions, the ongoing expertise, the partnerships with these corporations' partners, the connections all these organizations make on the clubs' behalf, the leveraging opportunities—that add up to millions more.

For example, what began as a small Nike-sponsored Michael Jordan essay contest mushroomed into a multimillion-dollar commitment, prime-time television advertising support, the construction of two new clubhouses, the installation of new gym floors and outdoor courts in dozens of local clubs, and much more. In return the partnership helped to further Nike's image as a good corporate citizen and provided Nike with a useful network—through one phone call to the national organization, Nike could gain access to a club in a community of particular importance to it for philanthropic activities.

A $15 million commitment from the Taco Bell Foundation to support teen programs and establish teen centers has been a win-win relationship if there ever was one. Taco Bell has a great interest in teens, as does Boys & Girls Clubs of America. After in-depth discussion it was determined that a relationship could be developed around this common target audience. A strategy evolved in which the Taco Bell Foundation agreed to support a national teen program and teen conference and the establishment of one hundred teen centers. The relationship promotes Taco Bell as a good corporate citizen and enables the company to give value back to its largest constituents.

A $1.5 million relationship with Major League Baseball to revive baseball and softball in the inner cities has evolved into a relationship worth ten times the original commitment. Two new Boys & Girls Clubs public service announcements were developed and are aired on every televised Major League Baseball game. MLB has brought Boys & Girls Clubs promotions with other corporations, relationships with the Major League Baseball Player's Association and Minor League Baseball, a special feature in *Reader's Digest,* and so much more. At a time when Major League Baseball was very concerned about reviving America's interest in baseball, Boys & Girls Clubs of America developed and expanded baseball programs for boys and softball programs for girls.

Once a company gets involved and becomes a champion on your behalf, things start happening that you might not even be aware of and often you cannot control. The company begins to spread the word through its ranks and with its strategic partners and the next thing you know even more marketing opportunities, professional development opportunities, and product donations come your way.

Strategy Is the Name of the Game

What all of these strategic partnerships—nonprofit and for profit— have in common is that they require a win-win relationship in which each party contributes something of significant value and gains something of significant value in return. What Boys & Girls Clubs of America has learned through experience is that there is a critically important process to follow in identifying strategic partners and preparing for the negotiations. To successfully target potential strategic partners and then negotiate relationships, you have to do your homework first. Here are the most important things you need to know:

Your mission, your vision, and especially your core beliefs and guiding principles—the values that you will not sacrifice no matter the benefits of the relationship. In negotiating strategic partnerships with corporations, Boys & Girls Clubs of America found that guiding principles were critically important. (See, for example, Exhibit 21.1 for the core beliefs of the Boys & Girls Clubs and Exhibit 21.2 for the organization's guiding principles in establishing corporate partnerships.)

Exhibit 21.1. Core Beliefs of Boys & Girls Clubs of America.

A Boys & Girls Club provides

- A safe place to learn and grow
- Ongoing relationships with caring, adult professionals
- Life-enhancing programs and character development experiences
- Hope and opportunity

Your strategic priorities—the specific targets and tactics established in your organization's plan. Your priorities define the areas in which the right strategic partnerships can help your organization take a quantum leap toward its goals. Conversely, strategic partnerships that do not support your strategic direction can drain your organization of energy and focus. Strategic partnerships take time and energy. They are only as good as the match between the proposed partner's goals and your organization's strategic direction.

Your core competencies. These are the things you do best, the areas of your greatest expertise. It is equally important to identify the areas in which your organization can benefit substantially from the expertise and core competencies of others. This knowledge will help you target potential partners who can provide that expertise.

The value you bring to the partnership. This might be your outreach to a specific population, your expertise, your brand equity, your presence in specific markets, or a combination of these assets. These are your selling points, the value added you bring to a relationship. They must be clearly articulated.

Your potential partner's mission, vision, core beliefs, strategic priorities, and core competencies. Be sure to read each potential partner's annual report, promotional materials, and strategic plans. Use your inside contacts to learn as much as you can about each partner. This information will not only help you choose partners well but will give you an important edge in the negotiating process.

**Exhibit 21.2. Strategic Philanthropy Guidelines
of Boys & Girls Clubs of America.**

Boys & Girls Clubs of America encourages corporate supporters to find
innovative ways to support our children while also achieving corporate
goals. However, to guarantee the integrity of its Cause Marketing program,
Boys & Girls Clubs of America has established guidelines to help corporations in their planning.

- Boys & Girls Clubs of America's Cause Marketing strategy has three
  goals:

  1. Build awareness for Boys & Girls Clubs of America and its partners

  2. Raise funds for local clubs

  3. Raise funds for the national organization

- Boys & Girls Clubs of America, locally and nationally, looks to the
  entire community for support. Its independence must be preserved in
  any alliance it creates. Boys & Girls Clubs of America reserves the right
  to determine what companies it will work with.

- It does not endorse products, promote the sale of products, or mandate
  clubs to endorse, purchase, or sell any product. It does not give "official,"
  "preferred," or "exclusive" status to any company, product, or brand. The
  national organization does not sell to or through club members.

- Boys & Girls Clubs of America seeks relationships with corporations to
  support its cause without a quid pro quo. The business benefit it offers
  is that consumers are more likely to buy a product if it is associated with
  the Boys & Girls Clubs cause. Also, by supporting Boys & Girls Clubs
  of America, corporations fulfill their social responsibility.

- Large strategic alliances must have financial benefit for local clubs and
  must include an appropriate philanthropic gift to Boys & Girls Clubs of
  America.

- All legal, tax, and public relations issues are thoroughly investigated.
  Major Cause Marketing relationships are reviewed by the Boys & Girls
  Clubs president and board marketing committee before implementation.

Negotiating the Partnership

Good partnerships do not happen overnight. The discovery process—getting to know each other—is the key to building large and far-reaching partnerships. This process enables each partner to learn about the other and to build the trust that is critical to success. Negotiating beneficial partnerships requires open, honest dialogue and mutual respect. Because trust and respect take time to develop, most good partnerships take a while to evolve. They often start small and grow. In the negotiating process it is important to be very clear about the following aspects of the partnership:

- Clearly define the purpose and the goals of the partnership.

- Be specific about the deliverables and the anticipated time line.

- Identify the specific responsibilities of each partner.

- If financial goals are part of the relationship, agree on the dollar figure. Also have an agreed-on guaranteed, or minimum, contribution.

- Discuss and agree on the acceptable use of each partner's service mark. Each party should have the right to review and approve the use of its service mark by the other.

- State the guiding principles and core beliefs that the partners must adhere to, so that everyone is clear from the outset on what is and is not possible.

- Have a cancellation clause in written agreements, so either party can cancel the relationship.

A Special Kind of Leadership

Although partnership opportunities sound very inviting—and they are—it takes a special style of leadership to make them work for your organization. It is important for the leadership in partner organizations to openly embrace the partnership and encourage its development. Indeed, such strategic thinking is a very important aspect of the leadership role in most organizations today.

The chief professional officer must also empower staff to engage in this thinking. At the same time it is equally important to communicate the platform on which your organization needs to negotiate relationships. That platform includes the strategic priorities of your organization, its core beliefs, and its guiding principles.

Your leadership must be strategic and proactive. It is important to know both your organization's strengths and the areas where it could benefit from the expertise of the right partner. These are the partners to seek out.

It is important to be flexible and willing to assume some risk. Remember, strategic partnerships are all about win-win relationships and may require your organization to engage in new and different activities.

Be prepared for the synergy that comes from good partnerships. A mutually helpful relationship is likely to grow and expand. Good relationships create excitement, and your partner is likely to identify new and exciting additions to the original plan. This can be very beneficial for both partners. At the same time, you and your staff might also see exciting possibilities for expanding the relationship. In an open and mutually supportive relationship, expect this kind of growth.

There are just so many relationships that your organization can manage. Each one requires staff time and attention. It is important not to overextend your staff. You may be approached by many organizations wishing to partner with you. Look before you leap. Make sure each partnership is consistent with your priorities and does not overburden your staff.

Last, you have to be willing to share power and responsibility. This is the leadership ability that ultimately makes partnerships work.

In this changing world it is more important than ever for nonprofit organizations to provide responsive and efficient services. In the future, partnerships will be an essential way of doing business. Instead of asking how we can improve all that we do, we need to ask what it is that we should be doing—what are our core competencies? Once we answer this question, nonprofits will be in a better position to come together in a seamless web of service delivery, helping the entire nonprofit sector become more responsive and efficient and engaging the for-profit sector in its support.

22 RICHARD E. CAVANAGH

BUILDING CIVIC COALITIONS

Richard E. Cavanagh is president and chief executive officer of The Conference Board and previously served as executive dean of the John F. Kennedy School of Government at Harvard University, as a consultant with McKinsey & Company, and in senior positions at the White House Office of Management and Budget. He is the coauthor (with Donald K. Clifford Jr.) of the best-seller The Winning Performance: How America's High-Growth Midsize Companies Succeed.

Since the end of World War II, in an increasingly important trend, society has been turning to the business community to join with government and the social sector to solve pressing social,

Note: I am indebted to many former McKinsey colleagues for their insights and the ways they helped shape my thinking. They were also present at the creation of four important civic partnerships (the New York City Partnership, the Cleveland Tomorrow Group, the Glasgow Tomorrow Group, and the Miami business community), and they include Jon Katzenbach, Katherine Lewis, Barbara Mullin, Ginny Day, Richard Shatten, Tom Tinsley, Bill Seelbach, Sir John Banham, Norman Sanson, Bob Irvin, and Rick Gross.

economic, and civic problems. In some locations, notably Atlanta, Cleveland, and Pittsburgh, business partnerships have made a real and enduring difference in the fortunes of communities. But just as many alliances that trumpeted business leadership and support have failed to achieve their goals, despite great effort and generous resources. In the course of a decade of professional experience helping business leaders create civic strategies and form partnerships with the other two sectors, my former McKinsey colleagues and I had the opportunity to study in some depth a score of U.S.-based civic coalitions. Although the problems they addressed were as diverse as the cities involved, we were able to discern seven rules of thumb that seem to distinguish the coalitions that work from those that try:

- Enlisting personal CEO commitment and leadership

- Engaging businesses that have an enduring stake in the future of the community

- Valuing business *skills* as much as business resources

- Conceiving doable projects with short-term measurable results

- Creating project-based coalitions rather than grand comprehensive and permanent general-purpose alliances

- Relying on volunteer leadership rather than professional staff

- Giving credit where it's needed (rather than simply where it's due)

In the remainder of this chapter, I explore what my colleagues and I learned about these seven key factors for success.

CEO Commitment and Leadership

The most effective partnerships, we found, were ones that enlisted the active participation of CEOs from each sector—especially from the business community. CEOs alone can commit resources, exercise influence, and weigh in on policy issues without having to check in with the boss. And by virtue of the resources they marshal and the respect they are accorded by leaders of the other two sectors, business CEOs command the attention of government, politics, education, labor, community-based organizations, and the media as few others can. This is not to say that others in the corporate structure do not have important work to do and contributions to make—they do indeed. But they need their boss's involvement to be most effective.

The catch of course is that business CEOs are typically the most difficult people to recruit. Their calendars are typically committed months, if not years, in advance. Their time is demanded by all manner of good causes, ranging from business associations and trade groups at home and abroad, to charities and nonprofit groups both locally and nationally, to their alma maters. And the job of CEO has become increasingly insecure as institutional investors demand more sooner from corporate top managements. But as difficult as CEOs are to attract and retain, they make all the difference between success and failure when it comes to civic partnerships. This means that partnerships have to be careful stewards of CEO time and that the staff work supporting the effort has to meet top-management standards.

Businesses That Care

Although everyone would like to think that every business has something to contribute to the work of community partnerships, the truth is that not all businesses are equally committed to or equally effective at building civic coalitions. Time and time again we witnessed a recurring pattern in who makes an effort and who makes a difference. First and foremost, enterprises with an enduring stake in the economic vitality and civic health of a region have usually been the top performers. Thus leaders in community partnerships have often come from banks and utilities and from companies whose headquarters are located in the region. Family-dominated companies with a tradition of community service have also figured prominently.

But given the recent trends of consolidation and conglomeration in key industries, most community partnerships now have to learn how to get the most out of yesterday's local company headquarters that is today's branch office of a far larger and often remote enterprise (sometimes headquartered on a different continent and with disparate customs and language). In addition, learning how to enlist the leadership and energy of smaller, and especially midsize, enterprises (which for two decades have provided the lion's share of new job growth) is a challenge of both high difficulty and high promise.

Real Business Skills—Not Just Money

The governments and nonprofits who populate successful civic partnerships have come to appreciate that their business partners bring far more to the table than just money (even though this resource is almost always critical). In particular, businesses can bring to bear real expertise in such areas as financial and project management and special insights on how to market a program or indeed a region. But for the best outcomes, the projects in which the business community is engaged must draw on *business* skills. It should not be surprising, for example, that many of the best-known successes of business-led civic partnerships are found in the areas of economic development, job creation, occupational training and development, and the use of technology. In contrast, most businesses have little expertise to contribute when the question is whether or how to teach the new or old math in elementary school or how to provide what kinds of social services for high-rise public housing buildings.

Doable, Results-Oriented Projects

Paradoxically, thinking small and pursuing a series of narrow, short-term projects seems to make far greater headway in addressing vexing community problems than grand, large-scale, comprehensive efforts do. Thus a series of efforts to, say, "train and employ one thousand at-risk youths" tends to achieve better results than an effort to "eradicate poverty in the greater metropolitan area." Not only are expectations held in check, but the majority of the effort is focused on execution rather than strategy and policy formulation—a refreshing way to tackle embedded community problems. And such doable projects can capitalize on business management skills.

Similarly, we found that partnerships that pursue a few, narrow, highly focused projects with limited duration have better results than those that set far-ranging, interdisciplinary agendas with long-term payoffs.

Project-Based Coalitions

Adhocracy works best when it comes to civic partnerships. Thus we found that project-based coalitions, in which each sector plays an active role and brings real expertise and energy to specific tasks, succeed far better than general purpose alliances aimed at setting broad social agendas. This is because real partnerships demand real work and genuine flexibility on important issues. However, when true ownership of the effort is syndicated among the key players in this way, the fewer players or partners the better—as less time can be spent talking and more time spent doing.

All this is to say that each project should begin with a careful analysis of who really needs to participate to make the project work, then the appropriate constituencies can be consulted and involved. In the end, ad hoc action beats full (and sometimes endless) discussion and debate.

Volunteer Leadership

As in all organized enterprise, success rises or falls on the quality of leadership. And in the case of community partnerships, volunteer leaders make the key difference. Indeed, it appears that the smaller (and more energized) the professional staff and correspondingly the greater the role of volunteers, the more successful the project. Thus membership-driven coalitions are more effective and productive than staff-driven ones. This is not to say that a small cadre of paid staff is not critical—it is. And the best staff for these coalitions are individuals who have had working experience in two or three of the sectors and who are seen by the volunteer leaders as equal to the best in the volunteers' own organizations.

Shared Credit

Although business leaders are increasingly the subject of press and media coverage, they are best advised to keep their public egos (and corporate public relations staffs) in check when it comes to awarding credit for community partnerships. This is because government officials (who often must face elections or be supervised by those who carefully follow the public opinion polls) greatly value the currency of media coverage. Similarly, leaders of community groups (and even of some nonprofits) need public recognition to survive. But business CEOs don't. We discerned that the most effective business partners are generous, indeed lavish, in covering their public and nonprofit counterparts in glory.

Conclusion

Golfers are sometimes advised that their game will improve if they try *not* to overachieve, because too great an effort can actually result in reduced performance. Similarly, trying not to overachieve permits community partnerships to accomplish a great deal. By setting short-term, measurable goals, focusing on results rather than planning, moving from limited project to limited project, and enlisting those constituencies necessary for success on a project basis, these alliances build credibility and momentum—and make a difference.

23 JOSEPH S. NYE JR.

NEW MODELS
OF PUBLIC
LEADERSHIP

Joseph S. Nye Jr. is dean of the Kennedy School of Government at Harvard University and the author of numerous articles and books, most recently Bound to Lead, Understanding International Conflicts, *and* Why People Don't Trust Government *(coedited with Philip D. Zelikow and David C. King). He has appeared on programs such as* Nightline, Good Morning America, *and* The NewsHour with Jim Lehrer *and has worked in three government agencies, most recently the Defense Department, where in 1994 and 1995 he served as assistant secretary of defense for international security affairs.*

W hat will public leadership look like in the new century, and how should we train people for it? Politicians tell us that the era of big government is over, but they say little about what will replace it. We do know that markets and nonprofit organizations now are filling functions once considered the province of government. For example, in the United States, Britain, and Australia, private security forces greatly outnumber police forces. We also see a trend toward devolution of authority for social programs from the federal to state governments, counter to the trends of most of the twentieth century.

The Erosion of Confidence in Government

The public's confidence in government has declined over the last three decades. In 1964, three-quarters of Americans said they trusted the federal government to do the right thing. Today, only a quarter express such trust. The figures are only slightly better for state and local governments. Government is not alone in losing public trust. From 1965 through 1995, public confidence in many major institutions dropped by half or more: from 61 percent to 30 percent for universities; 55 to 21 percent for major companies; 73 to 29 percent for the practice of medicine; and 29 to 14 percent for journalism (see J. S. Nye, P. D. Zelikow, and D. C. King, eds., *Why People Don't Trust Government*, 1997). And the United States is not alone in this— many other countries are experiencing a similar predicament.

These trends suggest a crisis of public confidence in institutional leadership that has significant implications for the future of U.S. public policy schools. Paul A. Volcker, the former chairman of the Federal Reserve Board, has suggested (at the Kennedy School of Government conference "Visions of Governance in the Twenty-First Century"; see also National Committee on the Public Service [the Volcker Commission], *Leadership for America*, 1989) a connection between the loss of public trust and the declining numbers of talented young people entering government service. Restoring public confidence in our institutions may require a new kind of leadership, and public policy schools have a crucial role to play both in defining the problem and in developing the skills to address it.

Leadership requires understanding how the world is changing, how the trends of globalization, marketization, and the information revolution are shaping democratic governance. In order to prepare leaders for service in the public interest, public policy schools must provide graduates with skills that will help them address the impact of these trends in diverse institutional settings. Today they are entering a job market that demands this ability. But even more, if effective leadership means persuading people to undertake adaptive changes, as Ronald Heifetz argues (in *Leadership Without Easy Answers*, 1994), the first step in leadership is reflection and analysis to identify the changes that are needed.

Students at public and international affairs schools across the country are shifting away from the public sector to the private and nonprofit sectors, although many will follow a revolving-door pattern in which they may alternate between sectors over time. For example, in 1980 three-quarters of Kennedy School graduates receiving master's degrees in public policy took government jobs. Last year less than half did. Overall only about one-third of all M.P.P. degree holders hold jobs in the government. The lure of private consulting firms that pay six-figure salaries is particularly strong. Moreover, as *U.S. News & World Report* (P. Longman, "Lure of the Private," Feb. 19, 1998) recently noted, "Even students who are more interested in doing good than doing well are opting for jobs with private firms or nonprofit organizations that do government work under contract."

Common sense says that if fewer bright young people choose government as a career path, then government's ability to deal with complex social problems will decline. And when the image of government as inept, distant, bloated, and corrupt is reinforced by the media, by popular culture, and paradoxically, by campaigning politicians themselves, it is small wonder that fewer graduates seek public service jobs.

A certain degree of mistrust of government and of centralized power is a long and healthy American tradition, arguably stretching as far back as Anne Hutchinson's and Roger Williams's religious-cum-political challenges to the leaders of the seventeenth-century Massachusetts Bay Colony. But all of our institutions are at risk when bad government becomes a self-fulfilling prophecy and government bashing becomes the self-serving pastime of politicians and pundits.

Redirecting Public Policy School Focus

The phenomenal growth of nonprofits suggests how increasingly we depend on them to address problems that governments and for-profit institutions find intractable. Roughly 25 percent of Kennedy School graduates now go into management positions in nonprofit organizations, and other public policy schools report similar trends. Those responsible for training leaders for public service need to address a variety of questions: How can nonprofits best be managed? How do corporations and nonprofits effectively collaborate? What accountability is necessary in return for public support?

Training for the nonprofit sector is one area where public policy schools need to redirect their focus. The Kennedy School, for example, has started a new center for the study of nonprofit institutions. In addition, those who enter the private sector will profit from an understanding of public policy, environmental issues, the global economy, the impact of the new technologies, and the development of public-private partnerships—training leaders in these areas will require a reformulation of the skills and knowledge we have offered students in the past. As mentioned earlier, at different stages in their careers individuals may work in each of the three sectors.

The real world of public service tomorrow will be multicultural and multidisciplinary. Public policy school graduates will need to think and analyze through the lenses of many academic disciplines—areas that have been traditionally segregated from one another in these schools. Leadership and management will also require a new practicum of teamwork and negotiation skills so that individuals can adapt to the distinct institutional cultures of the three sectors as they increasingly interact with one another. In addition, as markets become more global, leadership will require deeper understanding of various indigenous cultural and social milieus.

Public policy schools need to teach the essential skills, tools, and behaviors of policy analysis, managerial action, and democratic advocacy. Interdisciplinary curricula, case method teaching, and collaborative and project-based learning are all effective pedagogic means to that end. The Venn diagram in Figure 23.1 can help us conceptualize how a curriculum should combine leadership skills and roles. Successful leadership consists of the strategic exercise of three overlapping roles and actions: analysis—understanding a situation and thinking about what choices and changes will work out best; management—mobilizing individuals, groups, organizations, and societies to work together to undertake important challenges; and advocacy—fighting for a mission that involves values, ideas, and principles and persuading others to follow. In addition, effective leadership requires the application of substantive expertise. Schools can prepare leaders by fostering basic skills and teaching about real policy issues and impacts.

In the public policy realm, we can think of the diagram's inner core in terms of roles successful leaders play: the analyst assesses policy choices using economic, statistical, institutional, political, ethical, and historical modes of analysis and thinking. The manager

Figure 23.1. Essential Skills Are Interdependent.

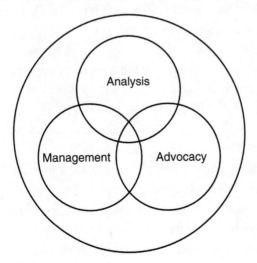

mobilizes his or her constituents to work together as teams by using information technology and organizational change as well as internal, financial, and human resource management. The advocate advances a mission by articulating a vision, organizing political action, participating in the electoral process, persuading, focusing media coverage, and polling. This model captures essential features of leadership that are relevant to the public, private, and nonprofit sectors beyond academia's walls.

Lessons in Responding to Change

But above all, the quality that defines good leadership, its strategic roles and activities, is the ability to understand and respond to change. Consider the U.S. military. Despite the fact that the armed services constitute a highly centralized government bureaucracy, leaders in the military over the past two decades have vigorously adapted to change. The results have been dramatic: according to a recent Gallup poll, our armed services are among the major government institutions that still enjoy the highest confidence ratings. Despite highly visible recent controversies involving sexual harassment and adultery, a full 60 percent of those polled gave the military high confidence marks. In contrast, Congress received 29 percent and the criminal justice system, just 19 percent.

The military's popularity is something of an anomaly in this era of declining public trust in government in general and in most major institutions. Why is the military different? Some say it is because the armed forces are associated with patriotism. But that was true in the 1960s and early 1970s when confidence in the military declined along with confidence in the rest of government. What is striking about the recent figures is the military's turnaround. After Vietnam the military was an institution that was drug-ridden, undisciplined, and divided by terrible racial problems. But in the mid-1970s, public confidence in it began to rise—well before its successful performance in the Persian Gulf War.

Why did the public image of the military change so dramatically? For a start, the end of the Vietnam War gave the services relief from the "baby killer" image that had resulted from the My Lai massacre, indiscriminate napalm attacks on civilian populations, and other battlefield catastrophes. But it was also incumbent on the military to take advantage of this change in circumstances. The end of the draft also provided the services with both an impetus and an opportunity to remake their public image in America. Without conscription, the military had to compete in the labor market. This required mass advertising, such as the army's highly successful "Be All That You Can Be" campaign. In an age when negative advertising in political campaigns and increasingly cynical press coverage is *demarketing* the rest of government, the military learned how to present itself in a positive light.

So, incidentally, did the U.S. Postal Service, another large bureaucracy and another example of a federal agency with high confidence ratings, one whose public image has benefited from mass marketing strategies and ad slogans like "We Deliver for You." Again, market competition helped. The Postal Service faced stiff competition from private companies like Federal Express and electronic mail systems.

But there is more to the military story than merely a tribute to the power of Madison Avenue. The military is an example of a government bureaucracy that fundamentally transformed itself. The U.S. automobile industry, another tradition-bound institution that fell on troubled times, changed in the 1980s under the impetus of intense market competition. The military, in contrast, changed because it learned from crushing defeat. After failure in Vietnam, not only did the military develop new doctrines and training that produced successful performance in war; it also developed one of the best records of any U.S. institution on the critical social problems of race, drugs, and education.

Americans like the military because they see it as a meritocracy. Individual effort, discipline, and commitment are the clear keys to advancement and success. The public can see dramatic examples of the military's meritocratic commitment, such as General Colin Powell's rise through the army's ranks to become chairman of the Joint Chiefs of Staff.

The military achieved racial integration not through rigid quotas but through promotion of minority candidates who met mandatory criteria. As Charles C. Moskos and John Sibley Butler have pointed out in their 1996 book *All That We Can Be: Black Leadership and Racial Integration the Army Way,* the army demands a high degree of accountability for "racial climate" from its officers. Not only is discrimination prohibited, but officers must also "resolve the perception of unfair treatment." This lesson in accountability should be portable to other institutional settings in all three sectors.

As for drugs, a zero-tolerance policy and random testing that includes everyone up through the chairman of the Joint Chiefs of Staff has produced a drug-free military. Some might object to transferring this example to other institutions or see structural problems in attempting to do so, but it is worth examining the military's experience to see what potential lessons there might be for society at large.

Another lesson from the military's success story is its commitment to its personnel to provide long-term training and education, even for those who do not intend to make the military a long-term career. Soldiers of the all-volunteer army now surpass nonveterans in education and earning power. For many of today's underprivileged youth, the armed forces have become a prime means to college education and job training—traditional high roads to increased earning power and the American dream.

Not every government agency can engage in massive advertising campaigns or demonstrate its performance in a televised war. But beyond its operational successes from Grenada to the Gulf War, the U.S. military has been able to change much of its own institutional culture. It did so by becoming labor market oriented and personnel sensitive and by stepping to the forefront of racial integration. Now it is beginning to cope effectively with problems related to gender. It is still grappling with difficulty with the issue of gay rights and participation, but even here it is arguably no worse than a reflector of the U.S. society's own deeply conflicted attitudes. The military's capacity to change is why so many people look on that institution as a success, a place where Americans can be what we all have the promise to be.

Conclusion

The U.S. military and the Postal Service demonstrate that even large bureaucratic organizations can evolve. Leadership can make a difference. But as the information revolution and globalization proceed, more change will be necessary for institutions. Bureaucracy itself is under challenge as the Internet and other networks increasingly facilitate unmediated communication and action. Schools of public policy must take the lead in understanding these changes and preparing people to adapt to them.

In our fractious political climate the problem of declining public confidence in our institutions has no easy fix. Therefore another contribution policy schools can make is to foster serious dialogue among academics, policymakers, and the public about what constitutes effective leadership and governance in a changing world. Such a dialogue would be a welcome departure from the rhetoric of government bashing, which in election years comes loudest from Washington, D.C., itself. And it would demonstrate the public policy schools' contribution to leadership beyond the (academic) walls.

INDEX

Lessons in Leadership

Peter F. Drucker

Over the span of his sixty-year career, Peter F. Drucker has worked with many exemplary leaders in the non-profit sector, government, and business. In the course of his work, he has observed these leaders closely and learned from them the attributes of effective leadership. In this video, Drucker presents inspirational portraits of five outstanding leaders, showing how each brought different strengths to the task, and shares the lessons we can learn from their approaches to leadership. Drucker's insights (plus the accompanying *Facilitator's Guide* and *Workbook*) will help participants identify which methods work best for them and how to recognize their own particular strengths in leadership.

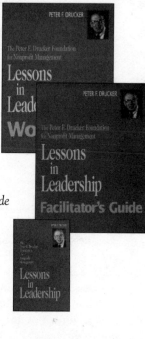

1 20-minute video + 1 *Facilitator's Guide* + 1 *Workbook*
ISBN 0-7879-4497-1 $89.95 US $134.95 CAN

Excellence in Nonprofit Leadership

Peter F. Drucker, Max De Pree, Frances Hesselbein

This video package is a powerful three-in-one development program for building more effective nonprofit organizations and boards. *Excellence in Nonprofit Leadership* presents three modules that can be used independently or sequentially to help nonprofit boards and staff strengthen leadership throughout the organization. The video contains three twenty-minute programs: (I) *Lessons in Leadership* with Peter Drucker (as described above); (II) *Identifying the Needs of Followers*, with Max De Pree and Michele Hunt; and (III) *Leading Through Mission*, with Frances Hesselbein. The video comes with one *Facilitator's Guide*, which contains complete instructions for leading all three programs, and one free *Workbook*, which is designed to help participants deepen and enrich the learning experience.

1 60-minute video + 1 *Facilitator's Guide* + 1 *Workbook*
ISBN 0-7879-4496-3 $129.95 US $194.95 CAN

FAX
Toll Free
24 hours a day:
800-605-2665

CALL
Toll Free
6am to 5pm
PST:
800-956-7739

MAIL
Jossey-Bass Publishers
350 Sansome St.
San Francisco, CA
94104

WEB
Secure ordering at:
www.josseybass.com

Leading in a Time of Change

What It Will Take to Lead Tomorrow

A Conversation with
Peter F. Drucker and
Peter M. Senge

Hosted by Frances Hesselbein

Share the wisdom of two great minds of modern management

How can leaders prepare themselves and their organizations for the changes that lie ahead? No question is more fundamental to the success of our business and social institutions. In this provocative video package, two of the most influential thinkers of our time—Peter Drucker and Peter Senge—explore the challenges of leadership and change. An ideal tool for executive retreats, management training, or personal leadership development, this remarkable dialogue offers insight on many issues, including:

- How to focus on opportunities rather than problems

- When to start phasing out established products or programs

- Why preserving institutional values and trust is key to change

- What businesses can learn from nonprofits in attracting and mobilizing knowledge workers

Enjoy a seat at the table with two thought leaders who are setting the agenda for business.

1 42-minute video + 1 *Viewer's Workbook* + 1 *Facilitator's Notes* in a library case.
ISBN 0-7879-5603-1 $195.00 US $292.50 CAN

FAX
Toll Free
24 hours a day:
800-605-2665

CALL
Toll Free
6am to 5pm
PST:
800-956-7739

MAIL
Jossey-Bass Publishers
350 Sansome St.
San Francisco, CA
94104

WEB
Secure ordering at:
www.josseybass.com

The Drucker Foundation Self-Assessment Tool

Since its original publication in 1993, the best-selling *Drucker Foundation Self-Assessment Tool* has helped and inspired countless nonprofit boards, executives, and teams to rediscover the direction and potential of their organizations. This completely revised edition of the *Self-Assessment Tool* now offers even more powerful guidance to help organizations uncover the truth about their performance, focus their direction, and take control of their future.

The *Self-Assessment Tool* combines long-range planning and strategic marketing with a passion for dispersed leadership. It allows an organization to plan for results, to learn from its customers, and to release the energy of its people to further its mission. The *Process Guide* by Gary J. Stern provides step-by-step guidelines and self-assessment resources, while the *Participant Workbook* by Peter F. Drucker features thoughtful introductions and clear worksheets. Participants will not only gain new insights about their organization's potential, but also forge strategies for implementation and future success.

Multiple Uses for the *Self-Assessment Tool*

- *The leadership team*—the chairman of the board and the chief executive—can lead the organization in conducting a comprehensive self-assessment, refining mission, goals, and results, and developing a working plan of action.

- *Teams throughout the organization* can use the *Tool* to invigorate projects, tailoring the process to focus on specific areas as needed.

- *Governing boards* can use the *Tool* in orientation for new members, as means to deepen thinking during retreats, and to develop clarity on mission and goals.

- *Working groups from collaborating organizations* can use the *Tool* to define common purpose and to develop clear goals, programs, and plans.

Process Guide   Paperback ISBN 0-7879-4436-X $29.95 US $44.95 CAN
Participant Workbook   Paperback ISBN 0-7879-4437-8 $12.95 US $19.50 CAN

1+1 SAT Package = 1 *Process Guide* + 1 *Participant Workbook*
ISBN 0-7879-4730-X $34.50 US $51.95 CAN **Save 20%!**

1+10 SAT Package = 1 *Process Guide* + 10 *Participant Workbooks*
ISBN 0-7879-4731-8 $89.95 US $134.95 CAN **Save 40%!**

FAX	CALL	MAIL	WEB
Toll Free	Toll Free	Jossey-Bass Publishers	Secure ordering, tables of
24 hours a day:	6am to 5pm	350 Sansome St.	contents, editors' notes,
800-605-2665	PST:	San Francisco, CA	sample articles at
	888-378-2537	94104	www.josseybass.com or
			www.leaderbooks.org

Leader to Leader

A quarterly publication of the Drucker Foundation and Jossey-Bass Publishers

Frances Hesselbein, Editor-in-Chief

Leader to Leader is a unique management publication, a quarterly report on management, leadership, and strategy written by today's top leaders *themselves*. Four times a year, *Leader to Leader* keeps you ahead of the curve by bringing you the latest offerings from a peerless selection of world-class executives, best-selling management authors, leading consultants, and respected social thinkers, making *Leader to Leader* unlike any other magazine or professional publication today.

Think of it as a short, intensive seminar with today's top thinkers and doers—people like Peter F. Drucker, Rosabeth Moss Kanter, Max De Pree, Charles Handy, Esther Dyson, Stephen Covey, Meg Wheatley, Peter Senge, and others.

Subscriptions to **Leader to Leader** are $149.00 US $179.00 CAN. 501(c)(3) nonprofit organizations can subscribe for $99.00 (must supply tax-exempt ID number when subscribing). Prices subject to change without notice.

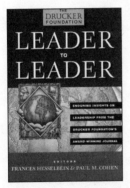

Leader to Leader

Enduring Insights on Leadership from the Drucker Foundation's Award-Winning Journal

Frances Hesselbein, Paul M. Cohen, Editors

The world's thought leaders come together in *Leader to Leader*, an inspiring examination of mission, leadership, values, innovation, building collaborations, shaping effective institutions, and creating community. Management pioneer Peter F. Drucker; Southwest Airlines CEO Herb Kelleher; best-selling authors Warren Bennis, Stephen R. Covey, and Charles Handy; Pulitzer Prize winner Doris Kearns Goodwin; Harvard professors Rosabeth Moss Kanter and Regina Herzlinger; and learning organization expert Peter Senge are among those who share their knowledge and experience in this essential resource. Their essays will spark ideas, open doors, and inspire all those who face the challenge of leading in an ever-changing environment.

For a reader's guide, see www.leaderbooks.org

Hardcover 402 pages   ISBN 0-7879-4726-1 $27.00 US $40.95 CAN

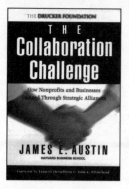

The Collaboration Challenge
How Nonprofits and Businesses Succeed Through Strategic Alliances

James E. Austin

Presented by the Drucker Foundation

In these complex times, when no organization can succeed on its own, nonprofits and businesses are embracing collaboration for mutual benefits. Nonprofits are partnering with businesses to further their missions, develop resources, strengthen programs, and thrive in today's competitive world. Companies are discovering that alliances with nonprofits generate significant rewards: increased customer preference, improved employee recruitment and morale, greater brand identity, stronger corporate culture, expanded good will, and innovations strengthened by testing.

In this timely and insightful book, James E. Austin demonstrates how to establish and manage strategic alliances that are effective and mutually beneficial. He provides a practical framework for understanding how traditional philanthropic relationships can be transformed into powerful strategic alliances. Readers will find key lessons drawn from more than fifteen collaborations, including Timberland and City Year; Starbucks and CARE; Georgia-Pacific and The Nature Conservancy; MCI WorldCom and The National Geographic Society; Reebok and Amnesty International; and Hewlett-Packard and the National Science Resources Center. From his analysis, nonprofit and business leaders will learn how to:

- Find and connect with high-potential partners

- Ensure strategic fit with a partner's mission and values

- Generate greater value for each partner and society

- Manage the partnering relationship effectively

Perceptive, powerful, and practical, *The Collaboration Challenge* offers valuable insights on the process of creating and sustaining successful strategic alliances between nonprofits and businesses.

Hardcover   216 pages   ISBN 0-7879-5220-6 $25.00 US $37.50 CAN

For a free reader's guide, see CollaborationChallenge.org

FAX
Toll Free
24 hours a day:
800-605-2665

CALL
Toll Free
6am to 5pm
PST:
888-378-2537

MAIL
Jossey-Bass Publishers
350 Sansome St.
San Francisco, CA
94104

WEB
Secure ordering, tables of
contents, editors' notes,
sample articles at
www.josseybass.com or
www.leaderbooks.org